A long-standing friendship and writing partnership has created this account of our national love affair with sport. **Douglas Booth** played Australian football for St Kilda between 1976 and 1982, is a dedicated surfer and teaches sport history and policy at the University of Otago, New Zealand. His book *The Race Game: Sport and Politics in South Africa* was published in 1998. **Colin Tatz**, who plays golf with some talent and much pleasure, is emeritus professor of politics at Macquarie University, Sydney. His sports books include *Obstacle Race: Aborigines in Sport*, the centenary history of the Royal Sydney Golf Club and *Black Diamonds* (with his son Paul).

Among the local and overseas newspapers and magazines in which Doug's and Colin's sport journalism has appeared are *Inside Sport*, the *Age*, the *Australian* and the *Sydney Morning Herald*.

Partisanship, verging on fanaticism, are hallmarks of the Australian way of sport, as this photograph of 'one-eyed' swimmers Ian Thorpe, Grant Backett and Michael Klim testifies. Here they are driving their team mate, Daniel Kowalski, to victory in the 1998 World Swimming Championships in Perth, totally oblivious to the world around them. NICK WILSON/APL

One-Eyed

A View of Australian Sport

DOUGLAS BOOTH
AND
COLIN TATZ

ALLEN & UNWIN

First published in 2000 by
Allen & Unwin
9 Atchison Street
St Leonards NSW 1590
Australia
Phone: (61 2) 8425 0100
Fax: (61 2) 9906 2218
E-mail: frontdesk@allen-unwin.com.au
Web: http://www.allen-unwin.com.au

National Library of Australia
Cataloguing-in-Publication entry:

Booth, Douglas.
    One-eyed: a view of Australian sport.

    Bibliography.
    Includes index.
    ISBN 1 86508 055 1.

    1. Sports—Australia—History. 2. Sports—Political aspects—Australia. 3. Sports—Social aspects—Australia. I. Tatz, Colin. II. Title.

796.0994

Internal design by Simon Paterson
Set in 11/14 pt Plantin Light by Bookhouse Digital, Sydney
Printed by South Wind Productions, Singapore

To our guides, Gaye and Sandra

Contents

Acknowledgements

Thanks to Paul Tatz for acquiring and selecting the photographs; to Sandra and Paul Tatz and George Parsons for their comments and criticisms; Stephen Alomes and John Loy for their suggestions and materials; Cathy Wilcox for the use of her cartoon; Venetia Somerset, Colette Vella and Dorothy Bransfield for their caring and excellent editing; Simon Paterson for the design of the book; and Les Williams, of the University of Otago, New Zealand, for that most precious of commodities—time.

Abbreviations

ABC	Australian Broadcasting Corporation (formerly, Commission)
ACB	Australian Cricket Board
AFL	Australian Football League (formerly VFL)
AIF	Australian Imperial Force
ALS	Aboriginal Legal Service
AOC	Australian Olympic Committee
AOF	Australian Olympic Federation
ARL	Australian Rugby League
ASC	Australian Sports Commission
ASU	Australian Swimming Union
CSC	Croatia Soccer Club
DLP	Democratic Labor Party
ICC	International Cricket Conference
IOC	International Olympic Committee
MCC	Melbourne Cricket Club/Marylebone Cricket Club
MCG	Melbourne Cricket Ground
MLA	Member of the Legislative Assembly
MLC	Member of the Legislative Council
NRL	National Rugby League
NSW	New South Wales
NSWASA	NSW Amateur Swimming Association
NSWLASA	NSW Ladies' Amateur Swimming Association
NSWRFL	NSW Rugby Football League
NSWRL	NSW Rugby League
NSWRU	NSW Rugby Union

NZAAA	New Zealand Amateur Athletic Association
OCAS	*Oxford Companion to Australian Sport*
OECD	Organisation for Economic Cooperation and Development
SCG	Sydney Cricket Ground
SLCOC	Salt Lake City Organising Committee
SLCBC	Salt Lake City Bid Committee
SLSAA	Surf Life Saving Association of Australia
SMH	*Sydney Morning Herald*
SRFU	Southern Rugby Football Union
VFA	Victorian Football Association
VFL	Victorian Football League
WACA	Western Australian Cricket Association Ground
WSC	World Series Cricket

Prologue

There is nothing so momentary as a sporting achievement and nothing so lasting as the memory of it.

—Greg Dening[1]

[Sport] was a wonderful, chaotic universe of clashing colors, temperaments, and emotions, of brave deeds performed sometimes against odds seemingly insuperable, mixed with mean and shameful acts of pure skullduggery, cheapness, snide tricks, filth, and greed, moments of sheer, sweet courage and magnificence when the flame of the human spirit and the will to triumph burned so brightly that it choked your throat and blinded your eyes to be watching it, and moments, too, of such villainy, cowardice, and depravity, of such rapaciousness and malice that you felt hot and ashamed even to find yourself reporting it.

—Paul Gallico[2]

There are any number of reasons why books are written. In this case, the publishers asked us for a history of sport. As one would expect, the reasons for accepting are complex.

First, we are familiar with other texts in this small field of writing. Most are anthologies, pieces long and (mostly) short put together by invitation of editors or conferences pulled together by their organisers. There is some excellent material amid much that is poorly researched and reasonably written, or well researched and badly crafted. This book, at least, has the merit of modest length by two authors who share similar views on sport.

Second, as Brian Matthews observes, Australian sports writing is seen, 'often with the best will in the world, as somehow second rate'.[3] He assigns two causes: the confinement to short newspaper pieces and hence the lack of suitable outlets for good extended writing; and the cultural factor, namely that sport in Australia 'has never been seen as intellectually or artistically respectable'. There is, in our view, another and more significant factor. All too often 'sports history' is about sport for the sake of sport, about sports trivia, leaving a legacy that concentrates on sport solely as sport, constituting a cocoon devoid of context. Even some of the newer writing—especially by commentators on Australian football— is euphoric.[4] Sport can be, and often is, fun; it is also a fiction, an illusion, and certainly not as real, let alone more real, than life itself. Sport doesn't end wars or great national animosities; it doesn't cure poverty or the ills of national or regional economies; it doesn't alter the nature of governance at various levels. The olympics is patently not what the president of the International Olympic Committee (IOC), Juan Antonio Samaranch, so absurdly claims it to be—'the most important event in the world, not just in sports'.[5] But sport *is* an important lens or mirror for examining the larger ideas and issues in a human society. These include nationalism, war, nationhood, elitism, patronage, civilisation and civility in society, inequity and inequality based on spurious criteria, international relationships and commitments, the nature of plural societies, democratic and autocratic processes, human rights, the exercise of authority without accountability, and so on. In this sense we are somewhat outside the tradition of what has come to be regarded as Australian sports history. Rather than being *into* sports culture, we try to look beyond.

Third, and arising from this, we want to see whether sports critics who happen to like sport—which is a more appropriate label in our case—can write effectively (as opposed to beautifully) about the subject, without being obsessed, besotted or merely in love with the activity. One of our *compadres* once complained that our problem was that we 'didn't love sport', or didn't love it enough. We don't. We play it, watch it, read about it, like it in general and praise or condemn it where appropriate. But it isn't a be-all and end-all, and there is much about sport, as Gallico says so elegantly at the start of this book, that is hardly lovable. There are those who see and feel virtue in vicariousness, even in voyeurism, who salivate over every technical or artistic twist of the wrist. We don't. We are not insiders or barrackers, nor are we—to use sport historian Max Howell's phrase—'sports patriots'. We dispute the views of John Carrol and John Harms that to be 'theorists' we 'must stand in the shoes of the outer fan if [we] are to understand fully the significance of sport'.[6] Neither do we share the views and visions of colleague Richard Cashman that Australia was once 'a paradise of sport', and that it may again be so.[7]

Fourth, we believe that there must be a genre of sports criticism as opposed to sports writing, sports history, sports culture, sports sociology and the like. Everyone accepts the validity of music criticism, literary criticism, art criticism. Why not sports criticism as an *adversary* genre that examines, assesses, questions, debates, praises quality, denigrates the shoddy—in short, that makes informed judgements? It strikes us that, unlike American writing, Australian literature and journalism on sport is essentially idolistic, jingoistic in many respects, celebratory for the most part, 'limp, ghost-written, chronology-enslaved autobiography'[8] in too many instances, and often exculpatory or 'excusatory' in defeat. Most often it is narrative or revelatory, as in unfolding a story. But it often stops short of analysing the story and rarely takes the next step, which is to evaluate critically. We like the approach adopted by (the often maligned) Lawrence Grossberg to cultural studies. He suggests a model that is always contextual, uses critical inquiry of both its subject and its context, and that is also political, 'guardedly authoritative', self-reflective, interdisciplinary, and theoretical.[9] So much of Australian sports history has no politics, insufficient context, and suffers from being ever so sanitised. American critic Greil Marcus calls much of this approach 'the smooth surface of history, looking backwards, making everything make sense'.[10]

Fifth, both of us are involved in teaching and researching in mainstream areas of politics, history and sociology, especially in the field of race politics. Sport is a major case study in racism: it is where most sportspeople don't expect to find it or where that important tenet of sport, to be 'sportsmanlike', should eliminate it, or at least transcend it. We tend to write about race with a degree of intensity. We feel much less passionate about sport as sport, or even as a means of writing about these other issues. American sociologist Brewton Berry once claimed in his book about race relations that he would write with the dispassion of a zoologist looking at a kangaroo or a palaeontologist looking at fossils.

Obviously we feel more about sport than Berry about his bones, but not all that much. Our 'problem'—and there are doubtless many who will consider that we have a problem—is that sport as sport is essentially ephemeral. Dening's opening quote is half correct: the essence of sport is its momentariness. It is 'an expressive form' that 'survives', in the words of anthropologist Clifford Geertz, 'only in its own present—the one it itself creates'.[11] But memory, let alone lasting memory, is rare, and recapture is even rarer—unlike art or film or recorded music. Unless, of course, one is of the legions of sports nuts, rabid fans, program and scarf collectors, people who can tell you the colour of Jack Dempsey's trunks the night he won the world heavyweight championship, or those arithmeticians who can tell you how many runs Michael Bevan scored in day–night matches at the WACA in Perth. We see no virtue in elevating such trivia, or 'memory', to a level of social significance. For us, unless there is a message of substance involved, sport is a little bit like the New Year fireworks over the Sydney Harbour Bridge: waiting for the (relatively) unexpected, *uncertain* about the quality and the outcome, then great fun for twenty minutes, remembered for possibly another ten, then gone, smoke and all. As many contemporary postmodern critics observe, we dwell in a present-tense culture. David Harvey contends that 'the horizons shorten to the point where the present is all there is'.[12] Indeed, there seems to be only the televisual present—one which, like the fireworks, is cramped, impoverished, transitory and often illusory.

Understanding the ephemeral, fictional and illusionary nature of sport is especially important, given the hype and wild claims made about the 'enduring legacies' of the Sydney 2000 olympics in the years preceding the games. Readers shouldn't find it strange that we have such limited discussion of this event. The games end on 1 October 2000. For most Australians, the memories will fade quickly, and it may well be that the pre-games scandals remain longer in the memory than the 'fireworks' on the track. Olympic venues carry no weight of tradition. Unlike Le Mans, Lords, the MCG, Augusta, Wembley and Wimbledon, olympic sites are merely grid references. When sports historians enshrine memorable olympic moments—the dramatic, beautiful, tearful and ecstatic, together with the dastardly, mean and disdainful—they inevitably ignore the venue. Location looms large only when the non-sporting aspects overwhelm—such as the Nazi 'triumph' in Berlin, the Israelis killed in Munich, the massive boycotts of Montreal and Moscow, the black American race issue in Mexico. When statisticians list Jamaican or

American 'Florence Foster' winning the 100m in 2000, the record books
will give her medal and time—followed by Sydney, in brackets. Most
social history texts barely refer to the venue, except perhaps as
'Melbourne (1956)' or 'world record (Melbourne 1956)'.

Is this is an anti-sport book? No. We believe that sport expresses
beauty and grace; there is joy in the essence of particular sports, in skill,
adroitness, in manipulation of the human body and its senses, in achievement, in opposition or adversity. We also believe that there is more room
for silence and imagination as one watches or reads, plays or indulges
in make-belief. But we are repelled by the noise, the hype, the 'charisma'
attributed to 10-second, 40-minute or 15-round heroes, the media treatment of audiences as intellectually challenged, the violation of sight and
mind by Coke and Fosters and Fila, the gross elevation of sport to
pedestals so often made of clay. We object to being told what to watch,
what to see when watching, what to observe in the umpteenth slow-
motion replay, what to think about what we've watched, and to marvel
at statistical trivia so mindless as to be a parody of sport. Blessed is the
remote control that allows us to watch the stroke-making of Tendulkar
or Lara, or all manner of football artistry, while muting Tony Greig or
the buffoonery of the two football Rexes—Hunt and Mossop.

One-Eyed is a social and political history of sport in Australia aimed
at students, journalists, sports fans, even those who dislike sport, and
the interested lay public. It is not a neutral, objective history; nor do we
claim simply to present 'facts' as incontestable truths. This is not the
historian's task. David Hackett Fischer reminds us that historians don't
'wander in the dark forest of the past gathering facts like nuts and
berries'.[13] They deal in interpretation. They must decide, in the words
of Edward Carr, 'which facts to give the floor, and in what order or
context'.[14] How do historians decide? They filter and select on personal
philosophies which have evolved through research, observation, and the
information that comes through the writings and theories, the rigour and
the standards, of others. Our perspectives rest on the foundations of
humanism expounded by liberal philosophers like Jean Jacques Rousseau
and John Stuart Mill, and by moral and ethical philosophers like Morris
Ginsberg and John Rawls. This book, however, explicates neither political philosophy nor theory; rather our narratives and examples, which
are far more interesting, illustrate the philosophy and theory.

Our sources are not new in the fieldwork or archival senses of 'original'. In all but a handful of cases we have used published writings for

the facts and interpreted them afresh. We have used the work of some Australian historians who are out of favour; however, what are called their 'distortions' are not momentous in our particular context. The purpose has been to present an overview of the issues rather than engage in deep debate about particulars. Our research and published works—on topics like South Africa, women in sport, racism and sport, Aboriginal sports achievements, golf and beach culture—are cited or repeated where relevant. Space prevented more quotation from those who provide the first draft of history, the journalists of the day. Harry Gordon calls them the eyewitnesses to Australian history.[15] In sport, long before there was sound and sight, the journalists conveyed fresh results, provided deep background, evoked the ambience, recreated the mood, painted what are now obvious, even trite pictures. Nat Gould, Frank Myers, Richard Coombes, J. C. Davis, Alfred Hales, W. F. Corbett senior, the rest of the Corbetts and the Palmer family were hardly 'second-rate'. But even they never quite matched the insights of the best of the Americans, like Gallico.

The title? 'One-Eyed' means, literally, blind in one eye. It also means an inability to see another point of view because one is partisan, intolerant, narrow and unreasonable. Many Australians believe they are fair-minded and generous-spirited; they believe they can see things, sporting and otherwise, for their true worth. Often they're not; often they can't. *One-Eyed* is a constant reminder of this. We hope it will encourage readers to question the emotions they invest in sport, why they approach sport in the ways they do—to look beyond themselves, to try to understand the objectives, feelings and passions of others.

Lastly, we do not subscribe to the convention that sports in general warrant the veneration of capital letters. Throughout this book we talk simply about rugby union, rugby league and so on. We take this one step further. The ancient Olympic games were at held at Olympia, hence the use of the upper case as a place name. The modern versions of these super sports festivals bear no resemblance to the ancient version or to the place called Olympia—thus the small 'o'. There may well be—or rather, there may well have been—a case for talking about a *philosophy* of olympism, but that gives it no greater claim to a capital letter than liberalism, humanitarianism, authoritarianism, fascism or utopianism.

1
Sporting Connections
1788–2000

From the earliest days in Sydney and Melbourne the [cricket] teams that met each summer were not mere collections of individual players who had joined together for recreation, but representatives of groups testing their skill against each other. Soldiers took on civilians. Currency took on sterling. The first contest between teams representing New South Wales and Victoria, at Melbourne in 1856, was also virtually an encounter between natives and immigrants, for ten of the visiting team were of colonial birth and all of the Victorians were born in the United Kingdom.

—Ken Inglis[1]

Bushies and Townies came to mingle in circumstances that enabled them to speak to themselves as Northerners, to join in ways comprehensible to all, the excitement of the race track, the bonhomie of the booze, the fraternal cavorting on the dance floor after the clod-hopping of their forebears... The spirit prevailing during the Races, from the moment the mob poured itself out of the trains (such being the way the alcoholic detrainments were described) on the Wednesday afternoon to that when, by those responsible for getting them home again, they were poured back on, was surely as near to Carnival, in its true sense of behaviour with riotous excess, as was possible in a community predominantly Anglo-Celtic.

—Xavier Herbert[2]

NOWHERE TO HIDE?

Sport is now an intrinsic part of the Australian landscape. Goalposts are signposts in leafy suburbs and in rural paddocks; squares of asphalt darken schoolyards and municipal playgrounds; steel stadiums tower in cities; mega-arenas dwarf other construction projects; rinks and courses green an otherwise urban ugliness; iron and wooden sports 'halls' dot farming communities; gravel tennis courts attach to station properties. English novelist Anthony Trollope observed in 1873 that 'there is hardly a town which has not its racecourse, and there are many racecourses where there are no towns'.[3]

Sport is an indelible part of the Australian home. It is ever-present and omnipresent on radio and television, in the papers: a succession of previews, reviews, interviews, team selections, live broadcasts, replays and post-mortems. For those who have no interest, or who detest the suffusion of life with sports mania, existence can be grim. At the height of recent saturation cricket coverage, including that by the Australian Broadcasting Corporation (ABC), Pilita Clark commented: 'just remember that there are thousands of us out here and we all know one true thing: a day without Shane Warne is a day full of hope.'[4]

Results, clearly, are the most important things in the world. Some years ago the marvellous 1934 version of 'Romeo and Juliet' was shown on the small screen. Grainy Romeo, finding an even grainier but still beautiful Juliet seemingly dead in the vault, slays the mourning suitor Paris and then swallows his poison: 'Here's to my love! [drinks] O true apothecary! Thy drugs are quick. Thus with a kiss…[flash on screen: CORRECT WEIGHT MOONEE VALLEY CORRECT WEIGHT MOONEE VALLEY]…I die [dies].' Par, one would say, for Australian commercial television—except that this was the ABC!

No longer confined to the back pages, sport now spreads from the front to the editorial to the features pages of nearly every quality broadsheet and mediocre tabloid. The 2000 olympics has been widely, and wildly, promoted as a Second Coming. Reporters, columnists and commentators dissect and analyse every facet of sporting life. Sport, it seems, has become our common language, our common and connecting denominator, the unifier of racial, social and class differences, the metaphor for life's experiences. In the following chapters we will focus on the social history and evolution of sport in the Australian experience—thematically and chronologically—especially over the last 150 years.

CONNECTING AUSTRALIANS

Sport seems an ideal way to connect Australians, to join disparate and similar people in a shared set of values, to provide a focus for group loyalties. Such relationships are, of course, essential to being human and to living in a society. We need to relate and to share. The easiest way to connect is through phatic speech, that is, meaningless breakers of the ice that may lead to deeper interaction. Thus, we—men, that is—engage in the phatic 'avagoodweekend', 'g'day', 'owyagoin' mate?', 'whatsa score?', 'who's gonna win?' and 'd'ya watch the game?'. Sport—and for men, the dirty joke—allows people to explore or test for common feelings, interests, qualities and traits. The important question is whether there is enough substance in sport—as an idea, an ideal, a set of actions, as a distinct culture—to claim that it both connects and unites some eighteen million people who are not all English-speaking, Anglo-Saxon, British-descended 'stock', and more than half of whom are women.

A major theme of this book is that historically sport only connected those who were and are already connected in a substantial sense by either class, religion, gender or race. This was because sport was peripheral, something secondary, distinct and apart from real life. More recently, sport has become increasingly a facet of everyday life, an activity much more interwoven with the other threads that make up the social fabric. That 'football is more than a game' is fast becoming a national cliché: 'it has become an integral part of the cultural life of many Australians.' Perhaps sport will come to play the crucial role of connecting the disconnected in a more ongoing, less fleeting way than hitherto. Perhaps. Then again, there is always the possibility, to borrow some phrasing from Shakespeare, that given an 'excess of it', 'the appetite may sicken, and so die'.

For the first hundred years of European settlement Australia was a society of emigrants, with Australian-born not reaching numerical majority until the 1880s. The colonies lacked a 'natural' ethnic base and faced the problem of drawing together people with divergent political, ideological, religious, ethnic and racial interests. Huge distances and small populations added to the problem. Very slowly some of these social groups began to cohere in the sense that they represented themselves in the past, or in the future, as if they formed a natural community. In short, divergent groups came to possess a 'national' identity of origins, culture and interests which is greater than their individual differences.[5] This process of nationalisation is both past and present tense. Sport is a wonderful example: groups of different classes, cultures, ethnicities, religions and even races become one under the banner of loyalty to the 'nation'.[6] Sport, then, is much more than mere speech contact. Examples abound from different periods of history and from a variety of geographic contexts. The success of its soccer team elevated dark, postwar Hungary living under a crushing communism: the Magyars thrashed England 6–3 at Wembley in 1953 and united the victorious nation as never before, or since, albeit fleetingly. Australia's victory in the America's Cup yacht race 30 years later had the effect of producing a great nationalist and patriotic fervour, albeit in the shortish term.

In England sport wasn't always the social cement that united rich and poor, the upper and lower classes. Australia was lucky to have missed the mother country's 'unrelenting friction between the landowners and the rest of rural society' in the eighteenth and nineteenth centuries.[7] Rather, egalitarianism and giving everyone a fair go are traits which Australians from early on have been proud to call their own, characteristics they consider the foundations of a national, social, cultural and sporting identity. 'The desire to enjoy the games of the rich became one of the most effectively expressed moods of Australian egalitarianism', observes Donald Horne.[8] These values help explain, for example, why the Melbourne Cup is Australia's true national day, the equivalent of America's fourth of July, the one day of the year when the 'half-crown public' and the 'half-guinea folk' across the continent focus on a single event.[9] An exceptionally long race, run by horses of various ages carrying different weights, the handicappers' brief is to ensure all entrants an equal opportunity, regardless of ability. Winners are notoriously difficult to pick, with the favourite coming home only once in every four races, and odds are 'long enough to encourage dreams of affluent leisure'.[10]

Sport also provides shared experiences that can help shape a 'common destiny'.[11] In the mid-nineteenth century, Anglo-Australians feared that 'emigrant stock, of doubtful origin... might have deteriorated' as part of the British 'race'. They eagerly seized any test to prove they retained 'the manhood and muscle of their English sires', that 'the manly qualities of the parent stock flourished as vigorously in the distant colonies as in the mother country', and that the English 'race' had not physically degenerated in the bright Australian climate. The almost universal fear of the 'convict taint' was both debilitating and a spur to a sporting jingoism. Victories over English cricket teams in the 1870s happily reassured Australians about their physical fitness and moral worth.[12]

Symbols, icons, anthems and songs of Australian national teams signify that Australians are a separate species. There is a distinct Australian sporting ethos or culture, one that at times evokes characteristics that really have little or nothing to do with sport. Harry Gordon—former editor, now historian and sports writer—described Sydney's bid to host the 2000 olympic games as 'wholesome'.[13] Australians, historian Richard White argues, have long considered themselves wholesome: a happy, cheerful, healthy, youthful, robust, honourable, upright and decent nation.[14] In the case of the olympic bid, and Sydney's touch-and-go victory over close rival Beijing, bid officials, journalists and politicians repeatedly compared Australian wholesomeness with Chinese underhandedness, deceit and dishonesty.[15] When the Chinese gave a priceless 2200-year-old terracotta soldier from the Ch'in tomb[16] to the International Olympic Committee (IOC) museum, Sydney's *Sun-Herald* roundly condemned what it called China's 'bribe' to the olympic movement.[17] In Sydney, an 'unofficial strategy committee' conspired to distribute around the world adverse material on China's human rights record. It was a 'dirty tricks campaign' that 'coincided' with a similar plan in the United States. The campaign ended only because one of Australia's IOC delegates, Kevan Gosper, feared 'it could backfire'.[18] (China, to its credit—or, in this tough world, its stupidity—never raised Australia's appalling Aboriginal record.) None of this was considered 'unwholesome'; rather it was a matter of national interest. Hypocritically, the press (initially) insisted that gifts of scholarships to the Australian Institute of Sport, university placements, holidays in luxurious resorts, and the occasional job for children of voting IOC delegates were not bribes but merely 'duchessing' and aid consonant with Australia's humanitarian programs abroad. Altruism and samaritanism are not in the mission statements of national and international sports organisations. John Coates, president of the Australian Olympic Committee (AOC), insists that the means justified the ends, and that profit from the games will provide 'a legacy for the [elite] athletes'.[19]

Despite the general confidence, and indeed the widespread faith, in sport as connecting and unifying Australians, phatic speech and national identities are too commonplace, too banal and too contingent to bond people in any deep, meaningful or enduring manner. Unlike class, gender, race and ethnicity, neither phatic speech nor national identities can achieve what sociologist Georg Simmel called 'organic' connections.[20] Rather, they tend to bring people together in a 'series', a term the French philosopher Jean-Paul Sartre used to mean a social collective passively and temporarily joined in some way. A crowd waiting at a bus stop is a series.[21] People at the stadium are little more than a series—but in neither case is there a lasting quality for the collectivity. That events can be significant and memorable, that they can and do produce unity and togetherness, is not in question: for example, the many thousands who watched Carbine win the 1890 Melbourne Cup, the 20 000 who sat at ringside to watch black heavyweight Jack Johnson demolish white hero Tommy Burns in 1908, the hundreds of thousands who attended boxer Les Darcy's funeral services in 1917, those who watched or listened to the first tied cricket Test against the West Indies in 1960, the nation hailing Lionel Rose's bantamweight championship in 1968, the nation (almost) as a whole cheering *Australia II* in 1983 or Kieren Perkins in his olympic 1500m swims in 1992 and 1996. But at the end of them all, the last real or metaphoric train or tram took them home and dispersed the series. Cricket is our one major cross-continental sport, yet it doesn't quite transcend a 'series' in the way that baseball does in America. Ken Burns says that baseball 'reflects a host of age-old American tensions—between workers and owners, scandal and reform, the individual and the collective. It is a haunted game in which every player is measured against the ghosts of all who have gone before'.[22]

One paradox of sport is that it both connects and differentiates at the same time. The rivalry between Australia and China to host the 2000 olympics is one example. While olympic rivalry could be said to connect Australians and Chinese, their respective histories, literature, language, social organisation, folk sanctions, standards of conduct, spiritual ideals and aesthetic preferences differentiate them and preclude an 'organic' connection.[23] Arrogant Australian jingoism and racism, like that uttered incessantly by talkback radio host and former Wallabies coach Alan Jones, means that there are few prospects of a positive connection between Australians and Chinese. After the Chinese women's basketball team beat Australia during their tour in mid-1994, Jones produced a tirade for his listeners, abusing the Chinese player Zheng Haixai. His xenophobia, as always, was excessive, crudely vilifying the player as a 'most grotesque thing', 'a heifer' and not his 'idea of sport'.[24] (In 1998 Jones was elevated to the deputy chairmanship of the board of the Australian Sports Commission, a matter discussed in Chapter 10.)

Even at the local level, sport connects and disconnects. Solo Melbourne mums from high-rise housing commission flats in Richmond and society ladies from across the river in Toorak mansions join in aerobics classes. But their different material circumstances, histories, manners, carriage, vocabulary, elocution, dress, adornments, grooming, punctuality and attention to detail thoroughly separate them in time, space and habits. Solo mums collect at the bare and dowdy local community centre; Toorak ladies 'meet' at their well-appointed and plush private clubs.

Sport certainly connects, especially on momentous occasions like Australia's victory in the America's Cup in 1983. The event produced a masterpiece of exaggeration from Prime Minister Bob Hawke, who called it 'Australia's greatest sporting achievement'.[25] The euphoria and rhetoric that day was thought by all to be frozen for mortality. A mere decade later, the common memory is the winning boat's connection with its disgraced owner and entrepreneur, Alan Bond. But whether sport unifies and forges a nationhood for Australians needs close scrutiny and careful analysis. As popular and even appealing as the idea is, we struggle to find any substance for it.

SPORT AND DIFFERENTIATION

Modern sport obviously involves social organisation. It also involves political and cultural decisions about what to play, how to play, when to play, where to play and who to play with and against. Different social classes, genders, races, ethnicities, religions and political groups have their own ways of playing their preferred sports. These differences are important. First, they tell others what the group represents, how it lives, its priorities and its values. Second, they reinforce their sense of exclusiveness and distinctiveness so as to enable groups to regulate their membership. Often this is to prevent the mobility of others who may want to join and to partake in the privileges they have built up over time.[26] For much of our history, women and Aborigines were seen as different, as being apart from the mainstream of sporting and social history. In several chapters we discuss their involvement in sport as separate entities, at least until the 1960s, because they were so often regarded as such. Briefly, we look at four categories of differentiation.

Class and status

In general, economic class and social status determine what sports Australians play and how, when and where they play. Brian Stoddart describes the effects of 'economic calculations' on the distribution and organisation of sports in the 1920s and 1930s:

> It was all very well to play in street versions of games like cricket, tennis and golf using primitive equipment, but to play regularly and seriously required the right uniform, good equipment, and the ability to pay entrance and subscription fees. For many at the lower end of the economic scale, especially in times of depression (along with its concomitant unemployment), such a purchase was simply impossible. For that reason many would 'choose' to play, say, football where the outlay was minimal rather than golf where the costs were prohibitive. Interesting divisions stemmed from such economic calculations. The early forms of trotting and pacing in all states were developed and run by butchers, drapers, grocers and other small businessmen who could not meet the high costs of thoroughbred horses that they would have needed to go racing.[27]

Yet difference of this kind is not based solely on economics. Sociologist Barry Barnes makes this point when he shows that many groups 'give more attention to other matters: for example, to religion or ritual or what is perhaps the same thing, to clubs and sport. And they may attach great importance to arbitrary and non-instrumental dimensions of dress and diet.'[28]

Stoddart's illustrations include 'penniless pastoralists' who gained membership of the Western Australian Turf Club more readily than 'prosperous publicans' during the Great Depression,[29] and the annual rugby match between students from the Australian National University and officer cadets from the Royal Military College at Duntroon. The match offers a classic example of the different senses of lifestyle, status and purpose within the middle classes:

> The university students are regarded by the trainee military officers as intellectual, radical, soft, socially privileged and frequently republican;

themselves they see as hard, disciplined and loyalist. The potential officers are seen by the students as militaristic, overly physical, intellectually
dull, lacking in flair and frequently right wing; themselves they see as
possessing flair, abiding by the rules and conventions, intellectually
progressive and natural future leaders.[30]

Even more conspicuous differences emerge when we compare the
ethical imperatives and aesthetic tastes of the middle and lower classes.
The former see themselves as valuing self-restraint, discipline, sobriety,
frugality and piety. The hallmarks of 'lower' or working-class spectators
are often roughness, rudeness, vociferous partisanship, an unashamed
premium on victory, a suspicion of, and often disdain for, constituted
authority.[31] Historical and contemporary descriptions of larrikin behaviour, colourful language, raucous barracking, vulgar hedonism and
challenges to authority by crowds congregating in 'Bay 13' at the
Melbourne Cricket Ground (MCG) and on 'the Hill' of the Sydney
Cricket Ground (SCG) are testimony to the class attitudes of Australian
spectators.[32]

At first glance such class differences may appear innocuous. To mock
or sneer at the mannerisms of the elite class who 'go to hounds', hunt
foxes and wear velvet caps is to misunderstand the symbolism of such
sports. Thorstein Veblen, an American economist and social scientist,
took much delight in poking fun at the courtly and pedantic sporting
manners of the upper classes as they galloped the fields or lounged round
tennis courts. But he ignored the military, economic and political realities that underpin these symbolic actions. The sociologist C. Wright Mills
argued that 'prestige buttresses power, turning it into authority, and protecting it from social challenge'.[33] French sociologist Pierre Bourdieu
shows how those at the top exert their authority through symbolic power
as a way of protecting themselves from social challenges by those at the
bottom. The fox hunts were and are powerful symbols—and symbols of
power.

There is no shortage of Australian examples to support these important insights. In the late nineteenth and early twentieth centuries,
anti-gambling laws closed the gambling dens and betting shops of the
lower classes, while allowing 'gentlemen' to continue gaming in private
clubs.[34] Similarly, amateur sporting associations and clubs excluded the
working classes from membership to preserve the distinct tastes and
lifestyles of 'gentlemen'.

Gender

Sport is probably the most significant area for distinguishing male and female identities. Colonial middle-class men, whom social commentator Marcus Clarke called 'a fretful, clever, perverse, irritable race' with an insatiable desire for 'out-of-door exercise', considered women victims of biology. In 1828 surgeon Peter Cunningham lamented that 'young females generally lose their teeth early...a calamity always commencing about the period of puberty'.[35] Clarke also believed it would be 'rare to find girls with white and sound teeth'. He saw women as those who grew thin, narrow, 'fond of dress and idleness, caring little for [their] children, but without sufficient brain power to sin with zest'.[36] There was little space for women's sport, especially among the middle classes, who, on the advice of medical practitioners, played gently for fear that hard exercise and competitive sport would cause infertility. For most of the nineteenth century, doctors advocated inactivity as the route to physical well-being and beauty. When languid lifestyles proved positively unhealthy, they advised women to partake in limited, gentle physical activity: tennis, croquet and golf were the perfect genteel sports, emphasising grace and sociability rather than competitiveness and exertion. Richard Twopenny depicted the Australian woman as 'bound to strum the piano', capable of cooking 'some kind of dinner' and 'making herself a dress'; she was 'good natured and fond of every species of fun' even 'if her accomplishments are not many'.[37] A few women acquired a 'second-rate masculinity' by handling horses well or by acting as 'tomboys'. Mostly, however, 'women were portrayed as a negation of the [male] type, at best as one who passively pined and waited, at worst as one who would drag a man down'.[38]

Significant numbers of women began to challenge these stereotypes before and immediately after the Second World War. Sport, especially in private schools, brought girls honour among their peers, helped alleviate the stress of study and provided enjoyment, entertainment and fun.[39] Yet most women continued to stress their sexuality and femininity at the expense of their sporting abilities. The fear of being considered 'an immoral and unnatural woman', or worse, being labelled a 'lesbian', afflicted sporting women. In the 1950s several olympic gold medallists—including sprinter Shirley de la Hunty (formerly Strickland) and swimmer Dawn Fraser—faced accusations that they were too aggressive and competitive. Rumours and innuendos about her sexuality haunted Dawn Fraser. In the weeks leading up to the 1960 olympic games in Rome,

> I learned for the first time that there were rumours suggesting that I was masculine. The rumours built up steadily over the next couple of years...and they did me irreparable damage. They were hurtful rumours, and the terrible thing was that I had no way of fighting against them. How can you combat a whisper? You can't walk around announcing to people, 'Look, I'm not masculine. I've got muscles, sure. But I'm not masculine.'[40]

Feminism swept across sport like a wave in the 1960s and 1970s, eroding old attitudes. Frailty was out; strength, power, speed and taut muscles were in. Women adopted male playing styles and strategies. But the fear of lesbianism remains as strong as ever in sport. Men accuse lesbians of being sexual predators, of stalking and pouncing on naive and impressionable young girls. 'Angus', a senior manager responsible for implementing affirmative action policies in sport, admitted candidly in an interview that he and his wife had 'stopped' their 'daughters going to softball—it's just a haven for lesbians. It's like cycling—it used to be blokes on spokes; now it's all dykes on bikes.'[41]

Sportswomen have responded with silence, denial, apology and overt heterosexual behaviour, and by attacking lesbians and hiring male coaches: Fraser 'stopped hugging girls who won races'[42] and the Australian Women's Cricket Council opted for culottes rather than trousers. In other sports, officials ban 'severe' haircuts, discourage public drinking and smoking, scrutinise social engagements and living arrangements, impose evening curfews, and hire chaperones and 'experts' who teach them how to look like the nice girl next door. Women who play traditional male sports, like cricket and football, suffer the most. They are labelled automatically. Unfortunately, Denise Annetts 'confirmed' lesbian domination of Australian women's cricket: in January 1994 she alleged selectors had dropped her from the national team because she was heterosexual and married. Women's cricket, which is all but invisible in the Australian media, suddenly became headlines. Nightly news, current affairs, 'infotainment' shows, radio and television sports programs and newspaper editorials seized the scandal. In the week after the story broke, 76 articles appeared in Australian newspapers; eleven of Australia's twelve metropolitan dailies (the *Australian*

Financial Review being the sole exception) covered the story, mostly in sensational style.[43]

Race

'There has been some rough work' is how Anthony Trollope described white treatment of Aborigines in 1873:

> We have taken away their land, have destroyed their food, made them subject to our laws, which are antagonistic to their habits and traditions, have endeavoured to make them subject to our tastes, which they hate, have massacred them when they defended themselves and their possessions after their own fashion, and have taught them by hard warfare to acknowledge us to be their master.[44]

A century later Richard White describes the exclusion of Aborigines from Australian national identity:

> As the idea of 'being Australian' developed among European inhabitants, the Aborigines became less and less representative of 'Australia' until in the end they were quite dispossessed. For most of the settlers they were pests, sometimes comic, sometimes vicious, but always standing in the way of a civilised Australian community. Eventually they were to reach the indignity of being 'Our Aborigines', their image no longer representative of Australia except as garden ornaments in suburban backyards and ashtrays in souvenir shops.[45]

Paternalistic approaches to 'our Aborigines' endure. In 1993, as members of the IOC gathered in Monaco to choose the host for the 2000 games, the Sydney olympic bid committee flooded the city with Aboriginal dancers and performers in an effort to showcase Aboriginal culture and to demonstrate sport's contribution to the reconciliation of white and black Australia. But as Aboriginal leader Sol Bellear sadly reminded us, they were 'tourist curios—like koalas and kangaroos'.[46]

What are Aboriginal conceptions of national identity and how has sport contributed to those conceptions? Geoffrey Stokes contends that in the 1930s and 1940s, when they were arguing for full citizenship rights, Aborigines 'relied on a conception of identity that suppressed notions of Aboriginal difference from Europeans'.[47] Certainly in the 1930s Aborigines asserted that their capacities and humanity matched those of Europeans but that white racism denied them opportunities of reaching their potential. In the late 1920s racial hostility and victimisation initially denied Aboriginal sprinter, boxer and footballer Doug

Nicholls an opportunity to play with Victorian Football League (VFL) club Carlton. While Nicholls could not conceal his Aboriginality, he desperately wanted to succeed in white society. He subsequently joined Northcote, in the Victorian Football Association (VFA), before signing with Fitzroy in the VFL. After his sporting career, he became a pastor of the Churches of Christ Aborigines Mission and co-director of the Aborigines' Advancement League of Victoria. Knighted in 1972, he was appointed governor of South Australia in 1976. Yet it was his football magic that gave him constant status in white society, not his religious or political attributes.

Conceptions changed in the mid-1960s when, as Stokes observes, 'Aborigines increasingly made political claims on the dual basis of equal citizenship and cultural differences'. The 1967 referendum paved the way for Aborigines to be counted in the census and for the federal government to make laws for Aborigines in the states. Thereafter Aborigines became more confident about expressing their Aboriginality and about emphasising the differences between Aboriginal and European cultures. Two quite graphic expressions of Aboriginal identity occurred in the early 1990s. First, in 1993 the Collingwood football crowd gave victorious St Kilda's Nicky Winmar a torrid time:

> The Collingwood cheer-squad had decided to remind Nicky Winmar, an Aborigine...that he was one of them rather than one of us, and they did so in the manner for which they are justly notorious...After the final siren he gave the Magpie cheer-squad as good as he had received, lifting his jumper and pointing to his skin. As spectacularly talented as he is with or near a football, Winmar has never been more eloquent or effective for his cause or his colour than he was in that moment.[48]

Second, Aboriginal sprinter Cathy Freeman paraded an Aboriginal flag on a victory lap at the 1994 Commonwealth games in Victoria (Canada). Ignoring a rebuke from Australian team manager Arthur Tunstall, Freeman carried an Australian and an Aboriginal flag entwined after her next victory at the games. The Australian public turned on Tunstall, while lauding Freeman as a national celebrity.[49] What is so important about these two events is that the press and the public applauded these assertions of Aboriginality. Before the 1990s, such actions would have been harshly condemned.

Aborigines have also become more politically confident, a fact not lost on Sydney's olympic bid committee: it feared Aboriginal groups campaigning actively against the city on the grounds of Australia's poor race relations record. The committee moved to counter this by employing prominent Aborigines—including Charles Perkins, David Clark, Cleonie Quayle, Justine Saunders and Ricky Walford—in the bid effort. The media also assisted, publicising the views of sympathetic Aborigines like Bill Naird, former chairman of the (short-lived) National Aboriginal Conference. Mired in the government's intended legislative response to the High Court's *Mabo* decision,[50] Aborigines initially took little interest in Sydney's olympic bid. The lone exception was the Aboriginal Legal Service (ALS) at Redfern. In a letter to the IOC, the ALS said that 'mistreatment' of Aborigines—including police harassment, drug and alcohol dependency, high rates of imprisonment, unemployment and infant mortality, and racism in sporting institutions—'disqualified' Australia from hosting the games.[51] Members of the IOC didn't take the letter seriously. Some Aboriginal leaders—then Social Justice Commissioner Mick Dodson and lawyer Michael Mansell—became more outspoken and began to threaten boycotts after Sydney won the hosting rights. In the wake of the *Wik* decision,[52] calls by Aborigines for a boycott of Sydney 2000 intensified. In the end, leaders opted for a campaign of shaming white Australia by showing visiting media the people in poverty.

Community

Like international sport, community sport tends to encourage an 'us versus them' mentality. For much of its history, Collingwood Football Club represented the Catholic and right-wing Labor working classes of that 'lowly' inner Melbourne suburb. In the late nineteenth century, Collingwood's arch-rivals were the marginally better-off residents of Fitzroy. Later, supporters directed their animus at the silvertails and toffs from Carlton and Melbourne. Rough play and an air of electricity marked matches between Magpies and Maroons, Magpies and Blues, and Magpies and Demons. 'Pies supporters jostled their opponents and barracked loudly for their men.'[53]

When the Newcastle Knights won the 1997 Australian Rugby League (ARL) premiership, Novocastrians seized the victory to 'state the case' for their city and region. Despite a shadow of gloom hanging over the city—with its steelworks about to close, high youth unemployment, idle shipbuilding yards and memories of the devastating 1989 earthquake still fresh—the rugby league victory demonstrated their resolve to band together and forge ahead. The victory 'proved' that Novocastrians are masters of their own fate and captains of their own souls. Ten months after its fairy-tale victory, ignominy came to Newcastle in the form of three players who tested positive for performance-enhancing drugs.[54] Opponents were quick to insinuate that the club's 1997 success had been drug-induced. The accusations bonded Novocastrians. According to the Anglican dean, Graeme Lawrence, Newcastle is the 'kind of town' that will look after 'our boys and...work through this together'. Novocastrian Mark Richards, a former world surfing champion, adopted a different tack: 'why are they [the ARL's drug-testing agency] picking on the Knights?' he asked.[55]

HISTORY AND CHANGING IDENTITIES

Identities constantly fracture, or undergo redefinition, as individuals and groups ask questions about long-held meanings. They also change when there are shifts in technology and changing patterns of urbanisation, migration and immigration. Each of these factors alters the interests of particular groups and their assumptions about others.

The suggestions by some Aborigines that they should boycott the 2000 olympic games offers one example of a group prepared to challenge long-held meanings about the subservient place of Aborigines in society and the cherished notions of olympism. Recent protests against racial abuse on the football field are another example. Their actions— in particular the Winmar incident—forced the Australian Football League (AFL) to introduce a 'Racial and Religious Vilification' rule in 1995. By expressing dissatisfaction with that rule's lack of bite, Aboriginal players subsequently forced the AFL to impose tougher penalties on players who violate the rule. In 1998 the ARL judiciary, which has no formal vilification code, fined a Canterbury player, Barry Ward, $10000 for racial abuse of St George's Anthony Mundine. Despite the Canterbury cry that this was 'unfair and unAustralian', the penalty stood. With substantial fines and embarrassing disclosures now hanging over clubs and players in at least two codes, one can reasonably expect changes in the behaviour of those who sledge Aborigines.

These are political changes. But other changes reshape identity, such as population shifts. Carlton, an inner-city suburb of Melbourne, offers a good example of how demographic changes can effect community identity and formation. Close to the main workplace in the inter-war years, Carlton developed as a dormitory for the working classes. The post-1945 economic boom conferred new prosperity on many workers who moved to Melbourne's outer suburbs in search of higher status. Poor migrant families, mostly Italian, who needed cheap and convenient housing, replaced the better-off workers. When petrol prices rose dramatically in the 1970s, middle-class professionals, academics, teachers, business people and artists moved to Carlton as a strategy to reduce transport costs. Property prices went up and forced the migrants to cheaper outer suburbs. Each of these groups became involved in the Carlton Football Club, and over three generations they radically changed the club's supporter base and 'the cases' they choose to make: to win for Carlton today means something quite different from what it did half a century ago.[56]

Similarly, Murray Phillips notes that the New South Wales Rugby League's (NSWRL) decision to expel the Glebe Club in 1929 stemmed in part from the industrialisation of the area, which robbed the suburb of its residential base. On the other hand, the addition of Canterbury (1935), Parramatta (1947), Cronulla–Sutherland (1963) and Penrith (1967) to the NSWRL 'reflected demographic changes as many from the working classes left the inner areas of Sydney and moved [outward] with the expansion of city limits'.[57]

Two other factors have radically changed sporting identities in Australia: citizenship, and mass markets and technology.

Citizenship

Thomas Marshall has argued that social citizenship—entitlement to basic social necessities such as education, health care, housing and minimum level of income—has evened out class and status inequalities. What matters, he concludes, is not the equalisation of incomes but rather that

> there is a general enrichment of the concrete substance of civilised life, a general reduction of risk and insecurity, an equalisation between the more and the less fortunate at all levels—between the healthy and the sick, the employed and unemployed, the old and the active, the bachelor and the father of the large family. Equalisation is not so much between classes as between individuals within a population which is now treated as though it were one class. Equality of status is more important than equality of income.[58]

Equality of status doesn't mean that all are automatically equal and therefore political and legal action are not necessary. McKay cites the case of sports manager 'Erica'. She threatened legal action after her boss 'refused to ratify her promotion to a senior position'. In her words, 'suddenly, because I was in a position where legal action was a threat, it was amazing how they reversed rudder. Up until that stage I had not taken much interest in the [affirmative action] legislation, but I suddenly appreciated being in a position of having some back-up'.[59]

Social citizenship has changed the nature of poverty, a point well made by Helen Epstein: 'In the past poverty meant leaky roofs, exposed sewage, poor nutrition, and risky workplaces, and the diseases of poverty included tuberculosis, cholera and scarlet fever. Today poverty means not being able to entertain friends, buy children new clothes, eat out or have holidays.'[60] Social citizenship has changed the nature of sports consumption. Today's middle and lower classes now pursue a far greater range of pursuits than in the Great Depression, when the choice was between cheap football and expensive golf. Similarly, the state's commitment to welfare provision allows a significant number of youth to pursue, full-time, different recreational lifestyles on unemployment benefits.

Mass Markets and Technology

Technology is a good illustration of how changes in objective conditions can influence sport. In 1858 an electric telegraph joined Adelaide with Sydney via Melbourne. The line helped bring the three cities closer as newspapers in each place began to regularly 'publish a few inches...of telegraphic intelligence about the others, including the weather, the business of parliament, the movement of ships and the price of goods, and seasonal news of racing and cricket'.[61] More important were the mass circulation papers that emerged in the late nineteenth century. They gave businesses a new medium in which to advertise their products to larger and increasingly better-educated audiences. Sport was a popular topic for newspapers: they kept fans informed about their team's progress and their players' exploits. To improve their public profile or to boost awareness of products, businesses quickly learned to associate their wares with popular sports and star players. Some companies found it profitable to sponsor specific sports and underwrite particular events. Dunlop, for example, supported cycling, motor racing and tennis. Radio increased advertising and sponsorship opportunities, but television, and colour screens in particular, created a totally new game—for the broadcasting and communication industries and sport. Television increased advertising and sponsorship opportunities and multiplied a hundredfold the number of corporations seeking to invest in sport. Television loved sport: it drew large audiences, was relatively cheap to cover, and generated huge revenue from advertisers. Sports associations loved television: it laid 24-carat eggs.

Television did not flock to every sport. It restricted coverage to the 'main' popular games—cricket, Australian football, and league—to the detriment of 'minor' sports like cycling and swimming, which, because they couldn't attract coverage, lost sponsorships. Sports thus found themselves competing for limited coverage. Survival depended on restructuring. In 1983 the NSWRL underwent a thorough overhaul: professional administrators replaced volunteers, a board of nine directors (only two represented the clubs) replaced the general committee of 52 club representatives, and a specialised bureaucracy developed employing financial, development and marketing managers. Clubs replicated these centralised bureaucracies, employing business managers, public relations and promotional personnel and legal services. Murray Phillips attributes this restructuring to the impact of television. New teams—such as Canberra, Illawarra, Brisbane, Gold Coast, Newcastle, Townsville, Auckland and a second team from Brisbane—'had little to do with accommodating major junior nurseries, Labor Party affiliations, Catholic connections or working-class demographic patterns but, rather, had to do with a desire to maximise television sponsorship potential'.[62]

Income from the media, sponsorship and marketing thus replaced gate receipts as the main source of income. This effectively changed many of the fundamentals of sport: players increasingly looked on sport as an avenue to financial security; corporate sponsors seized the images, insignia, symbols and uniforms that were once proudly owned and displayed by local communities and social classes; league officials changed the rules to make games more conducive to the logic and timing of television; billionaire moguls transferred events from free-to-air television to subscription television; and league officials forced clubs to amalgamate and relocate to bigger population centres. The fundamentals also changed in other ways. Sponsors began to dictate, on penalty of withdrawing their support, who would or wouldn't play; they began to demand tailor-made sport, faster cricket, slow-motion golf, tenser, shorter tennis matches, fewer scrums in rugby, more time-outs for ads. Even after several decades of televised sport, sponsors and television executives neither know, love, like, respect or care about the games they show. Sport, like sitcoms, is a product, a commodity, to be shaped and shifted as the financial bottom line dictates.

On the other hand, television has clearly benefited some sports and made them more popular by insisting that games be exciting and entertaining. In 1977, after the Australian Cricket Board (ACB) refused to grant Kerry Packer's Nine Network exclusive television rights to Test matches, Packer signed most of the world's leading cricketers and created a new limited-overs competition. His actions outraged cricket officials, former players, journalists and many academics, who accused the media mogul of hijacking Australia's national game. World Series Cricket (WSC) may have dismayed cricket purists, but 'bumper crowds' were testimony to immense popular support. Richard Cashman concludes that 'the WSC upheaval' caused 'a remarkable shift in the culture of Australian cricket. [It] helped strip away many of the Anglicist, clubby, gentlemanly vestiges of the game' and ensured that cricket became 'more Australian (and less Anglo-Australian) and more plebeian'. Packer gave cricket a more 'appropriate' culture, one better suited to 'a Republican and multicultural Australia'.[63]

However much the media act as the source of revenue for advertisers, for particular sports and celebrities, they nevertheless represent a rather false picture of what constitutes life in Australia. 'Sport', claims a *Sydney Morning Herald* editorial, 'has a cathartic and redemptive power that is often disregarded by uninformed critics'.[64] The editor postulates that competitive Test cricket in the West Indies and Australia 'goes beyond ideology...to an expression of the validity of the politics, lifestyle, the culture and aspirations of the people'. We believe these qualities are quite exaggerated by 'uninformed' editors: if Australian ideology, politics, culture, lifestyle and aspirations are indeed contingent on the values and behaviour of the severely 'compromised' Mark Waugh and Shane Warne and the spitting, petulant Glenn McGrath, the nation is in jeopardy.[65] To watch and to listen is to believe that perhaps 60 to 80 per cent of our lives is consumed with, for, or about sport. Worse, perhaps, is the belief by those who promote or play sport that the entire nation shares their values and interests. Football is, indeed, more than a game—for those who are passionate about the activity. For those who lack the agonies and ecstasies that come with 'fanhood', for those who are not 'true Australians', it is a blight. Pilita Clark is wrong when she says there are 'thousands' out there with no interest: the figure is hundreds of thousands, probably millions. The noted British television critic Milton

Shulman once said of the BBC that it had 'become a giant dope-pedlar doing its best to fix the nation on some sort of drug which offers togetherness and happiness through sport'—and by so doing, it encourages an unhealthy preoccupation which 'diminishes awareness of other activities life has to offer'.[66] That was said in the mid-1970s of what has been well described as 'the least worst television in the world'. What would he say about the Australian industry at the century's end?

The last words on sport and television come from Brian Cooney, a director of the world's largest sports managers, International Management Group. The context was a report which showed that while there are twice as many arts followers as sports watchers, Australian business invested $282 million in sports sponsorship in 1996–97 and only $29 million in arts and culture. Cooney explained: 'Sponsorship is about building relationships and with sport, blokes can do blokey things. You are with your mates having a few beers and a talk. The problem with the theatre is you can't talk during it.'[67]

In the next chapters we trace the development and transformation of sport in Australia from the colonial era to the present day. The primary function of sport, we argue, is to connect individuals, but in practice this usually means connecting with other 'pre-sorted', like-minded individuals and groups. Connection always involves sorting, separating, and differentiating others.

2
Currency and Sterling
1788–1868

The twelve years from the founding of the colony to the turn into the nineteenth century were largely a history of a tightening of the alcoholic grip on the little settlement, a grossness of sexual mores and practices, indulgence in some blood sports and the first crude manifestations of the theatre... Official celebrations and entertainments in the first couple of decades were little more than some formal flotsam on a turbulent society.

—J. W. C. CUMES[1]

[Newspapers are] stuffed almost to nausea, with advertisements and accounts of races, cricket matches, boxing matches, and regattas; with challenges to fight, to run, or to row, addressed by one obscure candidate for notoriety to another; and with the lengthy descriptions of contests, either by land or water, between the colonial youth and natives of England, or to use the phrase of the colony, between currency and sterling.

—THE REVEREND JOHN DUNMORE LANG[2]

EARLY SPORT

Despite the isolation, hardships and depravity associated with the convict settlements, games and pastimes quickly became important in
colonial culture. In 1880 James Hogan, a Victorian essayist, speculated
on 'The Coming Australian'. He didn't particularly like his vision. For
him, the three main characteristics of the 'native Australian' were 'an
inordinate love of field-sports', 'a very decided disinclination to recognise the authority of parents and superiors', and 'a grievous dislike to
mental effort'.[3] There was a certain prescience about Hogan, though he
was roundly criticised at the time. Henry Ling Roth, an essayist and
contemporary of Hogan, countered by questioning whether Australians
had 'already fallen so low that the Melbourne Public Library is becoming a useless institution'?[4]

We didn't have the sharp and often violent cleavages of Mother England, especially of the kind where the Game Laws gave hunting
prerogatives only to the wealthy ruling classes. Yet sport didn't connect
Australians in any organic sense. Among the upper classes, which largely
consisted of government officials and regimental officers, 'entertainment
was "genteel". Public entertainment was of a traditional, mostly formal
kind. Private dinners, suppers, cards, water-parties, some subscription
dances and, for men, cricket and hunting (mostly kangaroos) provided
a fair range of entertainment'.[5] In contrast, life among the lower classes
was 'all riot, revelry and drunkenness'.[6] Early colonial sport, in short,
expressed the dispositions, values, tastes, aesthetics and lifestyles of different social groups.

Social groups are never static. They exist in a state of constant flux,
with values and interests shifting in response to new economic, political
and social conditions. This is particularly true in immigrant societies
such as Australia. In many respects, migration is a simple process of
cultural transplantation. But this is truer for the upper classes, who have
the capital to simply transport their styles and tastes. When George
Watson of Ballydarton, Carlow, in Ireland, arrived in Victoria in 1852,
he brought with him some 'hounds from his father's kennels', which

'formed the first pack to make war on the kangaroos'. He became Master of the Melbourne Hounds. The hunting establishment then bought hounds from 'some of the best kennels in the United Kingdom, including those of the Duke of Buccleugh and the Duke of Grafton, and also from the famous Belvoir pack'. In 1857 the Chirnsides of Werribee Park imported some red deer and later they invited Mr Watson to 'bring his pack along'.[7]

For the middle and working classes, migration invariably involved compromise with other groups from different backgrounds. The Irish, who brought Gaelic sports to Australia, generally found it difficult to establish permanent clubs and associations because they found themselves constantly moving in search of work. Thus they preferred to 'Australianise rather than opt out for a sporting ghetto'.[8]

Change was certainly a hallmark of early Australian society. In the 1820s the development of the wool industry, together with assisted migration, shifted the balance of economic and political power away from the military and merchants to large landowners and graziers. The discovery of gold in the 1850s shifted the balance again, this time towards professionals and the urban middle classes. Gold brought about the largest middle-class migration ever seen: it was Victorian, respectable, temperate, religious and driven by money.[9] 'A complete mental madness appears to have seized every member of the community', wrote an unknown *Sydney Morning Herald* reporter in 1851.[10] Gold finds in the 1850s enabled some diggers and traders to transform themselves into a bourgeois establishment.[11] Australians have proudly equated social change with social mobility. Certainly there were success stories.[12] While some convicts remained trapped in the deprivations of the lower orders, the majority 'flourished modestly', as Ken Inglis notes, in trades or as small traders. A few emancipated convicts accrued great wealth, while others became influential in politics. From the 1830s, some 'assisted emigrants and sons of convicts' gained mobility through election to the Legislative Council and later to the Legislative Assembly. Relative comfort, however, doesn't necessarily confer economic, political or social independence. Economically, the colonies were 'not so much a new world as a capitalist extension of the old'. It was no coincidence that limited numbers of Irish Catholics, few Chinese and no Aborigines experienced social mobility in Australia: the victims of Australia's 'colonial enterprise' simply never enjoyed social power.[13]

In the early period few Australians challenged long-established ideas about social rank and order, an order the British expressed in the cricketing metaphor of 'gentlemen' (aristocratic amateurs) and 'players' (working-class professionals):

> Few contested the idea that the [social] ladder was necessary and appro-
> priate. There were enough visible differences in ways of life and manners
> between rich and poor, educated and uneducated, landowners and labour-
> ers, to make it easy to see them as different kinds of people. Clothing,
> cut of hair, bearing, manners, accent and even the weathering of the skin
> distinguished a poor working man from a gentleman employer. Educated
> observers tended to dwell on the lack of restraint on the part of the poor:
> their voices were louder, their gestures larger, their tastes cruder. Their
> conversation was stained with profanity and sexual allusion. They were
> quick to violence especially when drunk.[14]

COLLECTIVE TEAMWORK?

Sport is an ideal way to assess social relationships in the first 80 years of settlement. As Europeans arrived, governors, officers, ranks, convicts, free settlers, emancipists, Irish Catholics, Chinese and Aborigines pursued their own sporting tastes and social relationships. The crucial point, as Cumes notes, is that the general provision of recreation and sport 'lay in private hands'. The reason was simple: sport is one area where people chose (and choose) to come together to be with others of their own kind. Thus different groups catered for their own interests and tastes, to the exclusion of others, and they raised their own funds by subscriptions, entry fees and other dues.[15] Early governments occasionally made land available for recreation and sport, provided convict labour to build facilities, and promulgated public holidays.[16] In 1810 Governor Macquarie proclaimed Hyde Park as Sydney's first designated area for horse-racing, cricket, quoits, hurling and football. But in all other respects sport was essentially a private affair, although there was a reasonable coincidence of public and private sport.

We turn to the membership, history, and sporting relationships of the different 'teams' in early Australia, essentially to 1868 but with some references to Aboriginal cricket up to 1916. Most strikingly, there is precious little evidence of 'collective teamwork', of a nation forging connections, or connections forging a nation, of an over-arching patriotism and a common loyalty.

GOVERNOR PATRONAGE

At the apex of the social hierarchy sat the early governors. The first four governors of New South Wales were naval officers and their successors, army officers. All graduated through the ranks and most came from relatively humble lower-middle-class backgrounds, advancing 'through dint of application and benefit of patronage'.[17]

Cumes argues that the governors generally saw their role as supporting rather than providing, controlling or funding private sport. But Cumes doesn't distinguish between 'provision' and 'control'. This is somewhat strange because later he describes the first horse-races in Sydney in 1810 as an occasion for convicts to 'metaphorically doff their iron collars'. Further on he observes that staff took 'utmost care' when deciding 'the guest lists for dinners and balls at Government House [in Hobart Town]' and 'only acceptable ladies and gentlemen received a card'.[18] John O'Hara considers early horse-racing carnivals a classic example of social control:

> The building of a racecourse close to the town was a deliberate part of Macquarie's recreation policy. Race meetings at Hyde Park were part of a program of annual recreations which included an Easter fair and Whit-suntide celebrations. In promoting such leisure activities, Macquarie was simultaneously bringing some order to colonial recreation by confining it to specified periods and he was defining the role of the colonial governor as something akin to the rural landlord of early eighteenth-century Britain.[19]

A song at a commemoration dinner in 1820, recorded in the *Sydney Gazette*, shows much of these interrelated values: the first verse toast was to 'OLD ENGLAND FOR EVER!'; the second verse toast was to 'OUR KING, BOYS, FOR EVER!'; the third, 'THE PRINCE REGENT FOR EVER!'; the fourth, 'AUSTRALIA FOR EVER!'; and finally, but ambiguous as to the ascending or descending order, 'MACQUARIE FOR EVER!'[20]

In Britain rural landlords used wakes, fairs and carnivals to control the lower orders. Such events were unrestrained merrymaking in the lives of ordinary people. They were 'temporary liberation from the prevailing truth and from the established order', a time marked by 'the suspension of all hierarchical rank, privileges, norms and prohibitions'. The social order was so strong that such 'temporary liberation' posed no threat.[21] Such thinking, O'Hara concludes, was undoubtedly 'responsible for Macquarie's decision in 1811 that all mechanics and labourers in government service should enjoy holidays on all three days of the annual race carnival'. According to the political logic of the time, 'it was better to have such events carefully controlled, patronised and concentrated into celebrations under the control of the government and the elite than to permit the continuance of haphazard spontaneous race meetings which might not be so controlled'.[22]

THE OFFICER CLASS

Military and civil officers were granted land, used convict labour, and stumbled upon a monopoly of trade because the British government neglected to provide the colony with a treasury. Sterling salaries gave them economic power, which was supplemented by patronage links, social position and the all-embracing code of honour. Military officers played an important role in organising several sports, especially those associated with eighteenth-century gentlemen, such as horse-racing and cricket. They bred horses and promoted racing and hunting. Officers of the 73rd regiment organised the first official race meeting in New South Wales—a three-day event in October 1810. The racing carnival was an annual event until the army command transferred the regiment to Ceylon (Sri Lanka).[23] One of the earliest accounts of a hunt also involved officers from that regiment. They had brought packs of hounds to New South Wales and early in 1811 killed a kangaroo 'after an exciting run of two hours'.[24] These things had been done much earlier by the New South Wales Corps: for example, Colonel George Johnston was into private racing in the early 1800s.

Among officers, regimental teams and sporting competitions served three functions: to cement relationships within the 'caste', to define social status, and to show individual bravery, the latter again emphasising honour. Ensign Best's account of a cricket match between two regiments at Norfolk Island in 1838 illustrates these 'functions':

> There was great excitement; in the Barracks men rushing violently about and betting figs of Tobacco on the result of the game, on the cricket ground a pitching of wickets and tents. At half past twelve the playing commenced and lasted till five when the 50th were declared victorious; this was a result I had expected, few of our men having taken a bat in

hand since leaving England while all our adversaries had had at least two years practice. At the men's request I challenged them to play again on that day fortnight. A Pig with a soaped tail was then turned loose and afforded great amusement after which the men ran races in sacks. All these diversions having ceased, we returned the men with their Pig to their barracks and we to my room where dinner was ready; when this was disposed of we adjourned to the mess room and danced all night.[25]

Officers did play civilians, but as the nineteenth century advanced they organised sport around the regiment and barracks. Much of their status derived from their exclusivity, their championing of pre-industrial ideals in an increasingly bourgeois world. David Mann, a transported forger who received a pardon in 1802 and then worked as a clerk, recorded that officers in Sydney 'built a private billiard room, by subscription, for their own use'.[26] Here it is important not to confuse status with morality, as Rickard makes clear:

> Governors, officers and free settlers often waxed loud about the moral failings of the convicts, particularly their drunkenness and sexual proclivities. Yet they, the rulers, were hardly paragons. In the early years many found it easy to overcome their distaste and took convict women as mistresses. A young surgeon arriving in Moreton Bay in 1830 remarked that 'all the officers here are desperate grog-drinkers and cigar smokers'... Archdeacon Scott, returning to New South Wales, complained more generally that he saw 'the same persons, pursuing the same licentious and profligate lives still in authority, setting forth all their bad examples of vice [as] they did when I was here before'.[27]

THE LOWLY RANKS

Sitting between the officers and convicts were the rank-and-file soldiers. Not a distinct status group, they typically shared common class and lifestyle positions with their convict charges. This was especially true after the formation of the New South Wales Corps in 1789. 'Most members of the Corps had been labourers, and in social background were not so very different from the convicts, except that more came originally from the country and smaller towns. Many were bludgeoned into enlistment by the same social and economic conditions which had educated the convicts in the ways of crime.'[28]

THE CONVICTS

Three-quarters of the (approximately) 168 000 convicted men and women who arrived in the Australian colonies were sentenced in Britain, and the majority were, in Rickard's words, 'products of a growing urban criminal subculture'. The ultimate source of that under-class was 'the industrial revolution, and the corresponding dislocation of rural life [that] swelled the ranks of the migratory poor'. Rickard makes three claims in support of his 'criminal subculture' thesis. First, possibly two-thirds of those transported to Australia had previous convictions. While often 'the offences appear trivial', the courts tended to consider 'the offender's reputation and other crimes of which he or she was suspected'. Second, probably no more than 300 of the rural convicts 'were convicted of poaching, and these were more likely to have been members of organised poaching gangs than hungry labourers'. Lastly, three out of five convicts were transported after 1830, during a period of penal law reform, and 'they tended to be more serious offenders than those despatched earlier'.[29]

Whether in government service or on assignment to free settlers, convicts 'worked nine hours a day for five days of the week and a five-hour day on Saturday, with intervals on the weekdays for breakfast and dinner. After these hours [they] could sell [their] labour for wages to an employer'.[30] Long though these hours were, Tom Dunning contends that 'convict workers were no worse off than other early industrial workers and generally lived a better life'. Drunkenness and smoking may well have been the principal forms of recreation, but Dunning notes that many convicts spent their free time 'snaring meat and fishing'. While hunting and fishing were upper-class pastimes, among convicts they were 'survival activities' necessary to supplement their meagre rations.[31]

Observers frequently commented on the lower orders' 'reckless addiction' to gambling. George Barrington, a thrice-transported pickpocket who rose to the position of superintendent of convicts at Parramatta, wrote about the 'excess' of that 'pernicious vice of gaming' among convicts in the mid-1790s.[32] David Mann agreed, charging convicts with carrying gaming to 'the most deplorable excesses'. 'Next to drinking', he said, 'this unprincipled practice' was 'the chief pleasure and amusement of the lower classes of the prisoners'.[33] In 1819 Lord Bathurst, Secretary of State for the Colonies, appointed John Bigge to assess society in New South Wales. In a report that would determine the future of transportation to Australia, Bigge described convicts at the Hunter River settlement gambling with their food ration and convicts in Sydney who 'spent their free time at the Rocks practising "every debauchery and villainy", including gambling'.[34] In 1858 William Jevons wrote a series of articles on the 'social cesspools of Sydney'. Of The Rocks, he wrote: 'I am acquainted with most of the notorious parts of London…but in none of these places, perhaps, would lower forms of vice and misery be seen.'[35]

THE FREE SETTLERS

While initially only a small minority, the number of free settlers steadily increased after 1820. By 1851, when the total population of Australia was under 440 000, convicts comprised only 1.5 per cent; former convicts added another 14 per cent. The Colonial Office preferred men of capital and genteel birth as emigrants.[36] The results were new political alliances and social distinctions.

The wealthier emigrants quickly established themselves as large proprietors of land and as substantial merchants. Politically, they aligned themselves with governors. Wealth gained by trade didn't ensure social acceptance: 'respectability' resided with officials of the colony—soldiers, judges, clergy and administrators—and 'older landed families whose pedigree in the colony extended beyond one generation'. Thus merchants who hoped for invitations to the governor's levee and ball on the monarch's birthday were mostly disappointed.[37] Large property-owners were known as 'pure merinos', a sneering term (since it linked the graziers to their animals) particularly associated with John Macarthur and his family. He arrived as an army officer in 1790, became a landowner and trader and flourished as a pastoral magnate after colonial officials in Britain gave him 5000 acres on which to experiment with growing wool from Spanish merino sheep.

Officers and 'pure merinos' considered themselves a colonial gentry. They affirmed their status by excluding from social intercourse all convicts who had served their term—called emancipists—and their children, even when rich and successful.[38] The new ruling classes were 'not only free and unconvicted' but they 'could boast of having no collateral relationship or distant affinity with those in whose escutcheon there was a blot'.[39]

Sport, especially hunting, horse-racing and cricket, helped distinguish the upper classes and reinforce their status and feelings of social superiority. For those members of the upper classes who formed the Adelaide

Kangaroos in Danger: *an 1822 book by Van Diemen's Land surveyor-general described one of Tasmania's great attractions—flocks of 'roos waiting for the slaughter. George Watson, from Ireland, arrived in Victoria in 1852 with some hounds 'to make war on the kangaroos'.*
TOWN & COUNTRY JOURNAL, 14 APRIL 1877

Hunt Club in 1842, 'the baying of the hounds, the sound of the horn and the wearing of "the pink"...reassured them of their status in the antipodes'.[40] Early sporting clubs also offered the ruling classes an opportunity to 'meet and fraternise with gentlemen of similar social standing'.[41] In principle, gentlemen were 'men with aristocratic connections in England', who pursued 'the leisured way of life' on large estates. Few actually met these criteria, and so they settled for 'good education, passable manners and financial success in an occupation that gave the appearance of leisure'.[42]

In Sydney, Sir John Jamieson proposed the creation of the Sydney Turf Club. The first patron was Governor Brisbane and first chairman was John Mackaness, sheriff of New South Wales. Prominent members included Captain John Piper and William Wentworth, tribune, barrister and pastoralist. To ensure social exclusivity and status, the club's founders set an entrance fee of £5 and an annual subscription of £4.

Similarly, the Melbourne Club offered members accommodation and indoor recreations, while the Melbourne Cricket Club catered for the outdoor pursuits of a small 'inner circle' that literally drove the social, business, charitable and philanthropic side of the town.[43]

Accounts of their pastimes suggest that the free settlers of lower class enjoyed considerable freedom. In the early years of settlement they celebrated traditional Anglo-Saxon folk festivals such as April Fool's Day, Easter and Whitsun.

[The] fun was often strident and guileless, full of practical jokes and ludicrous caperings. Pranksters yelled 'fire' on April Fool's Day. Seven girls ran a race for a chemise trimmed with 'British blue and scarlet ribbands'. Grimaciers grimaced through their horse-collars. A black (or blackened) man threw himself about like a crazed antelope, to the guffaws of the admiring throng.

Cockfighting and bull-baiting were part of the Whitsuntide celebrations in June 1810. Cumes cites an interesting story from the *Sydney Gazette* of the same month that recounts an incident during the bull-baiting:

The amateurs of bull-baiting were elegantly amused with that very refined diversion, in the course of which, we understand, a number of useless dogs were killed or crippled . . . In the end, the provoked animal, breaking from his tether, rushed in amidst the group of spectators [and almost gave] a tragical termination to the sports of the day.[44]

Publicans and public houses catered for the carousing, entertainment and sporting interests of the free settlers: cricket, foot races, billiards, bowling, quoits, skittles, pigeon-shooting, boxing and wrestling. The close association between sport, alcohol and gambling meant that public houses were a congenial location for sport. The first cricket clubs in Sydney were attached to public houses. Publicans organised teams, put up stake-money and hosted meetings and club dinners. By the 1840s, 'some publicans were organising, and investing, in sport on a substantial scale'.[45] In 1861 two enterprising Melbourne publicans, Felix Spiers and Christopher Pond, underwrote a tour of Australia by a team of English cricketers. It earned the backers a handsome profit of £11 000.[46]

Pedestrianism, the name given to professional athletics, was probably the most popular sport for gambling activity. The newspapers talked constantly about men 'running stiff' in order to gain a few yards from the handicappers, and those who so ran were always referred to as 'dead birds'. From the 1840s, much money changed hands on Saturdays and holidays after walking and running races. William Francis King, who sold pies from a tray in Sydney, was known as 'the flying pieman' for his pedestrian feats. In one event, which he won, King raced against a coach between Brisbane and Ipswich while carrying a pole weighing 100 pounds. On Easter Monday 1870, about 15 000 people filled Sydney's Albert Ground to watch three champion Englishmen compete in hand-icap races against local 'peds'.[47]

Occasionally leisure and sporting pastimes threw the different classes together. In 1838 Lady Franklin, wife of Sir John Franklin, the governor of Van Diemen's Land (Tasmania), organised a regatta to celebrate the anniversary of the discovery of the island by Abel Tasman. Several reports of the occasion commented that the 'high and low, rich and poor were commingled together apparently intent only upon the enjoyment of the animated and bustling scene before them'.[48] One should be wary of reading such accounts literally. Marian Aveling reminds us that such activities were 'usually organised so that different classes did not actu-ally mix. Colonists saw no contradiction in simultaneously celebrating the "commingling" of the classes and, like the elite of Hobart Town, sep-arating themselves from the throng by retreating to marquees and Persian carpets on the grass'. After all, 'church congregations divided into people with status and money enough to rent high-backed pews, and people who knelt on the floor or sat on benches at the rear. Theatres segre-gated their audience by purse and reputation, providing separate entrances so that the patrons of their more expensive seats could avoid rubbing against poor people and prostitutes'.[49]

EMANCIPISTS, CURRENCY AND STERLING

In the 1820s Colonial Office policy sharply distinguished free settlers from emancipists and their Australian-born children, to whom the upper classes referred by the derogatory name 'currency'.[50] The policy favoured the former with respect to political, economic and social advancement.[51] It also gave rise to rancorous divisions. Charles Darwin observed 'much jealousy between the children of the rich emancipist and the free settlers'.[52] Neither emancipists nor 'currency' welcomed free 'bloody emi-grants', who they considered had 'come to take the country from us'.[53] Clark reminds us that 'this xenophobia of the native born was the first of a long line of claims to exclusive possession, and the forerunner of later slogans such as "Australia for the Australians", or "Australia for the white man"'.[54]

Sport did not ameliorate matters. Popular recreational activities in the 1820s and 1830s 'were in large part a series of sporting contests between representatives' of 'currency' (Australian-born) and 'sterling' (born in Britain or Ireland). For the participants, the matches were serious: it was a 'matter of keen interest to discover how the natives compared with men born at home when their speed, strength and skill were put to the test'.[55] Moreover, relationships often soured. In 1826 a group of emancipists formed the Australian Cricket Club. A decade later the club split after John and William Hardy, two British-born, Cambridge-educated brothers joined. Ostensibly the cause of the split was the brothers' round-arm bowling style. But 'the public heat generated by the split suggests that the more educated and refined Hardy brothers did not get on well with their colonial club-mates'.[56]

Emancipists and currency were an important lobby for democracy and liberalism. Their champion was William Wentworth, who famously set himself against the 'exclusives'—the men of rank in the military or the colonial administration. He called them 'the yellow snakes of the Colony' and urged his supporters and followers to 'deprive' them 'of their venom and their fangs'.[57] Wentworth developed an intense hatred of the despotic and arrogant Governor Darling, who in turn described Wentworth as 'a vulgar, ill-bred fellow, utterly unconscious of the Common Civilities, due from one gentleman to another'.[58] The antagonism spilled into the sporting arena. In November 1827 Wentworth, in a speech at a dinner of the exclusive Sydney Turf Club (of which he was a founding member), attacked Darling. Robert Wardell, editor of Wentworth's *Australian* newspaper, continued the denigration of Darling at the next Turf Club dinner in December. Darling retaliated: he 'withdrew vice-regal patronage' from the club, 'forbade all officers or employees of the government membership of the club', and he punished those who continued their association in defiance of his ban. The Sydney Turf Club thus 'lost its position of importance, with those members who found it necessary or profitable to court the governor's favour' establishing rival clubs. The 'ultimate victor in the struggle' was the Australian Racing and Jockey Club, founded in 1828, known as the Governor's Club.[59] 'Rejoice, Australia! Darling's reign has passed', wrote Wardell in 1831, as the unpopular governor left Australian shores.[60]

By the 1850s the terms 'emancipist', 'currency' and 'sterling' had nearly disappeared from common use. Settled residents became known as colonists. But the new term did not miraculously erase social divisions. On the contrary, political, social and economic divisions between Irish Catholics and Anglo-Saxon Protestants intensified.

The Irish

About a quarter of the convict population came directly from Ireland, with another 6000 born in Ireland but arrested in England. Unlike their English counterparts, 'the majority were rural offenders' and many were convicted for 'agrarian protest' against British domination.[61] Irish convicts and their descendants never forgot that the law which sentenced them was an alien British law; even in Australia 'a sense of cultural protest' tended to 'fortify' them.[62] As emancipists, a smaller portion of Irish Catholics achieved social mobility. Protestant mistrust of Catholics, whether Irish or English, travelled to Australia on convict transports, and in the new land it persisted and grew:[63]

> The Protestants mocked at the Catholics' low standard of living, their stooping to their priests, their superstitions, the tinsel and ornament surrounding their acts of religious devotion. The Catholics grieved at the Protestants for sundering the unity of Christendom, for performing ceremonies that were but a pale shadow of their own rich liturgy, and for seeming to condemn a portion of God's children to a perpetual position of inferiority in society.[64]

By the 1850s Irish Catholics constituted between a quarter and a third of the population of New South Wales, between a quarter and a fifth in Victoria, a fifth in Van Diemen's Land and a tenth in South Australia. Like the emancipists, the vast majority of free Irish emigrants were Catholic and poor: 'they were people of peasant stock with little money, education, or skill, forced off their land by poverty and after 1845 by starvation.' And like the earlier generation of convicts, Irish free settlers retained a sense of cultural protest. St Patrick's Day was a time for the Irish to affirm communal solidarity and to talk of their achievements, hopes and grievances. On every anniversary Irishmen caroused in taverns and rampaged through streets indulging in what their critics liked to call pat-*riot*-ism. Peaceful St Patrick's Days even made news in the Protestant press. In 1836 the *Sydney News* reported that 'not a single head was broken, nor a hilelah was to be seen'; in 1837 the *Colonist* observed that St Patrick's Day had 'passed off very quietly, and there was less drunkenness than usual', while the following year the same paper was 'happy to hear that there were not many heads broken'; in 1849 the Hobart *Town Courier* commented favourably on the anniversary in Sydney, noting that it 'passed over in a manner highly credible to the lower orders of the Irish population'.[65]

THE STATUS OF WOMEN

It is necessary to correct some points in the literature on women's participation in colonial leisure, recreation and sport. In general this body of writing has 'hidden and down played both the nature and extent of women's physical activity'.[66] Like men, European women in Australia participated in the leisure pursuits, games and sports of their respective classes. But while acknowledging the extent of women's physical activity in the early colonial period, historians should not exaggerate its nature. Marion Stell conveys the erroneous impression that early colonial women engaged in recreation and leisure independently of men. She refers to Annie Baxter, who 'went on a picnic-type expedition which lasted several days, in the course of which she climbed Ben Lomond Mountain'; she describes Ann Dixon, who 'absconded from her employment as a housemaid and was later apprehended enjoying a game of cards and a drink'; and she reports on Jane Eliza, 'who sat in on a card game at the Governor's Ball in Perth in 1832, first lost heavily and then regained her finances during the course of the night'. Closer scrutiny of her sources shows that these women closely identified themselves with their male partners' attitudes and activities and that they were engaging in mixed activities. Baxter climbed Ben Lomond as a member of a party; Dixon enjoyed her drink and cards with 'her swain', convict and rope-maker Samuel Drew; and Eliza and her husband had their 'revenge at cards'.[67]

This, of course, raises the question of why we treat women as a separate group. Our answer is simple: the early colonial period laid the foundations for a particular view of women that increasingly discriminated against those who didn't conform to middle-class ideals. Rickard makes this point well with respect to convict women, who comprised a sixth of British convicts and a quarter of the Irish: 'the colonial gaolers saw the female convicts as a bad lot but this condemnation often seemed to derive from the shocked realisation that these women contemptuously disregarded middle class notions of femininity.' Here Rickard refers specifically to marriage and family:

> Most of the women claimed to be single, and nearly all were listed as domestic servants; they were usually convicted of some form of larceny. Some were noted as being... 'on the town', but prostitution itself was not an offence carrying transportation. The society in which they moved had placed little store on marriage and family, but a disdain for such values was more reprehensible if exhibited by women than by men. If, in the colonies, the female convicts aspired to marriage it was for decidedly prac-tical reasons.[68]

Such views persisted after the introduction of assisted female immi-gration in the mid-1830s. In lending its support to one scheme, the NSW Legislative Council said that the women 'should not work beyond a short stint as domestic servants'. Rather, they 'should marry and raise large families, restore the equilibrium of the sexes, raise the value of female character and produce virtuous homes for the labouring classes'. In real life, few female assisted immigrants 'accorded with this ideal'. Most were working-class, impoverished, and poorly educated and trained; many were Irish Catholics. Like their convict predecessors, these women were judged harshly by a middle-class ideal that found them 'lacking in refinement and respectability and economically and industri-ally useless'. The denigratory comments given below in Chapters 3 and 4, and the emphases on trivia such as teeth (see page 10), testify to these perceptions. This same model also offered limited 'economic opportunities outside the home or beyond the farm, other than in low paid and low status domestic service, and later in manufacturing'. Not surprisingly then, most free women 'sought marriage as the only socially sanctioned career for a "respectable" woman'.[69]

GOLD, GAMBLING AND THE CHINESE

Gold enticed male Chinese workers to Australia, just as it attracted Euro-peans. Some 3500 Chinese had arrived in Victoria by June 1854, 10000 by the end of that year, 18000 by the middle of the following year, and 42000 by the end of 1858. Chinese constituted about 15 per cent of the male population in 1858, and Governor Hotham's commission of inquiry into the goldfields predicted further arrivals. There was no welcome mat. On the contrary, anti-Chinese sentiment prevailed on the back of feelings that, in the words of Hotham's commissioners, they 'tend to demoralise colonial society by the low scale of domestic comfort, by an incurable habit of gaming and other vicious tendencies, and by the examples of degrading and absurd superstition'. Unfortunately for the Chinese, they began arriving as the surface gold ran out, and their mere presence incited resentment and rivalry. At several fields, many diggers advocated driving the Chinese home. In mid-1857 at Buckland River in north-east Victoria, 'between fifty and hundred men carrying pick-handles' attacked Chinese miners, who

> fled down the gorge. Their tents and joss-house were burned, and their bedding was thrown into the river. Three of the aggressors were wounded by shots from the Chinese. An unknown number of Chinese were drowned or died later from wounds or exposure. Policemen from Beech-worth...persuaded Chinese diggers to return from hiding in the bush and arrested a number of white men, most of whom were acquitted by juries in Beechworth and cheered as heroes when they left the court house.[70]

The Victorian government espoused the white miners' cause and resolved, in the words of John Pascoe Fawkner, a member of the Legislative Council, to 'control the flood of Chinese immigration...and effectually prevent the Gold Fields of Australia Felix from becoming the property of the Emperor of China and of the Mongolian and Tartar hordes of Asia'. Ken Inglis comments that the Chinese emperor, 'labouring to resist the intrusion of European powers, would have been amazed to know of his alleged designs on Victoria'.

Fear prevailed. The government of Victoria imposed inordinately heavy taxes on Chinese arrivals and miners. Appeals and protests earned Chinese diggers no sympathy, and in the 1860s their numbers declined in Victoria. Many fled to New South Wales where 'Chinkies', 'Chows', 'Celestials' and 'John Chinaman' met precisely the same reception.[71] Fear took on a particularly interesting form in relation to gaming. Widespread gambling occurred on the goldfields, although, O'Hara notes, 'in a less prominent and less boisterous way' than on the Californian fields.[72] As we saw earlier, the commission of inquiry into Victoria's goldfields associated the evils of gambling with the Chinese. This became a major issue later in the decade when evangelists mounted their anti-gambling campaign. Chinese who did not return to their homeland moved to the cities, where many established gaming houses. According to the 1891 NSW Royal Commission, which examined Chinese gaming, almost 16 per cent of the 287 dwellings occupied by Chinese in Sydney were gaming houses. Drawing on an account by the nineteenth-century social observer Nat Gould, O'Hara describes Chinese gaming houses as 'foul-smelling, vicious dens which catered mainly for enthusiasts of dominoes, fan-tan and pak-a-pu, and which were most unpleasant places to visit, due largely to the aroma of opium'. Such pictures, 'when combined with the tendency of the European settlers to dismiss the Chinese as a lower class of being, with disgusting habits and unacceptable values', provided the grounds for middle-class groups to challenge gaming. The decision to appoint the Royal Commission into Chinese Gaming arose after a group of businessmen from the northern end of Sydney's George Street accused Chinese gamesters of destroying legitimate businesses. The group lobbied the police, local members of parliament and the premier. Chinese gaming dens survived in New South Wales until the early twentieth century, when the *Vagrancy Act 1905* declared unlawful the favourite Chinese games of pak-a-pu and fan-tan. O'Hara comments that 'a society which had applauded the Commonwealth parliament's *Immigration Restriction Act 1901* and a tightening of other regulations applying to the Chinese, particularly in the aftermath of the Russo–Japanese war, which illustrated the possibility of an Asian nation's military superiority over a European one', was hardly going to support Chinese gamesters.[73] Nor even Chinese footballers. The selection of Wally Koochew in 1908 raised the ire of at least one Carlton Football Club supporter, who returned his membership ticket asserting that the Chinese player's inclusion was 'a death blow to the White Australia policy'.[74]

An Empty Land—Except for Aborigines

Aboriginal civilisation on the Australian continent varies in age from 20 000 to 60 000 years. Much work has been done in prehistory and archaeology, and both early and modern Aboriginal art forms have become a major facet, and asset, of present-day Australian cultural life. Aboriginal art is now celebrated. Not so pre-colonial sport. The material is slim: we have a Master's thesis by Canadian Michael Salter in 1967, two peripheral theses (by an American and a German), and a book, *Bush Toys*, from Claudia Haagen in 1994. Traditional games and pastimes remain something of a mystery—generally unresearched, unremembered, unplayed, unworthy, it would seem, of the researcher's attention. Ken Edwards of Brisbane is embarking on a major work in this area, one that will, we hope, emulate Stewart Culin's famous classic, *Games of the North American Indians.*

There is a fascinating glimpse of something important in the work of Victorian writer Jim Poulter. He argues that the strongest influence on Australian football was neither rugby (Tommy Wills went to Rugby school in England), nor Gaelic football (which has a style and format similar to the Australian version) but a traditional game played by Aborigines in south-western Victoria.[75] Geoffrey Blainey mentions such an influence in his *A Game of Our Own.* While rejecting the idea that Victorian football owed anything to the traditional Aboriginal game, he did think that the mark came from the indigenous people: 'It is conceivable that several of the early exponents of what became a distinctively Australian form of marking had seen Aborigines at play in rural areas, gained confidence from watching them, and even imitated their style of leaping.'[76]

Ken Edwards believes there are at least eight accounts—several from tribal legend—of an indigenous game involving a high mark but feels, on the weight of the evidence thus far, that the similarities are a coincidence rather than a derivation. Poulter contends that the Gunditjmara tribe played a game called *marn-grook*, or 'game ball'. A ball was made of possum skin, filled with pounded charcoal and bound with kangaroo sinews. Between 50 and 100 men a side played for possession for hours on end. Melbourne Church of England Grammar School and Scotch College, Melbourne, played a 40-a-side game—described as a combination of soccer, rugby and Gaelic football—on 7 August 1858, from noon till dark. If Poulter is right—and we are inclined to give his weightier evidence more credence than Blainey's dismissive conjectures—then the first 50 years of Australian football were less than kind to its founders.

From 1788 to 1992 Aborigines suffered the politico-legal fallacy, and indignity, of not being present in the *terra nullius*, the empty land.[77] Perceived as having no organs of government, Aborigines, who were real enough, were regarded as a 'state-less' society. From the outset, colonial relations between black and white were well intentioned at the official level but rent with strife in practice. Official instructions to Governor Arthur Phillip were underpinned by Enlightenment ideas about human dignity: thus he was 'to endeavour by every means in his power to open an intercourse with the natives and to conciliate their goodwill, requiring all persons under his Government to live in amity and kindness with them'.[78] But such instructions to governors were really benign utterances of far-away governments. The hard clashes of interest on the spot produced a different order. As the settlers spread out from the centres of administration, government control lessened, newly introduced diseases spread among the Aborigines, the birth rate dropped, the Aboriginal population declined markedly through disease and destruction by settlers, and law and order became impossible to maintain.

The genocidal period, from the 1840s to the 1890s, included hundreds of massacres, shootings and poisonings across the continent.[79] Elementary protective legislation began in the 1840s, but it didn't stop the genocidal impulses of the settlers and the murderous activities of the notorious Native Police, the white-officered but black-staffed units. In the circumstances, anything other than native sports seemed impossible. The Enlightenment wasn't transported to Australian natives.

Yet cricket, with all its notions of fairness, was a small, important yet aberrant part of Aboriginal life in this extermination period.[80] The first mention of an Aboriginal sportsman was in 1835 when Shiney, or Shinal, played cricket in Hobart Town. His story is significant because it ended a full 157 years later in a manner that was not untypical of the Aboriginal experience. On his death, Shiney was beheaded and the resident doctor sent the 'specimen' to an Irish museum for preservation. Recent agitation by Tasmanian Aborigines resulted in his remains being returned and ceremoniously cremated in 1992. After 1835 Aborigines played talented and enthusiastic cricket at a time when, while 'free' legally, they experienced geographic isolation, rigid missionary control, settler animus, poor diet, rampant illness and, of course, killing.

The Reverend Matthew Blagden Hale's vision in 1850 was to protect Aborigines from 'a vicious portion of the white population' at Poonindie, 19 kilometres from Port Lincoln in South Australia. He would 'train them in the habits of civilised life'. To overcome a 'native temperament', said to be distressed by 'continuous labour', illness, and 'flagging spirits', he introduced cricket. The team did well, winning all but one of its local matches. In Adelaide in 1872 the Anglican Bishop attended a match between Poonindie and 'the scholars of the Collegiate School of St Peter'. Cricket, wrote Bishop Short, proved 'incontestably that the Anglican aristocracy of England and the "noble savage", who ran wild in the Australian woods, are linked together in one brotherhood of blood—moved by the same passions, desires, and affections'. Not so. Legal and physical separation of Aborigines were already under way.

Increasing ill health, white complaints, and pressure from farmers to acquire Aboriginal land saw the mission close in 1895.

Victoria's Coranderrk people proved themselves as farmers, musicians, political demonstrators, Christians and cricketers. Successful crop-growers, especially of hops, white neighbours always coveted their land. A royal commission (1877) and a parliamentary board of inquiry (1887) listened to their plight. The conservative *Age* newspaper viewed them as happy, virtuous, and industrious amid the carnage that saw others 'shot down, starved, poisoned, corrupted in body and soul'.

The famous British naturalist H. N. Moseley visited the reserve in 1874. He saw them as 'incorrigibly lazy', gleeful when the plough broke down. However, 'we found the cricket party in high spirits, shouting with laughter, rows of spectators being seated on logs and chaffing the players with all the old English sallies: "Well hit!", "Run it out!", "Butter fingers!" etc...The men were all dressed as Europeans; they knew all about Mr W. G. Grace and the All-England Eleven'.

The Coranderrk people won the land war but lost their hop harvesters. The expulsion of 'half-castes' from reserves—the 'forced assimilation' policy—had begun. By 1895 more than 60 adults had been expelled and all dependent children were sent away at the age of 14. By the 1920s Coranderrk was finished. (Coranderrk is but one of several instances of successful Aboriginal farming—giving the lie to the prevalent and prevailing proposition that Aborigines shouldn't be granted land because they never tilled its soil.)

Cummeragunja (Cummera) on the Murray River began as a private mission in 1874. Daniel Matthews, an Echuca merchant, ran the original Maloga Mission on strictly religious principles. For him, cricket was 'an uncivilising activity'. The Aborigines saw things differently. Matthews' biographer wrote: 'They had discovered that their prowess in sport, particularly in cricket and running, gave them a passport to the white man's world, even to his respect and friendship.' He tried very hard to stop that passage.

A Spanish Benedictine monk, in contrast, saw cricket as a civilising force. At New Norcia Mission in 1879, Abbot Dom Salvado—ignorant of English as a language and a culture—introduced the game to the people of Western Australia whom he described as 'these poor natives, so hideous to look at'. Daisy Bates was moved to write, 'Cricketing patrons and lovers of the sport gathered in their hundreds to watch the aboriginal players; and wherever the team went it was treated as a body of sportsmen and gentlemen, for such is the Kingdom of cricket'. Nick-named 'The Invincibles' and coached only by a local grazier, they walked 120 kilometres each way to Perth and Fremantle to play. By 1905 it was all over. In 1904 the Queensland Protector of Aborigines, Dr Walter Roth, had proposed legislation for the West: it was time 'to bring Aboriginal–white relations more securely under the rule of the law'. Rule of law came a year later with the *Aborigines Act 1905* and all its restrictions.

Queensland settlers killed some 10 000 Aborigines between 1824 and 1908. Yet amid the carnage, there was freedom to play cricket. In the 1890s a number of Aborigines were playing cricket at Deebing Creek, near Ipswich. Townspeople felt that 'every encouragement should be given to our ebony brethren'. Slaughter notwithstanding, people came to watch. They 'behaved like white gentlemen', said the *Queensland Times*. The Deebing Creek team won a major trophy in 1895 and then played the National Cricket Union in Brisbane. Then followed an astonishing episode in the annals of genocide: the Colonial Secretary, shortly before he received a report from Royal Commissioner Archibald Meston on the urgent need to stop the wholesale killings, sent the Aborigines two bats 'in appreciation of their excellent behaviour and smart turn-out'.

Strict isolation was Meston's solution to the genocide. The *Aboriginals Protection and Restriction of Sale of Opium Act 1897* followed. Despite his love of sport, this royal commissioner and first Protector of Aborigines didn't like cricket or Deebing Creek. The second Protector, Roth, began isolating Ipswich men, dispatching them far and wide: they were 'malcontents' who had 'evidently been too much encouraged in competition with Europeans in the way of cricket matches…and have been treated socially far above their natural station in life'. Deebing Creek came to an end in 1916. The cricket had stopped long before that. What began as a high note ended on the lowest. In February 1906, the Normanby team refused to play the Railway team 'on account of the latter including aboriginals, and had stated that they would take a similar stand again'.

John Mulvaney and Rex Harcourt have described the 1868 Aboriginal cricket tour to England—the first team ever to represent Australia abroad—as a 'dignified episode in race relations'.[81] It was to be a short episode, occurring in the gap between the major massacres in Victoria and the establishment of the Aborigines Protection Board in 1869. The story behind the tour is that an Edenhope grazier sent pictures of 'his' Aborigines to the owners of the MCG refreshment tent. They had been

'A dignified episode in race relations': the Aboriginal cricket team that toured Sydney before a famous tour of England in 1868. Rear, left to right: Tarpot, T. W. Wills (captain and coach) and Johnny Mullagh. Front row: King Cole (leg on chair); standing, right: Dick-a-Dick; seated, left to right: Jellico, Peter, Red Cap, Harry Rose, Bullocky and Johnny Cuzens. This was the first team from Australia to tour abroad, and it did so twice. In both of its tours, the team suffered from sickness and, in 1868, even death. Only Johnny Mullagh achieved fame. AUSTRALIAN NATIONAL LIBRARY

taught the game by the sons of pastoralists in the Lake Wallace district of western Victoria. A match was arranged against the MCC and 'with the sympathies of the whole of the population of Melbourne behind them', and before 10 000 spectators at the MCG on Boxing Day 1866, 'these children of the forest', as the *Age* called them, lost by nine wickets.

Amid talk of commercial exploitation and associated skulduggery, and despite much illness among the players, hotelier Charles Lawrence agreed to coach the team on an English tour. In the pre-tour fund-raising, the team played well in Victoria and New South Wales. The team landed in England in May 1868. They played 47 matches, for nineteen draws, fourteen wins and as many losses. Of the 1868 cricketers, only Johnny Mullagh achieved fame. The 'black W. G. [Grace] of the team' was an early comment; 'a kind of early [Garfield] Sobers' was a later assessment. In England he played 43 matches, scoring 1679 runs at an average of 22.51 and took 237 wickets at 9 runs each. He later played for Victoria against Lord Harris's English team and continued playing in western Victoria's Murray Cup until 1890. His repute, personality and dignity kept him out of reach of the Protection Board. 'The Western district', wrote the *Sydney Mail* in 1891, 'will regret his death'. A memorial, engraved with his cricket averages, was erected to this 'virtuous exemplary man' on the local Harrow ground, later named the Mullagh Oval. Mullagh's playing partner, Johnny Cuzens, was not far behind in skill and repute. A tiny man, he had an outstanding tour in England, and was then, with Mullagh, employed as a professional by the Melbourne Cricket Club.

The predecessor of the Aboriginal Welfare Board, the Board for the Protection of Aborigines, had feared that the team might be abandoned in England. They were concerned that they could not compel the tour organisers to guarantee the safety of the Aborigines. King Cole died during the tour and Sundown and Jim Crow became so ill that they were sent home. The *Aborigines Protection Act 1869* came into force one year later. But had the Act been operative a year earlier, concerns for the safety and well-being of the team would have prevented the tour taking place.

These cricketing episodes were something of an aberration in Aboriginal life. They promised a degree of freedom and social relationships with mainstream society, even amid genocidal massacres. But the need to protect Aborigines from the depredations of white society was overwhelming, and the ensuing legislation produced both legislative fences and the administrative decisions to physically locate Aborigines as far away as possible from whites. The exclusion of Aborigines from Australian society had begun in earnest.

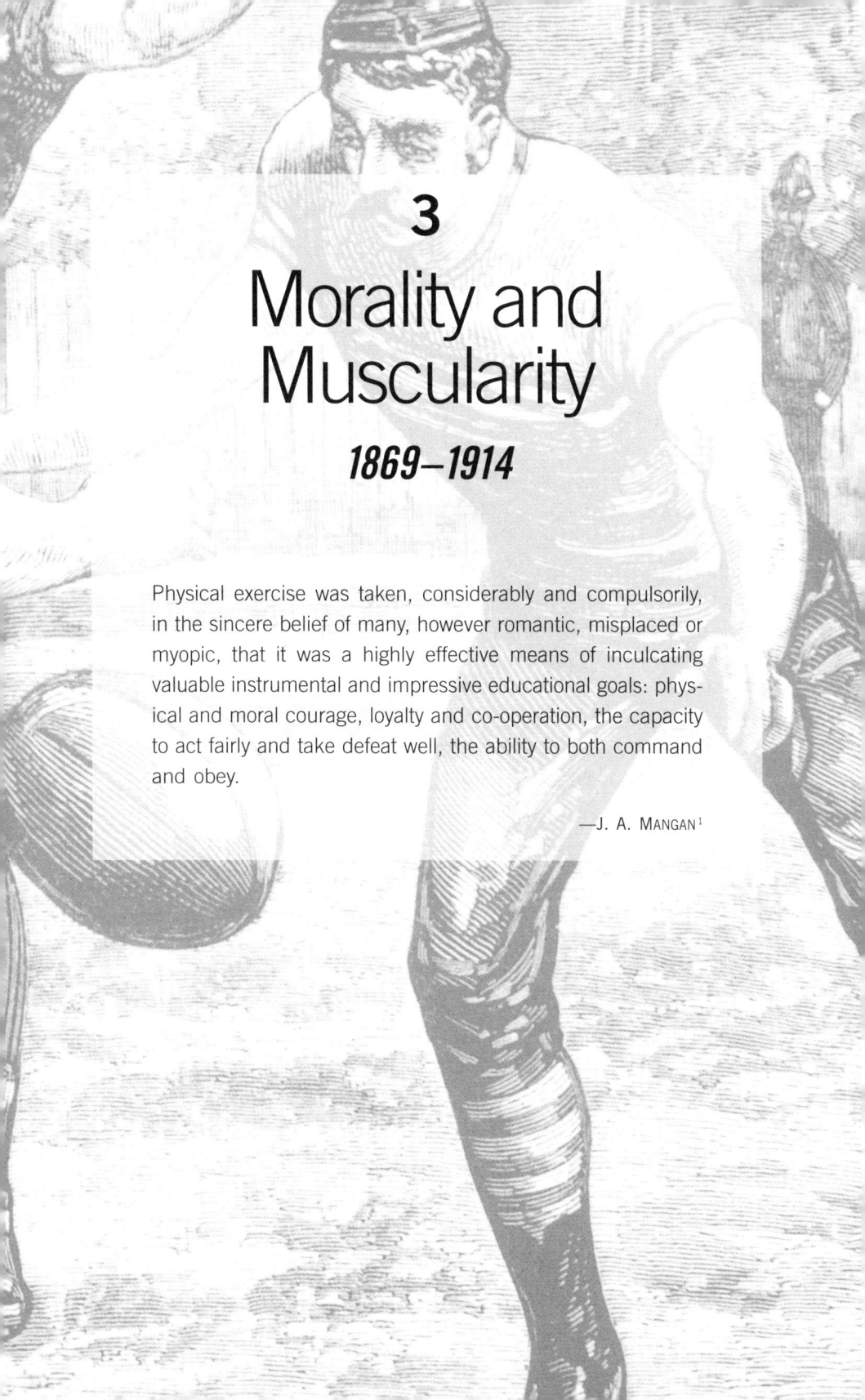

3
Morality and Muscularity
1869–1914

Physical exercise was taken, considerably and compulsorily, in the sincere belief of many, however romantic, misplaced or myopic, that it was a highly effective means of inculcating valuable instrumental and impressive educational goals: physical and moral courage, loyalty and co-operation, the capacity to act fairly and take defeat well, the ability to both command and obey.

—J. A. MANGAN[1]

A NEW SOCIAL FORMATION

Gold was discovered in the 1850s. The nuggets brought a fresh wave of immigrants, mostly labourers, artisans and small businessmen, who swelled the middle and skilled working classes. For the most part, the new immigrants were 'humble' and their 'manners...quiet and restrained'; they 'coveted respectability and were determined to better themselves through self-help'. Most 'had learned...self-discipline in churches and chapels in Britain'. These 'respectable', essentially middle-class, new arrivals did not simply add a new stratum to the old social order. Rather, they changed Australia's colonial social formation quite profoundly, making it 'harder to distinguish' one class from another. In the mid-nineteenth century, Australia's middle and skilled working classes 'turned deaf ears' to earlier rigid Georgian notions of social exclusivity and the belief that people could not gain respectability beyond their own occupation.[2] Anthony Trollope visited in the 1870s. An astute observer of Australian society, he commented favourably on the absence of 'humble-ness', 'hat touching' and 'servility' in the colonies. Certainly immigrant artisans 'were determined that no man would treat them as if they were convicts or paupers'. Trollope also found popular 'the idea that Englishmen'—that is, the new arrivals—'are made of paste, whereas the Australian, native or thoroughly acclimatised, is steel all through'.[3] John Galloway, a radical unionist stonemason who arrived in 1855, declared: 'we have come 16 000 miles to better our condition, and not to act the mere part of machinery.' Nor, he added, did they seek 'excessive toil, a bare existence, and premature grave'.[4] Melbourne's stonemasons led the struggle for the eight-hour working day, a battle they won in the mid-1850s.

These respectable immigrants helped build positive images of Australia as a working man's paradise, as a tolerant society, as the land of the 'fair go'. As early as 1852 the *Sydney Morning Herald* would enthuse, 'we are all middle class here'. Sadly, reality never quite matched the ideal. Only a minority of the working class—those belonging to the skilled, white, male workforce—encountered paradise. The benefits never extended to 'men out of work', 'women and children', 'lower white collar workers', 'clerks and shopmen', '*kanakas* in the sugar industry', 'Chinese in the laundries', farmers 'scratching hopelessly at poor inadequate land'. Neither did they extend to Aborigines in the pastoral industry, who often worked for no money and for 'less than subsistence rations'.[5] Yet in the struggle against a numerically small and relatively weak colonial elite, the rising middle and skilled working classes had little trouble gaining political equality. Gold fuelled the growth of an urban-based commercial capitalism that undermined the political and economic power of the conservative landed classes.

Democratic innovations introduced in the mid-1850s deprived the upper classes of majorities in the legislative assemblies of New South Wales, Victoria, Queensland and South Australia. New democratic systems included adult male suffrage, vote by ballot, and the abolition of property qualifications for members of parliament. Yet political reforms did not erase long-standing social divisions. The old colonial gentry tried to maintain their status and to distinguish themselves socially. They adopted exclusive lifestyles based on conspicuous consumption and inordinate use of free time. In this, sport was crucial. In Adelaide, for example, members of the upper classes established large estates where, alongside orchards and vineyards, they

> developed tennis courts and croquet fields. Inside, the homes boasted rooms for billiards and dancing. In the absence of 'proper game' the new gentry imported the fox, the rabbit and the sparrow to provide quarry for the sports man (and future problems for the farmer!). Not only were packs of hounds kept on a number of large estates but also stables of polo ponies.[6]

The colonial elite established the hunt, golf and, later, tennis clubs as 'sanctuaries' in which 'like-minded' people socialised. Clubs employed any number of strategies to preserve members' status. The gentlemen who formed the Charters Towers Hunt Club (Queensland) in 1888 set a high subscription fee of five shillings per quarter and agreed that members should wear a distinctive uniform of scarlet coat, top boots or gaiters and breeches.[7] Mid-week hunts were effectively declarations that the activity was 'reserved for the leisure class'; the governor's attendance at hunt club balls, hunt races and steeplechases 'further confirmed' exclusivity.[8] In Brisbane, Sydney and Melbourne, exclusive golf clubs served the same function.[9] Members insisted that their club was 'a home away from home', a place only for those with the right social pedigree and therefore eligible for dinner invitations.

Rather than mimicking their social superiors, the middle classes adopted a different approach, based on a distinct ethos, towards sport and recreation.

MUSCULAR CHRISTIANITY AND ATHLETICISM

In the 1860s and 1870s Australia's middle classes enjoyed a golden age. Opportunities increased through new clothing, printing, food-processing, brewing and tanning industries, new trades, especially in the building industry, new commercial and financial ventures, and new professions in law, medicine and the civil service. The middle classes would accumulate much wealth, but unlike their hedonistic social superiors, they sought respectability through the virtues of self-restraint, discipline, sobriety, frugality and piety. They believed, as did their British counterparts, that sport was a moral endeavour and that 'sportsmanship' arose solely from the competitive process. Nothing better expressed their values and morality than their sports and games.

In the mid-nineteenth century the middle classes adopted a physical form of Christian morality. The roots of what became known as 'muscular Christianity' lay in the English public schools and university colleges. It reflected 'the old chivalric and ascetic belief that the body was to be trained and brought under control to protect the weak and advance the cause of right'; and the belief that games suppressed sexual urges—especially masturbation—and produced Christian gentlemen.[10] Australia's elite and upper middle classes sent their sons to private schools,[11] many of them established to perpetuate these British-derived moral, muscular and religious values, although the popular diffusion of these values owed more to the literature of novelists and social commentators. Especially influential were Charles Kingsley's *Westward Ho!* (1855), Thomas Hughes's *Tom Brown's Schooldays* (1857), and the magazines *Bell's Life in Victoria* and *Sporting Chronicle*. In *Tom Brown at Oxford*, some of the 'young bloods who fought in the Battles between Town and Gown saw themselves in fancy as modern versions of the [Homeric] epic heroes'.[12] These texts, argues David Brown, 'augmented' prevailing notions of Christian manliness by adding 'a distinctive muscular or physical dimension' to the customary 'moral endeavours' by which men developed their 'character'.[13] Muscular Christians called this physical dimension 'athleticism'.

By the 1870s the pursuit of manliness had become a cult, and athleticism quickly became an ideology, as the following passages suggest. For Charles Kingsley, sport enabled boys to

> acquire virtues which no books can give them; not merely daring and endurance, but, better still, temper, self-restraint, fairness, honour, unenvious approbation of another's success, and all that 'give and take' of life which stand a man in good stead when he goes forth into the world, and without which, indeed, his success is always maimed and partial.[14]

In similar vein, Cyril Norwood, the distinguished early twentieth-century British educationalist, believed that games were essential training for life:

> A game is to be played for the game's sake...no unfair advantage of any sort can ever be taken, [yet]...within the rules no mercy is to be expected, or accepted by either side; the lesson to be learnt by each individual is the subordination of self in order that he may render his best service as the member of the team in which he relies upon the rest; and all the rest may rely upon him...Finally, never on any occasion must he show the white feather. If games can be played in this spirit, they are magnificent preparation for life.[15]

Muscular Christianity and athleticism assumed two quite distinct tones. First, in the elitist private schools—such as Melbourne Grammar, Scotch College, Xavier College, Wesley College, Geelong Grammar (Victoria), St Peter's College (South Australia), Sydney Grammar, Newington College, The King's School (New South Wales), and Brisbane Grammar School (Queensland)—athleticism encouraged cooperation, loyalty, courage, obedience to the rules, dedication and persistence. The aim was to prepare boys for leadership roles in government, business, the professions and family life. In this sense athleticism was an exclusive ideology intended to separate the classes. It was also the basis by which Victorians could disparage female participation in athletics. Although less zealous than British evangelists, who used organised sport to discipline and civilise the working classes, Australia's middle classes clearly recognised the power of sport. In 1872, for example, Sir James Ferguson, Governor of South Australia, told a meeting of the Sydney Amateur Athletic Club that amateur athletics in Adelaide had exerted a positive influence on the working class.[16] Second, athleticism offered the embryonic nationalist press a means of fostering nationalist sentiments. Below we look at the antagonistic class dimensions of muscular Christianity and athleticism; Chapter 4 explores the role played by athleticism in 'nationalising' nineteenth-century Australians.

AMATEUR GENTLEMEN AND PROFESSIONAL WORKERS

No sooner was muscular Christianity established than it became associated with another ideology, Social Darwinism. Based on crude interpretations, and misinterpretations, of ideas in Charles Darwin's *On the Origin of Species by Means of Natural Selection* (1859), Social Darwinism had a profound influence on how the middle classes viewed life and, ultimately, how they related to each other and to people of other classes. According to this doctrine, the laws of nature meant that different social groups competed against each other in a permanent struggle in which only the fittest survived. This narrow view of society—regrettably, still alive and well—justified vicious forms of class and gender discrimination and of racial hierarchy and racial oppression.

Social Darwinism injected class and race prejudice into muscular Christianity. Among the middle classes, amateur sport served a higher role to teach the 'essential elements of character' and 'imbue its participants with the traits of fair play, modesty in victory, dignity in defeat and sportsmanship'. In contrast, 'professional sport was primitive, unworthy, and dangerous'. Its close association with gambling exposed it to 'cheating, bribery and corruption', with professionals employing a range of 'sharp practices'.[17] The founders of the Adelaide Amateur Athletic Club cited the example of the English professional Albert Bird, who toured South Australia in the 1870s, to justify their stance against professionalism. They accused Bird of 'mismeasuring the distances over which he ran demonstration races' and with 'not trying against local runners if he had been paid before the event'.[18] The middle classes also identified what they saw as an inherent 'unfairness' in the professional approach. According to *The Sportsman*,

> it was hardly fair that young players—who, perhaps, had no other opportunities of practising than in the matches played on Saturday afternoons —should be expected to compete against men especially trained to keep

in first-class condition, and whose livelihood depended on their efforts to win a match.[19]

Similarly, 'Fairplay', football writer for the *Australasian*, condemned systematic training by the Albert Park Club in the 1870s as 'not altogether laudable'. In middle-class eyes, regular training amounted to cheating.[20]

The ideal sportsman was, therefore, an amateur. Defenders of this faith were never at a loss to describe the qualities of the ideal amateur. In 1897 John Blackman, correspondent for the *Sydney Mail*, portrayed the model of the amateur rower as 'a person of education, refinement, leisure and means', as someone who 'does not count the cost, nor... question the gain' but who rows 'because he likes to'. Moreover, when an amateur wins 'he is fully satisfied with the acknowledgment of his relative merit and seeks neither money nor goods with which his victory may be magnified in the eyes of others and his fame sustained in after years'.[21] In 1886 Britain's Amateur Athletic Rule stated that 'an amateur is a gentleman who has never taken part in a public competition open to all, has never competed for money, has never been a teacher or trainer of sport and is neither a working man nor an artist or a journalist'! Many middle-class Australians swallowed the entire 'philosophy' as summed up in Sir Henry Newbolt's prissy poem in 1892, 'Vitaï Lampada':

> And it's not for the sake of a ribboned coat
> Or the selfish hope of a season's fame,
> But his Captain's hand on his shoulder smote—
> 'Play up! Play up! and play the game!'

We must, sermonised the poet, 'set the cause above renown' and 'love the game beyond the prize'! As we will see later, he was the only notable British poet who persisted in seeing a glorious connection between sport and war. In the second verse, the sand of the desert was sodden red, the gatling (gun) was jammed and the Colonel dead, the river of death had brimmed its banks, but the voice of a schoolboy rallied the ranks with his cry of 'Play up! Play up! and play the game!'

The working classes had a very different set of values. Their sports were rough; they were rude, vociferous and partisan. The working classes set a premium on victory, were suspicious and disdainful of constituted authority and lacked veneration for official rules.[22] These values stemmed from their material conditions. While the urban middle and skilled working classes lived in five-room villas with verandas, iron-lace edging, plaster urns and stained-glass windows, the lower classes of Melbourne and Sydney 'lived in abject poverty':

> Few of the houses had such domestic conveniences as indoor sinks, pantries, stoves and clothes closets. The high rents caused overcrowding... [with] as many as seven men and women squeezed somehow into two rooms... In their daily lives the people were surrounded by ignorance and squalor, while their children, it was said, 'floated about the streets and lanes like fish in a pond'. Vagrant children infested the streets of Sydney; prostitution thrived as parents sold their daughters to supplement their incomes.[23]

Throughout the second half of the nineteenth century and well into the twentieth, the amateur issue divided the middle and working classes. Australian football and rugby showed just how sharp were these social divisions.

Australian Football

The founders of this unique brand of football were members of Melbourne's upwardly mobile middle class. For the first two decades the game belonged to the middle classes and the colonial elite. There was a simple reason for this:

> Nearly all men, whether miners or shopkeepers or farmers, worked on Saturday afternoon, and it was not easy to obtain leave merely to play football. Even then they usually lost part of their salary or wages if they gained permission to leave work early on Saturday afternoon in order to go to the football ground. Only a large town possessed a sufficient number of those bank clerks, school teachers, self-employed tradesmen, owners of gold claims and other men of property who had the freedom on Saturday afternoon to chase a football.[24]

It was not until the 1880s and 1890s that 'professionalism' and the 'gradual extension of the Saturday half-holiday from government offices and banks to include tradesmen and shopkeepers' allowed the 'lower' classes to play football in great numbers. Ironically, perhaps, Australian football almost immediately became the 'people's game'. The key was access: football was played in open parklands, and early in the game's

An early Australian football match: Carlton versus Melbourne. Australian football was founded by members of Melbourne's upwardly mobile middle class; not until late in the nineteenth century did the granting of the Saturday half-holiday allow the working classes to play football in great numbers. AUSTRALIAN SKETCHER, 18 JUNE 1881

development there were no entrance fees, as in cricket. In the early 1870s crowds of 10 000 watched some games.[25]

Later that decade, club administrators rearranged football. They transformed it from 'an enjoyable activity played among gum trees to a highly structured and organised competition played on enclosed grounds with admission charges'. Entrance fees helped improve grounds and facilities, but the Victorian Football Association (VFA), formed by seven leading clubs in 1877 to administer and control the game, couldn't decide how to distribute funds:

> Many administrators were aware that they were open to criticism for making money from an amateur sport played on public land. Their first response was to encourage donations to worthy causes by placing collection boxes around the grounds. Later the VFA nominated one or more match days per season as 'Hospital Saturdays' when all proceeds and collections would be distributed to hospitals and charities. The collections were soon replaced with a 5 per cent levy on net proceeds of all matches, to be distributed at the end of the season.[26]

Payment to players began in the 1880s. Middle-class opinion-makers—officials, administrators, pressmen, clergy and headmasters—attacked payments, calling them corrupt, unhealthy and evil.[27] Administrators, players and members knew that success in organised sport meant recruiting and retaining skilled players who knew their market worth only too well. Neither sport in general nor particular sports had any real or serious philosophy as starting points. Philosophy—in the sense of ideas, values, a coherent set of beliefs and principles—grew slowly under the weight of history and tradition and the hard-edged realities of places and peoples. Before a philosophy takes root and shape it undergoes argument, controversy and debate. Hence in the late nineteenth century, the middle and working classes vigorously discussed the role of sport in society, as Grow points out:

> 'Amateurs' saw sport as a leisure activity that had a higher purpose of 'providing training for life'. It should not provide a livelihood, and the outcomes of matches should be of no consequence. This view attracted much support from the middle classes who thought that any form of professionalism in football would eventually result in bookmaking, betting and match-fixing. They were also concerned about the effect of large amounts of money becoming available to football clubs, particularly if power became concentrated in the hands of a few wealthy clubs.

Many working-class enthusiasts took the opposite view. In an increasingly industrialised society, sport provided an exciting break from the monotony of daily work; many people thought that those who provided entertainment and took the risks should be suitably rewarded. The outcome of matches mattered greatly to them and would be constantly discussed through the week at work, in the pub and at social gatherings. Working-class communities' hopes and aspirations often came to rest on the performance of the local football team. Moreover, they wanted to be able to have a flutter on the result and could see nothing wrong with bookmakers operating at the ground.

The secretary of the VFA, Thomas Marshall, led the amateur campaign and issued frequent 'tirades against the evils of professionalism'. In 1886 the VFA, under Marshall's direction, decreed that any player found receiving payment would be disqualified for the rest of the season, and the offending club would be fined as well as 'losing' the match in which the offence occurred.[28]

Marshall's best efforts failed to derail creeping professionalism and the determination of clubs to make football more commercially viable and appealing to spectators. Increasingly, crowds packed grounds and drinking and gambling became more common. Respectable fans faced streams of curses, blasphemies, personal attacks (including racist slurs) and incitement to violence and brutality. Middle-class officials tried to solve the problem by building grandstands and pavilions to separate the classes. Respectable supporters and club members happily paid extra to sit in the grandstands to 'avoid the fearful crushes' and enjoy 'superior standards of behaviour and language'.[29]

In 1897 eight clubs left the VFA and formed the Victorian Football League in protest at having to carry economically non-viable clubs. Thirteen years later the VFL voted to legalise payments to players. (The original VFA continued as a separate competition, and in 1990 the VFL changed its name to the Australian Football League, the AFL.) It is interesting that middle-class concern was muted. Perhaps they realised that the social distance between amateur and professional was really not that far. When St Kilda ruckman Dave McNamara, a crowd favourite in the early twentieth century, defended payments to players in his memoirs, he wrote that all footballers required essential qualifications: 'strength', 'brain application', 'obedience', 'self restraint' and 'courage'.[30]

Rugby

Tight networks of middle-class 'influence and patronage' throve in Melbourne and Sydney in the mid-nineteenth century. As well as their sheer economic power, the interests of these networks

reflected their role as part of the upper and middle class which established
the parameters of the commercial, political and cultural development
[of the two colonies]. They were trustees and on the boards of the major
commercial and governmental organisations...forming the strong pro-
tectionist group within the political sphere. They were on the governing
bodies of the universit[ies] as well as on councils of...various private
schools. They were at the forefront of the arts...they were commissioners representing the colon[ies]...at international and intercolonial
exhibitions. They served and upheld the prevailing legal system as
barristers and solicitors, justices of the peace, magistrates, and judges.
They were on the boards of hospitals.[31]

Exclusive clubs such as the Sydney Turf Club, the Albert Cricket
Club (Sydney), the Melbourne Cricket Club and the Port Phillip Turf
Club provided for middle-class sporting interests. The next chapter
shows how population growth in the 1850s had a profound effect on
these networks and ultimately on the rapid organisation and codification
of football in Melbourne. Between 1850 and 1861 Melbourne's population grew from 29 000 to 125 000. By contrast, 'stagnant growth' in
Sydney, combined with limited public playing space and disagreements
about the rules by which to play, meant that in the third quarter of the
nineteenth century the men who promoted rugby, athletics and rowing
remained highly committed to the amateur ethos.[32]

In 1874 an 'alliance' of clubs from the private schools, the University of Sydney and gentlemen's clubs formed the Sydney-based Southern
Rugby Football Union (SRFU), later the New South Wales Rugby Union
(NSWRU).[33] All keenly promoted 'the ideology of athleticism', which
their upper-middle-class clientele considered integral to their 'status and
respectability'. These clubs dominated the SRFU until the 1880s. Thereafter, clubs representative of the lower middle classes and the working
classes began to join. But the middle-class amateur orthodoxy of the
game initially held firm, despite the inclusion of other classes which contributed to the popularity, and perhaps even the 'democratisation', of
rugby in Sydney in the 1880s and 1890s.

Class tensions erupted in 1907. The popularity of rugby had
increased the wealth of the NSWRU but, paradoxically, this wealth
became a source of discontent. In 1907 the NSWRU paid £15 000 for
the Epping racecourse, near Glebe. At that time the Union owned no
grounds and had to lease playing fields at considerable expense. The

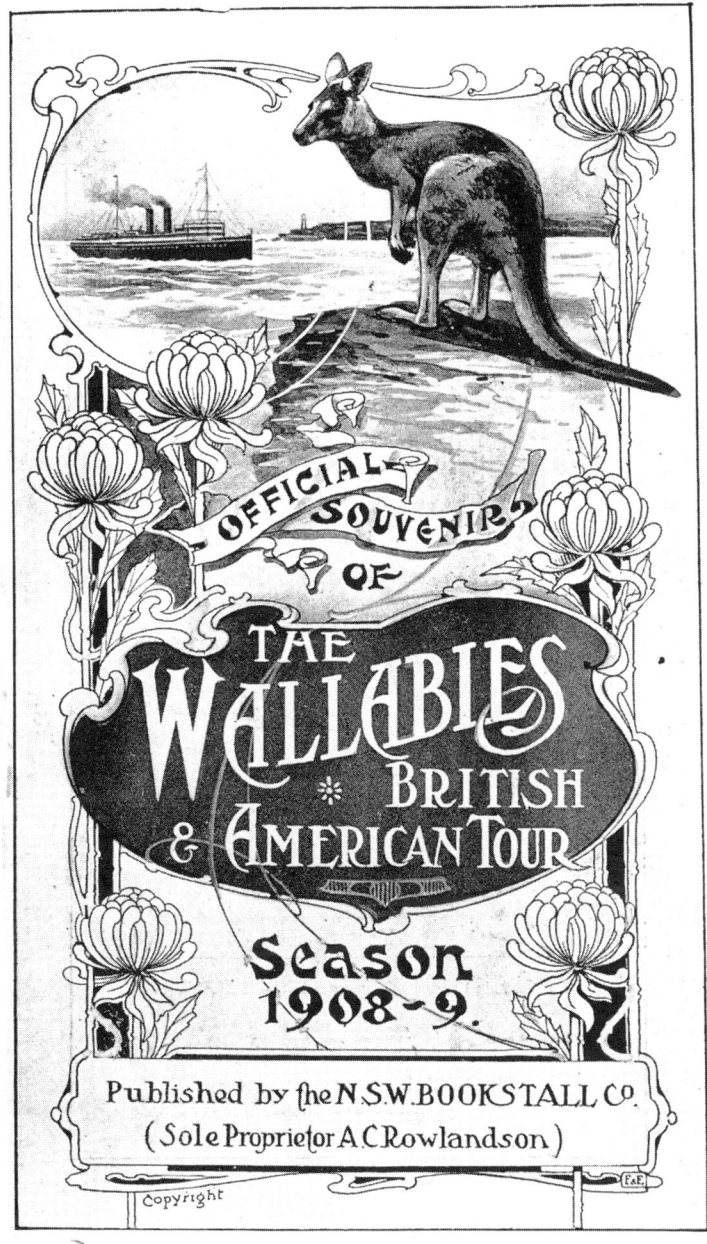

The first touring Wallaby rugby union team won 25 matches, lost five and drew one. Their 32–3 win over Cornwall, the English county champions, was for the olympic medal. In 1874 an alliance of upper-middle-class clubs formed the NSWRU and keenly promoted the ideology of athleticism, which members considered integral to their status and respectability.

purchase galled many people, especially the players. They 'drew the crowds and created the profits' and they resented the fact that administrators reaped the benefits. The previous season the Union had withdrawn its medical-aid scheme and handed responsibility for players injured in representative games back to the clubs.[34] Injuries were a crucial issue among working-class players because they meant lost time and lost wages. Middle-class officials were adamant: under the amateur code, money was a source of 'evil' in sport.

Professionalism, warned the *Sydney Morning Herald* in 1907, 'destroys the instinct of legitimate sportsmanship very quickly for the player and it teaches the onlooker as quickly to mistake the "play" for a contest of gladiators—hired at that'.[35] Blinded by their vision, amateur officials saw neither reason nor compassion. A case in point was Alex Burdon, a barber by occupation, who was incapacitated by a shoulder damaged while playing for New South Wales. Refusing to assist Burdon, these amateur ideologues sent a clear message: the game held no place for working-class men who couldn't afford to meet all their own costs.[36]

Business interests and representatives of organised labour joined forces against this middle-class amateur intransigence. Three men took the initiative and met a group of players in August 1907: James Giltinan, a businessman, Victor Trumper, the legendary cricketer and sports shop owner, and Henry Clement Hoyle, who had been dismissed in 1890 by the railways for agitating strike action and who would later join the Labor Party and eventually earn a place in cabinet. They formed the New South Wales Rugby Football League (NSWRFL). The League's initial aim was to organise matches against a group of professional New Zealand rugby players, sarcastically known as the All Golds. At Giltinan's invitation, they stopped in Sydney *en route* to England to play professionally. Played according to rugby union rules, the All Gold tour of Sydney made money. The Union retaliated by expelling all 22 players: four labourers, two painters, a storeman, a waterside worker, a boat-builder, an athlete (later fireman), a cleaner, a compositor, a clerk, a fishmonger, a boilermaker, a journalist, a draper and a tailor. These important details tell us much about the working-class composition of rugby league.

During the summer of 1907–08, Giltinan, Trumper and Hoyle organised a new competition based on nine working-class district clubs (Balmain, Cumberland, Eastern Suburbs, Glebe, Newcastle, Newtown, North Sydney, Western Suburbs and South Sydney). Rugby union, however, remained the more popular game in Sydney until hotelier James Joynton Smith, publisher of *Smith's Weekly* and later Lord Mayor of Sydney, transformed league's fortunes. In 1909 Smith financed a series of exhibition matches between the Wallabies (a representative union team) and the Kangaroos (a representative league team). Kangaroo players received five shillings each; the majority of Wallaby players received £100 each. At the time most workers earned only £2 per week. The matches secured a 'new crop of crack players' for league. By the end of the 1910 season, rugby league had clearly won the battle for the hearts and minds of most Sydneysiders. This in turn caused more footballers to 'desert' union.[37]

Rugby league's emergence reflected working-class concerns about adequate and just compensation.[38] Subsequent growth of the game revealed 'the structures of working class organisation in Sydney', including the Labor Party and the Catholic school system. Although he followed the ousted Hoyle as the League's president, James Smith, the entrepreneur, was essentially a figurehead. The key administrators and organisers were active in the Labor Party. Edward Larkin, the first full-time secretary, was a former policeman and later Labor MLA; Fred Flowers, one of two vice-presidents, was a Labor MLC. Larkin had attended St Joseph's College, a Marist Brothers school at Hunters Hill, and in 1913 Sydney's Marist Brothers schools embraced rugby league as *the* football code; the NSWRFL provided the referees.[39] In 1920 other Catholic schools took up the game. As Gordon Inglis observed, schools are the secret of success: 'have the schoolboys with you and much has been gained already.'[40] Union remained the dominant game in state schools until 1920 when T. D. Mutch, the Labor Minister for Public Instruction, directed the state's Public Schools Amateur Sports Association to include league in schools.[41] This 'solid grounding in the working class was', in Chris Cunneen's words, 'the basis of the new code's strength'. Through rugby, league supporters could express their community and district loyalties and, most importantly, the payment of players did not infringe any particular moral code they might have held.[42]

MANLINESS AND THE GENTLE GENDER

The philosophy of muscular Christianity underwent constant revision. As the nineteenth century closed, the religious dimension receded and God increasingly 'received only token recognition'.[43] Further, the virtues of manliness shifted from 'seriousness, self-denial and rectitude' to 'robustness, perseverance and stoicism'.[44] One element of manliness remained constant: physical courage. Across cultures, classes and time, physical courage has been a prerequisite for honour and status among men.[45] In Australia in the second half of the nineteenth century, football was a litmus test of manhood and courage. Football demanded considerable bravery, as 'Leatherstocking', a correspondent for the *Sydney Mail,* made clear in his 1877 'list' of recent 'accidents': 'I have already mentioned the death in Adelaide of the unfortunate bank clerk, Poole, and we now have from Auckland the announcement of the death through football of a young player named Pilling. Two accidents are also reported in Sydney, one player having his shoulder put out, and another his thigh broken.'[46]

How did men measure their 'courage'? The answer is important because it reveals much about gender relations. Men measured their courage against its opposite, physical cowardice, a trait imputed to women and femininity. In 1870 observers accused the Melbourne player and one of the founders of Australian football, Henry Harrison, of ungentlemanly conduct. They accused him of 'taking out' an opponent from the Albert Park team and then 'jumping on him while he lay on the ground'. He didn't repent. Football, Harrison declared, 'is essentially a rough game all the world over, and is not suitable for men-poodles or milksops'. While most of the Albert Park players were 'fine manly fellows', Harrison added, there were also some 'old women in disguise'.[47]

In the nineteenth century no divide—not even that between the upper middle classes and the *lumpenproletariat*—was greater than that between the sexes. Nothing reinforced this gender and sexual division better than sport. Murray Phillips reminds us that sport 'helped define and confirm male sexual superiority':

Sport was promoted as a masculine activity in order to counteract fears of 'feminisation' caused by changes inherent in urbanisation and modernisation. It was also a response to the cultural and political challenges posed by the women's movement in the late nineteenth and early twentieth centuries that threatened the distribution of power and existing gender relations. These forces help to explain the evolution of some forms of sport.... violent ['combat' sports like rugby and boxing] enhanced male dominance not only by denying access to females but also by associating sanctioned use of physical prowess with masculinity.[48]

If Victorian Australians considered physical prowess a Christian virtue capable of teaching modesty, truth, honour and obedience, why did they restrict these virtues to men? And why did the girls' schools take so long to discover the games field as a means of inculcating the Christian message among their female charges? The answer lay in a mixture of ideas associated with Social Darwinism and the natural and social sciences.

In the second half of the nineteenth century, ideas about the physical inferiority of women, emanating from the emerging natural sciences and sociology, reinforced Social Darwinist beliefs about motherhood and evolution. This hotchpotch of concepts consigned women to care and nurture.[49] Victorian women could pursue gentle physical activity as a means of producing healthy and well-proportioned bodies, but rigorous physical exertion was too dangerous. This 'common sense' translated into social customs in which hard physical activity was the antithesis of respectable femininity. In 1885 *Australian Etiquette* listed the following activities as suitable for middle-class women: dancing, private theatricals, twirl-the-platter, forfeits, schoolmaster and cotton flies.[50] It also

An intercolonial lawn tennis tournament, Association Ground, Moore Park, Sydney. Tennis was considered a genteel form of sport, and was the only arena besides croquet where men and women could play together. The absurdly restrictive garments gradually gave way to something more sensible. TOWN & COUNTRY JOURNAL, 14 MAY 1887

Callisthenics: 'training women in graceful and charming movements'. The grace of the female body was an important social consideration of the time, and callisthenics, unlike more strenuous sports, was believed to be non-injurious to women's reproductive organs, motherhood being all-important. AUSTRALIAN SKETCHER, 16 JULY 1881 approved of lawn tennis on the grounds that it afforded 'ladies a training in graceful and charming movements'.

Given that the upper classes defined social respectability, their patronage was crucial in defining acceptable physical activity. Lady Roma Bowen, wife of the Governor of Victoria, hosted archery parties at Government House in the 1870s. Lady Bowen and Mary Moorehouse, wife of the Bishop of Melbourne, both supported Harriett Rowell, who used the professional name Harriett Elphinstone Dick, and Alice Moon, who opened the Melbourne Ladies' Gymnasium. Lady Bowen also presented Dick with a gold bracelet 'in recognition of her successful efforts to promote the art of swimming among the ladies of Victoria'. Fashionable women followed Lady Sybil Brassey at Government House in Melbourne and Lady Mary Lamington in Brisbane when they took to cycling.[51] Dame Edith Walker's Yaralla estate at Concord was the first venue of what was to become the Royal Sydney Golf Club. There she hosted gatherings for croquet, an appropriate feminine sport. Moving to Rose Bay, it was not surprising that Royal Sydney began life as a golf course for men and a croquet club for women, who, as females, could not be 'full' members: women remained 'associates' of men. The term 'associates' for women golfers has endured for over a century, and for longer in Australia than in any other country.[52]

Most female exertion, it must be stressed, occurred in private. Women played tennis on private tennis courts. What society condemned in public it ignored in private. When Lady Roma Bowen, a competent markswoman, opened the Victorian Rifle Range in 1878, organisers 'rigged up a stand to which the rifle was attached and aimed at number 24 target on the new range'. Concerned officials even saved Bowen the physical effort of touching the rifle: 'she pulled a ribbon attached to the trigger'![53] Such conservative attitudes explain why cycling 'spearheaded the female liberation movement in recreation' in the 1890s. Daring, active women seized the relatively cheap 'safety cycle' as an instrument of female revolution: they showed that ladies could sit astride their bicycles as well as wear 'revealing' bloomers and blouses.[54]

Undoubtedly the key sites of sporting emancipation for women were the girls' private schools. But developments were slow. When the pioneers of female education championed physical programs for girls in the 1870s, they found it impossible to 'allay the fears' of concerned middle-class parents—people who believed physical activity would 'destroy' their daughters' 'bodily health' and ultimately 'reduce their

The Melbourne Bicycle Club opening meeting. The penny-farthing gave way to the modern bicycle in the late 1880s, and cycling became a highly popular means of both recreation and transport, used by all classes, with women gaining a new mobility and defying convention by sitting astride their machines. BULLETIN, 14 FEBRUARY 1885

chances of marriage', their 'capacity to manage a home' and their ability to function as mothers.[55] It wasn't until the late nineteenth and early twentieth centuries that the girls' schools incorporated sport into their curricula. In 1901, in a radical departure from accepted practice, Mary Morris, co-principal of Melbourne Church of England Girls' Grammar School, spoke of 'the great importance of sport in schoolgirl life': 'Our girls need open-air exercise just as boys do, especially if they are doing good mental work. More especially they need the discipline of the playground which boys get and which enables them to understand the value of co-operative effort in later life.'[56]

Yet, as several historians have suggested, much of the initial impetus and initiative for games came from pupils. In 1876 pupils at the Presbyterian Ladies College in Melbourne 'petitioned the principal, the Reverend George Tait, for the use of the gymnasium for roller skating practice' which they claimed was 'a much more healthful', albeit more risky, amusement than croquet.[57]

THE BLACK SIDE OF CHRISTIAN MORALITY[58]

The exclusion of females from sport was unreasonable, but at least men provided a rationale: strenuous sport endangered reproductive organs and motherhood. The Judaeo-Christian ethos of paternalism, in its true chivalrous sense, meant that men fought, earned, protected, foraged and provided for their women. There was no such rationale for those imbued with both Christian and secular notions about the inferiority of the cursed 'children of Ham', those with black skins.

Good Aboriginal athletes found themselves barred from amateur competition, even where they were keen to participate. The Queensland Amateur Athletic Association tried to disbar all Aborigines from athletics, first because they allegedly lacked moral character, then because they had insufficient intelligence, finally because they couldn't resist white vice. Unable to sustain any of these ludicrous 'reasons', in 1903 the Association simply deemed them all permanent professionals.[59] Other attempts at exclusion were just as ugly. In 1888 at Thargomindah in Queensland, white runners refused to compete against blacks in an important Sheffield Handicap, causing a special Aborigines-only race to be run. The Queensland Home Secretary wrote in 1897 that 'the whites complained of the superior capabilities of the blacks at Fraser Island, and asked me to stop them competing with the whites'. In 1889 three Aborigines competed at Blackall in central Queensland: Colin won three flat races and the running high jump; Bill won putting the (35-pound) stone and Charlie won two other field events. The local paper commented: 'It is very sad that our coloured brethren should have scooped the pool in this easy fashion, but it says a great deal for the generosity of the other athletes of Blackall that they did not attempt to bar aboriginal competitors.'

Charlie Samuels was undoubtedly Australia's greatest athlete of the nineteenth century. Yet even in tribute, the leading sports paper of the day, the *Referee*, was a little awkward about the loss of 'white' face:

> Thus it is that I am about to claim for an aboriginal runner what an overwhelming majority of foot racing critics will concede is his due—the Championship of Australia. It might be more pleasant reflection to Australians, perhaps, if a white man...could be quoted as champion; but as we are sizing up the sprint runners on the 'all-in' principle, a black aboriginal has to be accorded the laurel crown...Samuels has, in a long course of consistent and brilliant running, established his claim, not only

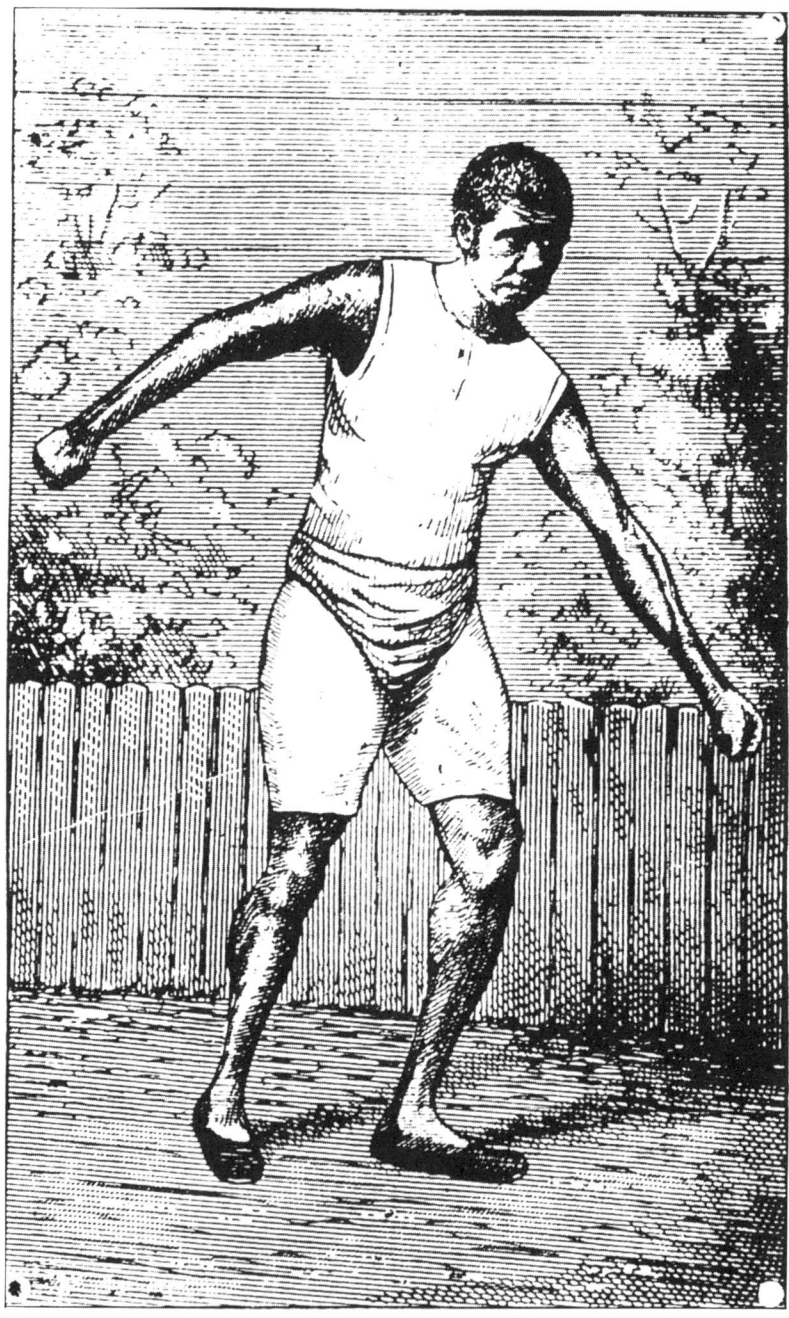

'He is a rather peculiar made sprinter, having little or no calf and a tremendous thigh at the top of the leg': the Referee's comment on Aboriginal 'ped' Patrick Bowman, winner of a prestigious Carrington Cup in Sydney in 1887. Pedestrianism (professional athletics) was the main avenue for Aboriginal sports achievement in the nineteenth century. REFEREE, 2 JUNE 1887 to be the Australian champion, but also to have been one of the best exponents of sprint running the world has ever seen.

Fortunately it was the tolerant Blackall rather than the racist and regressive Fraser Island approach that held sway, at least until 1904. In that year the Brisbane press published Dr Walter Roth's opinions. The Chief Protector of Queensland's Aborigines, quoting the philosopher Herbert Spencer, argued that it was imperative to give those in contact with whites 'every legal protection' but to 'make isolation complete' when removed from such society. Spencer, after all, had written that the only permissible forms of intercourse between the strong and the weak races were 'the exchange of commodities' such as 'physical and menial products'. Thus while purporting to have 'a sincere regard for their preservation and welfare', Roth proposed banning blacks from running:

> This kind of thing disorganises the work, demoralises the people and destroys our influence over those whom we are seeking to uplift and make a self-supporting people...They are being gradually turned into good farm workers, but the racing men will not work. They will not be subject to authority, but go away to their supporters for a time, and then come back and loaf on the station. If we deny them rations, they become a kind of martyr, live on the others, and spread discontent. Their friends have to be maintained, and they themselves, making plenty of money for a few years on behalf of the betting fraternity...come back to us wrecks, as a rule, and a nuisance and a burden upon the rest.

He then banned all 'peds' from earning their living by the simple strategy of prosecuting trainers who employed them and race promoters who 'harboured' them.

Even when officials sanctioned interracial competition, the morality of the time still demanded separation of black from white. On race programs there were dozens of Aboriginal competitors, each with an 'a' (for Aboriginal) or an 'h.c.' (for 'half-caste') after their names; occasionally 'c.p.' (coloured person), appeared. The last description gained appeal, suggesting an attractive American or West Indian runner. Fred Kingsmill began his running career in 1887 as 'a half-caste from Toowoomba'. By 1891 he was the celebrated 'coloured Adonis whom nature created and threw away the mould', hailing from somewhere or other in the United States; he was in fact a Toowoomban. Officials contended that 'without these distinguishing marks…the public are misled'. Misled about what? Their abilities, or the social, legal or biological class of the runners concerned? The initials began to disappear from about 1912.

ENTREPRENEURIAL INFLUENCES

In 1907 the *Bulletin*—discussing the New Zealand All Golds' visit to Sydney—commented that 'the idea of professional football proves very alluring to a number of people in Sydney and some New South Wales capitalists are considering the question of organising three or four professional teams to play in and around the big Australian cities'.[60] Indeed, 'capitalists' like James Giltinan, Victor Trumper and James Smith confirmed that not all middle-class sporting interests subscribed unwaveringly to the amateur ideals of muscular Christianity and athleticism. On the contrary, substantial middle-class interests saw sport as an economic opportunity. They not only undermined the narrow ideas of muscular Christianity but also laid the foundations for the social and economic development of sport.

Publican entrepreneurs had provided and distributed sporting games, especially to the working classes, since the penal era. It is true that voluntary sports associations, comprising largely amateur enthusiasts who were determined to 'safeguard their young parishioners' spiritual and physical well-being',[61] organised most sport in the second half of the nineteenth century and 'raised the large sums of capital needed to establish permanent facilities'.[62] But sporting publicans and entrepreneurs didn't vanish. Spiers and Pond brought the first All-England XI to Australia in 1861 (see page 31).[63] Rowland Newbury and Bryant, owners of the MCG refreshment tent, organised the first Aboriginal cricket match at that ground on Boxing Day 1866, an event that led to the famous Aboriginal tour of England in 1868. George Coppin, a theatrical producer, brought the world champion sprinter, Frank 'Scurry' Hewett from Ireland, to Melbourne for five races against the colonial champion, John Gregory Harris, in 1870. Twenty thousand people attended the first event at the MCG, the biggest crowd since the All-England XI.[64] In 1884 Frank Smith, another theatrical entrepreneur, became the proprietor of the Sir Joseph Banks Hotel at Botany (Sydney) and established the first professional running track in Australia, complete with 'cinders separated by grass lines and ringed by gaslights'. Followers bet hundreds and hundreds of pounds on a single race.[65] Hugh

Snowy Baker, the all-round sportsman, was the essence of 'muscular Christianity'. After considerable success as a boxer, he bought the Sydney Stadium and promoted boxing. In the issue of his magazine pictured here, note the articles on Jerry Jerome and on the women's physical culture course, operated by Annette Kellerman, the great Australian swimmer who was once arrested in Boston for wearing a one-piece costume. MITCHELL LIBRARY

'Huge Deal' McIntosh began his first business at age sixteen in the 1890s—selling pies at racetracks and prize fights. Around the turn of the century he began promoting sports events such as cycling and boxing. In 1908 he staged and refereed the historic world heavyweight bout between Jack Johnson and Tommy Burns at Rushcutter's Bay. That day was 'Australia's day of shame', the day, as poet Henry Lawson penned it, the 'nigger smacked [our] face'. The legendary writer Jack London said it wasn't a fight: 'No Armenian massacre would compare with the hopeless slaughter that took place in the Stadium.'[66] 'Huge Deal' earned £26 000 from the gate and £80 000 in film rights. In 1916 McIntosh took over the *Referee* and the *Sunday Times*.[67] Jimmy Sharman senior organised boxing tents at country shows. Many prominent boxers began or ended their careers in the shrewd entrepreneur's tents.[68]

Female entrepreneurs also played an important role in distributing sport, especially to middle-class women. As noted above, Harriett Dick and Alice Moon opened the Melbourne Ladies' Gymnasium in Collins Street. Pupils paid 29 shillings a quarter to learn callisthenics, Indian clubs, ring resistance, dumbbell exercises, free-exercises and marching.[69] Dick and Moon also organised classes in several private schools in Melbourne and Ballarat, while Dick conducted swimming classes for women at St Kilda.

Paradoxically, by organising sport, voluntary associations developed its commercial potential and paved the way for a more systematic involvement by business. While ideological fanaticism forced some amateur sports associations to hold a tight rein on finances, and to tread cautiously when dealing with commercial and professional interest groups, this didn't mean that amateur volunteers lacked understanding of the business side of sport. They, too, followed the 'laws' of commerce. The formation of the VFL in 1897 is one example. The VFL clubs wanted a financially viable competition and changed some rules to make football faster and more appealing to spectators. They introduced 'behind' goalposts, reduced the number of players on the field from twenty to eighteen per side, and stipulated that the ball travel at least ten yards before being 'marked'.[70] Nor could amateur ideologues ignore financial realities. Lack of sponsorship meant that players had to fund their own tours. Australian cricket tours of Britain in the last quarter of the nineteenth century, and in the lead-up to the Great War, 'were organised along joint-stock lines with each cricketer buying a share in the team and later earning a dividend from any profits accrued'.[71]

The press were the means by which business forged greater links with sport and developed sponsorship arrangements. In the late nineteenth century new publishing and newspaper interests recognised the potential for entertaining the increasingly 'independent', 'self-confident', 'literate', 'technologically competent' and 'sports-mad' lower middle and working classes.[72] Crucial to the 'liberation' of these classes were the free and compulsory education systems enacted by the colonial parliaments, beginning with Victoria in 1872. Advertisers seized sport, and especially 'star' players, as a means of selling all manner of products, thus helping reinforce sport's popularity. Dick's advertisements, for example, promised schoolgirls 'gradual gymnastic development of the whole body by exercises carefully adapted to each individual, calculated to counteract the effects of constant study, and ensuring good health, ease of movement and graceful carriage'.[73]

Complex internal contradictions and entrepreneurs were not the only factors to undermine the class structure of Australian sport. 'Community' and 'national' interests also intervened.

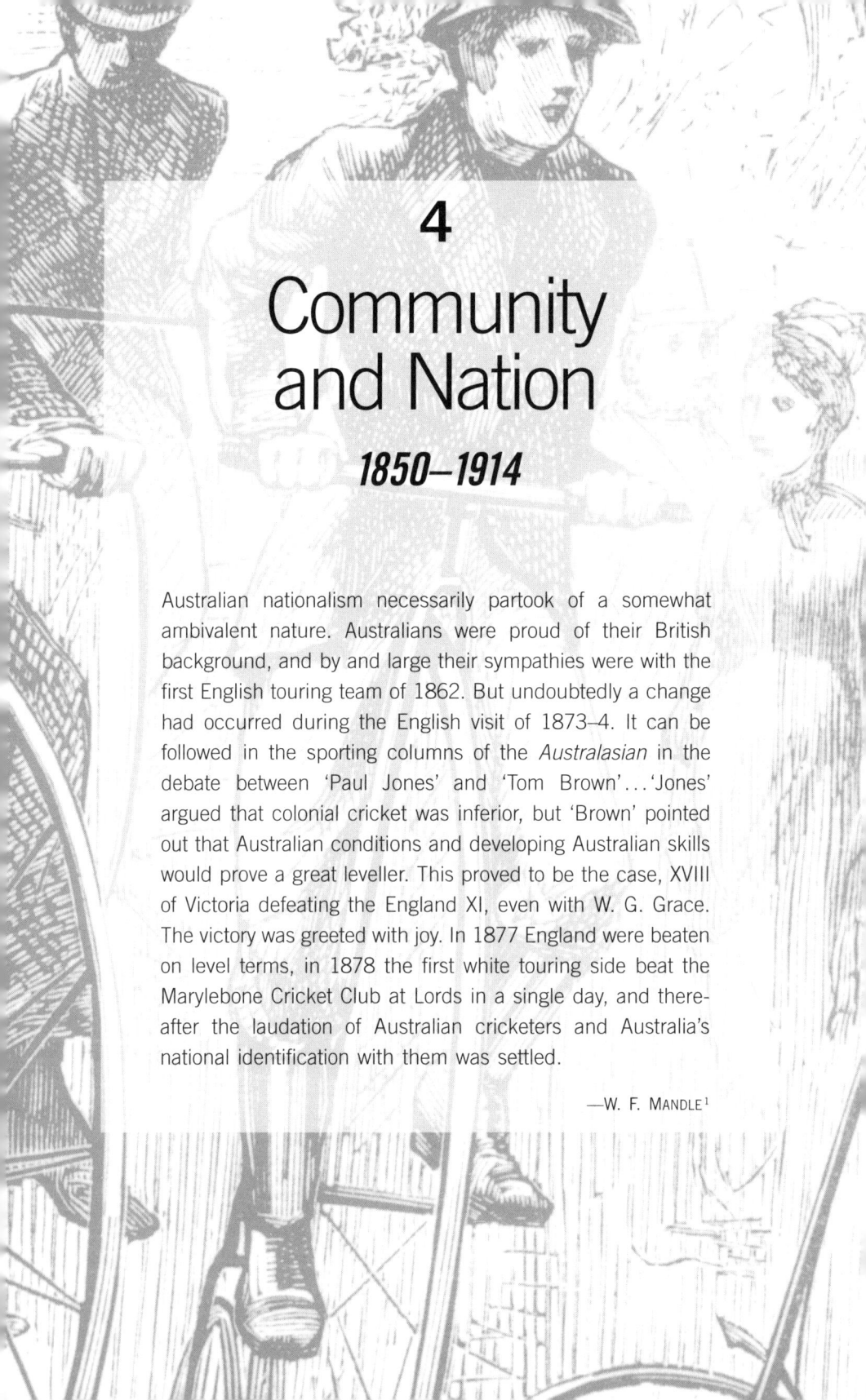

4
Community and Nation
1850–1914

Australian nationalism necessarily partook of a somewhat ambivalent nature. Australians were proud of their British background, and by and large their sympathies were with the first English touring team of 1862. But undoubtedly a change had occurred during the English visit of 1873–4. It can be followed in the sporting columns of the *Australasian* in the debate between 'Paul Jones' and 'Tom Brown'…'Jones' argued that colonial cricket was inferior, but 'Brown' pointed out that Australian conditions and developing Australian skills would prove a great leveller. This proved to be the case, XVIII of Victoria defeating the England XI, even with W. G. Grace. The victory was greeted with joy. In 1877 England were beaten on level terms, in 1878 the first white touring side beat the Marylebone Cricket Club at Lords in a single day, and thereafter the laudation of Australian cricketers and Australia's national identification with them was settled.

—W. F. Mandle[1]

COMMUNITY IDENTITY AND RIVALRY

Several forces fashioned sport in the second half of the nineteenth century. Social Darwinism, as we have seen, justified sharp divisions of class, gender and race, while entrepreneurship leavened these social cleavages. In addition, the growth of suburbs in Australian colonial cities introduced local community rivalry to sporting culture, and later, sport helped 'nationalise' colonial Australia.

Suburban development had a major impact on sport. New suburbs—typically based around a railway station, post office, retail stores and, in some cases, industrial manufacturing—generated local jobs. They also attracted like-minded socio-economic groups. Voluntary associations—churches, political associations and cultural organisations—further connected these groups, nurturing a strong spirit of community and local identity. Suburban rivalry also contributed to local identity and, ultimately, to a vibrant sporting culture. Robin Grow describes the development of football in colonial Melbourne:

> There were often bitter rivalries between neighbouring suburbs over issues such as the placement of public transport routes, the development of shopping centres, the location of post offices, courts, police stations and schools, waste disposal and road maintenance. Inter-suburban conflicts were fought out in local newspapers, at council tables, in parliament and cabinet, across the desks of government bureaucrats, and sometimes in the courts. Soon they were fought on the football field as well. Supporters rallied to watch their 'score of representatives' turn out to 'do battle for the honour of the locality'. Some of the fiercest on-field battles occurred between teams from neighbouring suburbs such as Collingwood and Fitzroy. Perhaps it did not matter so much that the council next door was dumping night soil on your side of the municipal boundary if your team could defeat theirs on the football field next Saturday.[2]

The very range of sporting rivalry explains how sport became entrenched in Australian culture. It included everything from 'light-hearted banter between supporters at local shops and hotels to pitched battles fought out with fence pickets in the streets'. 'Inner-suburban clubs and their supporters', writes Grow,

> often found themselves embroiled in disputes with two or three neigh-
> bouring clubs over issues such as on-field incidents, player transfers and
> the state of the grounds, and emotions were often fuelled by parochial
> local newspaper reports. The development of widespread, reliable and
> cheap transport systems made it possible for thousands of supporters to
> accompany their teams to away matches, and there were numerous dis-
> putes over visiting members' rights to enter the home teams' grounds and
> grandstands.[3]

Suburbanisation was not an even process in colonial Australia. It began in Melbourne in the mid-nineteenth century, preceding Sydney by a quarter of a century. The suburban sporting club was an early feature of Melbourne's history, but in Sydney sporting clubs remained predominantly class-based, that is, 'formed by gentlemen of similar background' with 'common interests' and who supported 'a common cause'. Members were invited because they too 'shared...common bonds'.[4] The differences between the two cities lay in geography and in gold.

Early Sydney was a commercial city, a spearhead of imperialism. But it developed haphazardly, with high-density housing and walking the commonest means of transport. Dense housing meant little surplus land for sport: access thus depended on how far Sydneysiders could walk. Hyde Park, Sydney's first recreation field, was an early venue for football, cricket, quoits and horse-racing. Determined to preserve the Park as 'common land', the government banned sport there in 1856. Horse-racing subsequently 'roamed' around Sydney between Bellevue, Camperdown, Parramatta, Homebush and Petersham before eventually settling at Randwick in 1860. Cricketers played in the Domain until 1861. A select committee—appointed that year by the Legislative Assembly to investigate management of the Domain—recommended the removal of a fence surrounding the cricket oval and the use of the Domain for passive recreation only. These decisions retarded organised Sydney sport for decades: without permanent enclosed home grounds, sports officials had no significant sources of revenue other than members' subscriptions.[5]

The government proposed Moore Park as the main sports venue. Most people still lived within a couple of kilometres of the city and as a prominent cricket player and official, Captain E. M. W. Ward, told the select committee, 'you could not possibly expect the large number of persons who live in Sydney and wish to have a little recreation at cricket in the afternoon to walk out that distance after their day's work is over'.[6] Finally, in 1878 cricket found a home at the Association Ground, later known as the Sydney Cricket Ground (SCG).

Complicating the space problem was the fact that competitive sport was organised by middle-class gentlemen's and officers' clubs, boys' private schools and Sydney University. Two issues arose here. First, historical internecine conflict between emancipists and exclusives divided the middle classes: they disagreed about the rules by which they should play cricket and football and they failed to build enduring sporting clubs. Conflict split the Sydney Turf Club and the Australian Cricket Club; the Albert Cricket Club, which succeeded the latter, also folded. Second, when Sydney's sporting clubs finally did begin regular interclub competitions in the 1870s, they excluded the working classes. It wasn't until the late nineteenth century, under the impetus of suburbanisation, that football and cricket became part of Sydney's popular culture.

By contrast, Melbourne, like Adelaide and Perth, developed as a new, urban, frontier city. Low-density housing and much space meant plenty of land for recreation. Melbourne's social and economic elite— unburdened by the weight of penal social divisions—formed a much more homogeneous group, working together and forming various sporting committees. In 1838, within three years of the city's founding, devotees had established the Melbourne Cricket Club (MCC); two years later, Melburnians attended their first race meeting at Flemington. In 1853 the MCC secured its own centrally located ground; gate revenue allowed the club to invest in and develop cricket. Footballers formed the Melbourne Football Club in 1858 and began playing regular games under the same rules in 1859. In 1866 a number of clubs further codified the rules.

Gold changed Melbourne from a pastoral town to a thriving city in the 1850s. Waves of immigrants had a profound impact on sport. Historian Andrew Lemon has traced the rapid growth of horse-racing in that decade to these newcomers: they turned 'an amateur enthusiasm and a rustic sport' into a 'flourishing industry'.[7] Trollope hated horse-racing: he couldn't distinguish the colours, he lost 'sundry small bets', and he didn't like champagne. But he attended the races at Launceston. What amazed him was the shiploads of Melburnians who sailed the Strait just for the meeting.[8]

Melbourne's geography also played a part. Some distance from its port, the city required an efficient transport system. Flat land assisted the development of tramways and railways, which quickly radiated into expanding suburbs. These utilities enhanced suburban identities, enabling local suburban teams and their supporters to move about. Suburban ovals were usually located close to railway stations. By the early 1860s, Collingwood, East Melbourne, Richmond, South Melbourne, South Yarra and St Kilda had suburban cricket and football teams.

Sydney didn't experience strong urban growth until the last quarter of the nineteenth century, when its population trebled. Yet even in 1890, when the populations were roughly equivalent, Melbourne covered twice Sydney's area. Suburban cricket and football competitions began in Sydney in 1891 and 1900 respectively. The Metropolitan Rugby Union's district competition stimulated a great deal of interest in rugby as teams increasingly expressed 'local district loyalties'.[9] But, as we have seen, the inflexible amateur structure of middle-class football discriminated against working-class players. These formed their own competition in 1907.

EMBRYONIC NATIONALISM

Intense intercolonial rivalry, especially between New South Wales and Victoria, was a feature of the nineteenth century. The 'first decades of self-government were marked by customs barriers, competition for investment and a short-sighted and expensive decision to build colonial railways on different gauges'.[10] Later, as young states in a federal system, they couldn't agree on whether Melbourne or Sydney should be the nation's capital, so they chose 'neutral' Canberra—amid nowhere!

Rivalry extended to sport. When Victorian cricketers visited Sydney in the 1860s, the locals apparently urged one another to ''eave arf a brick at them!'[11] In 1884 the *Sydney Echo* called the Melbourne Cup 'a sinful event bordering on the horrors of Sodom and Gomorrah'. The race, the paper insisted, led to 'murder, suicide, crime, despair and disgrace'. The *Sydney Morning Herald* agreed: compared to the 'fine and noble' festivals of Europe, the Melbourne Cup epitomised 'all that was rotten'. Melbourne's papers responded in kind: 'is there any racing in New South Wales?' asked the *Herald*. 'Yes, there is; something on a level with our "Wallaby Flat" or "Narracan Valley" meetings. Poor Sydney.'[12] Not surprisingly, Sydneysiders refused to play Victorian football. If the

The second intercolonial New South Wales versus Victoria cricket match, played at the Domain in Sydney, 14–16 January 1857. New South Wales won, but avoiding the cow pats was a problem for the fieldsmen. TOWN & COUNTRY JOURNAL, 1 JANUARY 1887

game had been called 'Scandinavian rules', suggested *Melbourne Punch*, it might have been accepted, but 'Victorian—perish the thought!'[13]

The Riverina was one area of New South Wales where Australian football did catch on: 'Melbourne was a major destination for many of the Riverina's products, and the rivalries between the towns for their share of the lucrative southern trade were intensified by contests on the football field.'[14] Similarly, economic links explain the early interest in Australian football among New Zealanders. Hess explains:

> Political and commercial ties with New Zealand were relatively strong in the middle and late nineteenth century, and improvements in steamship travel and telegraphic communication helped to foster an even closer relationship. The diffusion of the game received a boost with the Otago gold discoveries, which brought 64 000 Australians to the region between 1861 and 1863...and turn[ed] the west coast of the South Island into an Australian community.[15]

Intercolonial rivalry may have assisted the development of Australian football. E. C. H. Taylor argues that three losses in cricket to New South Wales in 1856, 1857 and 1858 were the catalyst for the foundation of Australian football. As a member of the defeated Victorian team, Tommy Wills, regarded as one of the fathers of Australian football, proposed 'a game that would keep cricketers fit during winter'.[16]

These rivalries and jealousies were an obstacle to a national culture. The very idea of an Australian nation, and a national culture, was a late nineteenth-century notion. Early in the century, 'the question of a distinctively Australian identity was not a burning issue' because most Australians recognised themselves as 'part of a group of new, transplanted, predominantly Anglo-Saxon emigrant society'.[17] As we will see, in many respects this common Anglo-Saxon identity would act as a millstone around the necks of Australians, who have consistently had difficulty accepting or even tolerating non-British immigrants.

A specific group of middle-class intellectuals, many of whom benefited from compulsory education and worked as professional journalists, fostered Australian nationalism. They challenged popular international views of the country as a cultural backwater—the 'dustbin of the unwanted and unsuccessful', in Eric Hobsbawm's words.[18] They promoted a positive image of Australia, arguing that its peoples constituted a unique and valuable culture.[19]

Negative images and feelings of inferiority derived from Australia's founding as a penal colony. Transportation carried with it images of brutality and depravity and tainted Australian settlement. In 1827 Peter Cunningham, who served as a surgeon on convict ships and then took up land in the colony, wrote that 'if you were conversing amiably in an English stagecoach with someone who discovered that you had been to New South Wales, your companion would move away, and under pretence of fumbling for a penknife or a toothpick assure himself that all his pockets were safe'.[20] Even when Australia promoted itself as a land of opportunity for everyone, many in Britain saw the emigrant as 'a failure whose economic difficulties…were caused by personal instability rather than an unjust system'. In 1852 Earl Grey, when Secretary of State for the colonies, told novelist Charles Dickens that emigrants were 'necessarily far below the average of the working population in respect to steadiness and strictly moral conduct…In every rank of life it is not the steady and well conducted that are the most disposed to emigration'. Even the more forgiving tended to see Australia as a haven for the

second-rate, a home for Britain's social and culturally inferior and its
'redundant population'.[21] A European visitor heard Melbourne people
say of Sydney in 1863, 'of course there are frightfully rich people there,
but mostly descended from convicts—and as for their behaviour…!'.[22]

Muscular Christianity helped kindle embryonic nationalism: sport
gave Australians a yardstick to 'measure' themselves. In 1864 *Bell's Life
in Victoria* described the Australian man as one who

> does not sit down to a small marble table, sip sugared water like the
> Frenchman, nor plant his back against the wall, and smoke innumerable
> cigars, like a Spaniard; nor bask dreamily in the sunshine and surrender
> himself to the *dolce far niente*, like a Neapolitan; nor booze away his brains
> in a beer cellar like a Bavarian. He demands motion and exercise. He
> engages in out-of-door pastimes which sometimes necessitate scarcely less
> physical effort than the ordinary vocations of daily life…rowing, racing,
> cricket and campaigning.[23]

Sport not only 'satisfied many commentators that a convict history
and climatic changes had not deleteriously affected the English race',
but it also inculcated a 'growing confidence that a more virile race had
developed in the Antipodes'.[24] Marcus Clarke, the great man of letters,
wrote enthusiastically about sport: 'read the accounts of the boat races,
the cricket matches, and say if our youth are not manly…deny, if you
can, that there is here the making of a great nation.'[25] In 1877 he fore-
saw that 'in another hundred years the average Australasian' will be a
man whose 'teeth will be bad' and who 'will suffer from liver disease,
and become prematurely bald'. But, despite these ailments, he will be
'a tall coarse, strong-jawed, greedy, pushing, talented man, excelling in
swimming and horsemanship'.[26]

Not everyone approved of sport as a foundation of national identity.
Melbourne Punch lamented the 'reign of muscle'. James Hogan inveighed
against it: 'to deify muscle, and degrade the mind, is a proceeding that
does not augur well for the future.'[27] The day was fast approaching,
wrote *Punch*, when the chief industry of the nation would be the production of athletes for export and the population of the country would
'only snatch an occasional hour or two from the prevailing rush for goals
to attend to the necessities of existence'.[28] Hogan, historian of the Irish
in Australia, ridiculed the 'nine out of ten' Australians who seemed to
'spend all their leisure in the practice of either cricket or football'.
Australians, he warned, were becoming 'rather selfish in conduct and

secular in practice; contented and easy going, but non-intellectual and tasteless'.[29] After a visiting dignitary reminded pupils at St Peter's College (Adelaide) that Australians are 'guilty... of the worship of those who shine in the performance of some manly sport', he offered some caution and advice:

> If this worship... is not controlled and checked we shall quite eradicate the pursuit of letters and literature, and of the arts and sciences, and create a false impression of ourselves. By all means let us admire those who love to indulge in healthy sports, but we must cultivate the mind and the body... There is a great deal more in this life than being able to run faster than anyone else, or to lift a greater weight, or to strike a heavier blow.[30]

Nor did commentators agree that a 'population besotted with sport' produced an 'athletic, healthy and moral nation'. Some thought it produced an 'uncivilised' nation 'given to the huzzaing of madmen'. Poet and storyteller Henry Lawson perceived the average Australian *boy* as a 'cheeky brat with a leaning towards larrikinism' and 'no ambition beyond the cricket and football field'; the average Australian *youth* was a 'weedy individual with a weak, dirty, and contemptible vocabulary, and a cramped mind devoted to sport': his god was 'a two-legged brute with unnaturally developed muscles and no brains'. As to the average Australian *man*, 'he has not been developed yet'! What angered him most was that while the unions might be crushed and the Labor cause abolished, 'these things would be of less importance to the towney than the fact that Bill Somebody sprained his (blanky) groin at football last Saturday and mightn't be able to play in the forthcoming match'.[31]

Sport should not be seen in isolation. In the late nineteenth century, a host of forces helped 'nationalise' Australia: confrontation with the outside world, such as German annexation of Eastern New Guinea and French proposals to annex the New Hebrides; economic development— for example the banks, financial corporations and pastoral companies had branches in every colonial city and some country towns; the formation of the Australian Federation of Employers in 1888; and intercolonial trade union congresses.[32] Moreover, sport was not always a panacea: combined intercolonial cricket teams frequently 'exacerbated' rivalries by promoting 'quarrels between colonial cricket associations, conflicts over the selection of umpires and disputes about the composition of Test teams'.[33]

Nonetheless, the euphoria and joy gained from sporting victories over England by combined teams from Australia's colonies in the 1870s and 1880s, two decades before federation, cannot be underestimated. They helped overcome feelings of inadequacy, lack of sophistication, second-ratedness, and were immensely 'important in fostering a sense of shared "Australianness"'.[34] Paradoxically, Social Darwinist notions of sport contributed to embryonic nationalism by shifting the focus of social divisions from class to nation. Increasingly, in the late nineteenth century, the middle classes condemned class loyalties as divisive and un-Australian.[35] *Bell's Life in Sydney* commented:

> Enable the...working man...to inhale the pure atmosphere of Heaven in some adjacent mead, and there indulge in a game of cricket, or any other rational pastime...and you will soon witness the change...The pot-houses of the towns and villages will no longer be inundated with swarms of sottish drunkards...in the purchase of maddening liquors; spouting obscenity...or endeavouring...to cut, maim, and mangle each other's bodies...and next morning condemned...by months of incarceration... Sports are the germs of sound morality and permanent happiness—of national prosperity, and of national honour.[36]

In the early 1890s some members of the working-class and a middle-class movement advocated federation of the six colonies; some labour parties opposed federation, seeing it as a conservative plot. In 1901 federation became a reality. But federation neither conferred immediate sovereignty nor 'nationalised' Australians instantly. Most citizens still considered themselves part of the British 'race'. Australia

> had no power to declare war or peace, it could not make formal treaties with foreign powers and it had no diplomatic status abroad. The head of state was still the British monarch; the governor general, her representative, retained wide discretionary power; Commonwealth law could be invalidated by legislation of the British parliament; the highest court of appeal was the privy council in London; the national anthem was England's.[37]

Australian participation in the olympic games of 1896 (Athens), 1900 (Paris) and 1904 (St Louis) shows just how embryonic was the nature of national sport at the turn of the century. Olympic records tell us that athlete Edwin Flack, who won gold in the 800m and the 1500m, was Australia's sole representative at Athens. But Australia 'did not even possess a national controlling union to administer the sport of athletics', and Flack's participation stemmed from a 'very private decision', initially based on the simple desire to see Greece. London had been his home and place of work in the year leading up to the first modern olympic games, and the London Athletic Club nominated him to compete. The Union Jack flew over the victory ceremonies, and official records, even as late as 1936, credited Flack's successes to Britain. It was five days after his first victory before Australians heard Flack's name. Three competitors—Freddie Lane (swimming), Stan Rowley (sprinting) and Donald Mackintosh (shooting)—represented Australia at the 1900 Paris olympics. But 'it would be wrong to consider them, in any but the loosest sense, as a team. Australia [still] possessed no national coordinating body, and no opportunity existed for any kind of comradeship, or even much sense of mutual awareness'. Money raised by public appeal in New South Wales helped Rowley, the colony's best sprinter. The Victorian Amateur Athletic Association refused to 'encroach' upon its funds, 'in view of various obligations in the near future', although it urged local amateurs to make donations 'as a fraternal gesture to our New South Wales friends'.[38] Australia's sole representative at St Louis in 1904 was Corrie Gardner. His inspiration derived not from a sense of national pride but from Flack. Gardner was a pupil at Melbourne Grammar when Flack presented his olympic olive wreaths to his old school.

As a case study in Australian sporting nationalism, Donald Mackintosh reveals much. 'Sports patriots' assert that Mackintosh won gold and bronze for Australia at the 1900 olympics, and in the 1980s they began a campaign to have the IOC officially recognise his achievements.[39] Mackintosh came first and third in two live pigeon-shooting competitions. No one disputes these facts. But was live pigeon-shooting an official olympic sport or a minor amusement? Confusion reigned in Paris and in St Louis. Both olympics were, in reality, merely appendages to world fairs. The athletic program at Paris was, in the words of olympic historian Allen Guttmann, a 'disaster': 'the competitions took place over a period of two months and were such a peripheral part of the world's fair that most visitors left quite unaware of them...Some of the athletes returning home were surprised to learn that they had just participated in the Olympic games.'[40] Mackintosh died quite unaware that he had ever been an olympian!

Among 'sports patriots', Australia's unbroken participation in the modern summer games demonstrates national credibility and Australia's place as a stalwart of the olympic movement. Only three countries—Australia, Britain and Greece—claim this 'status' and it is, says Harry Gordon, 'one of the proudest boasts Australia can make'. Gordon convincingly argues that Britain never sent a team to St Louis. While this trivial issue distorts so much of the historical period, in the context of Sydney's and Manchester's rival bids for the 2000 olympic games, it was a significant debating point.[41] Myths bedevil all history—and nowhere more so than in a country so obsessed with sport, sporting records, and sporting achievements.

THE INCLUSION OF WOMEN

In 1910 a correspondent to the *Argus* (Melbourne) praised 'the Australian girl', describing her as 'one of the finest types of young womanhood in this world'. According to the correspondent, 'this is largely due to sport in which she engages'.[42] Neither federation nor the enfranchisement of women miraculously changed the fortunes of Australia's sporting women, although both events coincided with growing acceptance of women's sport.[43] By the early 1900s most independent girls' schools 'had acquired the grounds on which to hold athletics meetings or were committed to levelling fields where necessary'. At the same time, an intense debate erupted about how sportswomen should present themselves in public. The 'establishment' refused to countenance public displays of women engaging in hard physical exercise or sport. Such activity violated prevailing notions about 'proper' female decorum. In 1907 the headmistress of Methodist Ladies College, Burwood (Sydney), supported a sports day at the school. Senior male clergy protested when it became clear that parents and friends would be present as spectators; they demanded that 'improper' and 'unfeminine' events, like the high jump and hurdles, 'take place before the carnival in the seclusion of the school's grounds'. Controversy arose when University of Adelaide students appeared in public wearing their hockey costumes:

> Their ankle length skirts, high necked white blouses with long sleeves, stiff collars and high waist earned them the title 'hussies'. An infinitesimal glimpse of their thickly stockinged ankles resulted in a rule...that, when in costume, hockey players should always carry their hockey sticks.

Only with this precaution could they hope to have their short skirts pardoned and outraged propriety mollified.[44]

Society simply wouldn't accept women compromising their gentility and decorum in the name of sporting pursuits.

In one sense federation did provide a catalyst for the resolution of women's sport. As the recently revived olympic games suggested, sport increasingly became an ingredient in the international comity, and Australia, as a new nation-state, could not ignore that reality. Swimming offers excellent insights into the changing role of sportswomen.

When the Frenchman Baron Pierre de Coubertin revived the olympic games, he did so with two political motives: first, to bolster the morale of French youth after the debacle of the Franco–Prussian War and to so develop character and vitality through (fighting) competition; second, to lessen—not end—tensions between *nations* through athletic competition. De Coubertin was essentially a militarist rather than a humanitarian philosopher. He was also the ultimate male chauvinist. He not only opposed women's participation, but 'fought against their admission for more than 30 years'.[45] According to the French aristocrat, 'equality must stop at the threshold of the family hearth'. So how did women gain entrance to olympic competition? Dennis Phillips argues that 'women took advantage of the confusion that marked the planning for early olympic festivals. They made a modest debut in a small number of "genteel" sports and then began a long struggle to wedge their way into other events'. Swimming was one such 'genteel' sport.

In 1910 the IOC added three events for women to the swimming program at Stockholm two years later: diving, 4 x 100m relay and the 100m freestyle. A political compromise ensured the inclusion of women's swimming: de Coubertin needed support from the newly formed International Swimming Federation to secure his favourite event, the modern pentathlon, in the 1912 program, and the Swimming Federation, or more correctly, Britain with its eyes firmly fixed on gold medals, wanted women's swimming. Much to the surprise of the British, Australians Sarah 'Fanny' Durack and Wilhelmina 'Mina' Wylie won the gold and silver respectively in the 100m at the 1912 Stockholm games. Although swimming was an old and popular Australian pastime, a long struggle preceded Durack's and Wylie's participation.

Inspired and motivated by prospects of financial gains, an obsession with good health and an increasingly garbled ideology of Social Darwinism, municipal councils and entrepreneurs began constructing pools and baths across the country in the last quarter of the nineteenth century. Swimming enthusiasts responded to the new facilities and established their own clubs. Competitions and umbrella associations to codify the sport followed. In New South Wales, half a dozen clubs formed an Amateur Swimming Association (NSWASA) in 1892.

These developments had an important ramification for women's swimming. In the 1830s and 1840s, in keeping with prevailing social mores, women wore pants, skirts, hats and shoes when swimming. The new pools and baths were segregated. This allowed women to remove these burdens and in the last quarter of the nineteenth century they wore short-leg cotton costumes. By comparison, cumbersome, body-hiding clothing continued to restrict their sisters in athletics, cricket, cycling and hockey. Equally important to the liberation of female swimmers was the aquatic medium. It removed a crucial 'ideological impediment' to women's swimming: 'no matter how hard the competitors pushed themselves, the watery medium minimised the outward appearance of effort and exertion.' Veronica Raszeja argues that segregation, enclosure and the medium of participation legitimised women's swimming by creating the impression of a non-threatening sport.[46] In March 1902, at the close of the 1901–02 swimming season, Sydney women competed in their first major carnival—in the presence of male spectators. The NSW State Ladies' Swimming Championships drew no adverse public reaction from moralists, the press, or medical and educational authorities. An enclosed venue which removed the swimmers from unrestricted public view, the medical profession's support for the scientific benefits of swimming, the popular press's enthusiastic reporting of swimming affairs, and the fact that female swimming had been part of the educational curriculum for some time, all contributed to social acceptance. As a result of the latter, a whole generation believed that women's competitive swimming was normal.

The next season NSWASA approved the affiliation of the recently established Sydney Ladies' Swimming Club, although it refused the club representation on the executive. By 1906 NSWASA included six women's clubs. However, NSWASA officials considered women's swimming an administrative burden and, rather than expand the bureaucracy and executive to include women, the men's association created a separate and subordinate women's controlling body, the Ladies' Amateur Swimming Association (NSWLASA).

Conservatives in the swimming establishment argued that 'improperly clad' competitors threatened the ideal 'images of middle class femininity—the modest and impeccably moral "angel"'. To 'restore decorum' and enforce its authority, NSWLASA instructed competitors to wear cloaks before and after events; it banned male spectators from women's carnivals and forbade women competing in front of men. Re-segregated women's swimming was short-lived. Men contributed to sociability and raised the number and quality of prizes; women rebelled against the exclusion of male relations, friends and members of the press. In November 1910 influential women competitors formed the NSW League of Swimmers to integrate the sport and offer money prizes; more than three-quarters of Ladies' Association members defected to the League. The League, too, had a brief life. NSWLASA revoked its 'no-men' regulation during the 1911–12 season amid the controversy over the selection of Durack and Wylie in the Australian olympic team.

Before Durack, the fastest female swimmer in the world, and Wylie could compete in Stockholm, the Ladies' Association had to rescind its rule forbidding women from swimming in public, and the Men's Association had to approve their selections. NSWLASA considered the motion at a meeting in mid-March 1912. Rose Scott, president of NSWLASA and a prominent figure in the history of women's rights, and A. C. W. Hill, secretary of NSWASA, opposed the desegregation motion: 'a girl who [is] in the habit of exposing herself at public carnivals [is] likely to have her modesty hopelessly blighted', Scott insisted.[47] While the *Bulletin* considered Durack a 'favoured sister', describing her as 'a fine, understanding miss, with the clear eye of perfect health, and a figure that shows no symptoms of ropes and athletic muscles, abnormal development, or any other nightmare', other sections of the press expressed doubts: 'The well-shaped girl might easily get over her qualms, no matter how modest she may be, but her less favoured sister is altogether differently placed. Men who have attended swimming shows where the other sex took part, could not help but notice the quizzing and guying girl contestants were frequently subjected to.'[48]

Delegates ignored the negative sentiments and voted to send the two women to Stockholm. Hill's warning to the Ladies' Association that the men's body would not ratify the decision proved wrong: NSWASA confirmed Durack's and Wylie's selection, subject to them paying £150 each to cover the Association's expenses, and to the appointment of respectable chaperones. Durack and Wylie were classic examples of the

Australia's champions at the Stockholm olympic games, 1912: Fanny Durack (left), Wilhelmina (Mina) Wylie (centre). At right is Jennie Fletcher, of Great Britain, world champion until beaten by Durack. Swimmers Durack and Wylie won the gold and silver respectively in the 100m. Before they could compete, the NSW Ladies' Swimming Association had to rescind its rule forbidding women from swimming in public. Swimmers were the first female athletes to be allowed to remove restrictive and body-hiding clothing. SMALL PICTURE FILE, MITCHELL LIBRARY

politics of female accommodation in international sporting competition. While reluctant to include women in what they saw as their domain, male sports officials also saw opportunities to bask in reflected national glory. Indeed, for Wylie, Australian men seized all the credit for which 'they really weren't due'.[49] Australia won two gold, two silver and three bronze medals at Stockholm, and as 'Natator', the *Referee*'s swimming correspondent, noted, 'had it not been for Miss Durack and Miss Wylie…there would have been little for Australia to hold her head up and stick her chest out over'. In short, Australia's chronic lust for olympic gold, and with it the opportunity to counter feelings of national inferiority, was stronger than gender prejudice.

Sporting success of this kind certainly didn't translate into social or political freedom. The warm welcome for Durack on her return quickly evaporated when she dared to point out that Australia remained one of the few nations where a significant proportion of the population still objected to mixed-gender swimming. The press was particularly quick to condemn what it saw as 'the favoured sister's' impertinence.

THE EXCLUSION OF BLACKS

Just as women were winning the battle for inclusion in national sports, so Aborigines were consciously excluded from sports previously open to them. For women, swimming was to be the leverage for inclusion and connection to the larger, male-dominated society; for Aborigines, cricket—as we saw in Chapter 2—was to be the basis of exclusion and disconnection from mainstream Australia. Just as women were becoming reasonably equal partners in the new nation, Aborigines were becoming ever more marginalised, a people not just different but 'other' than Australians.

By 1911 the exclusion of Aborigines was virtually complete: segregated, isolated, they were wards of the state, minors in law, with all the attendant disabilities of that status. Cricket had ended; the 'peds' were ever more controlled. Queensland prevented black runners from practising their profession. Joe Johnson, with 55 games for Fitzroy in the VFL between 1904 and 1906, was the only black footballer in a sport considered a 'bastion of colonialism and racism'. By the time of Durack's triumphs, Aborigines were excluded from the geography of mainstream Australia, from the franchise, from maternity and similar allowances, and, on the eve of Australia's coming of age, the Great War, the *Defence Act 1910* exempted from war service 'persons who are not substantially of European origin or descent'.

By the early Edwardian period, sporting entrepreneurs and broad social changes associated with both community and national development had begun to weaken earlier Victorian notions about the separation of the classes. War stalled this trend. Australian militarists, in the churches and public schools in particular, saw the Great War as a way to maintain the vigour of the British race. Sport was perfect training for this task. Since the advent of the de Coubertin 'philosophy', national pride has come to mean, in the main, the achievements of soldiers and of sportspeople as surrogate soldiers. That most ghastly of wars, the First World War, shows just how strong is the relationship between sport and militarism.

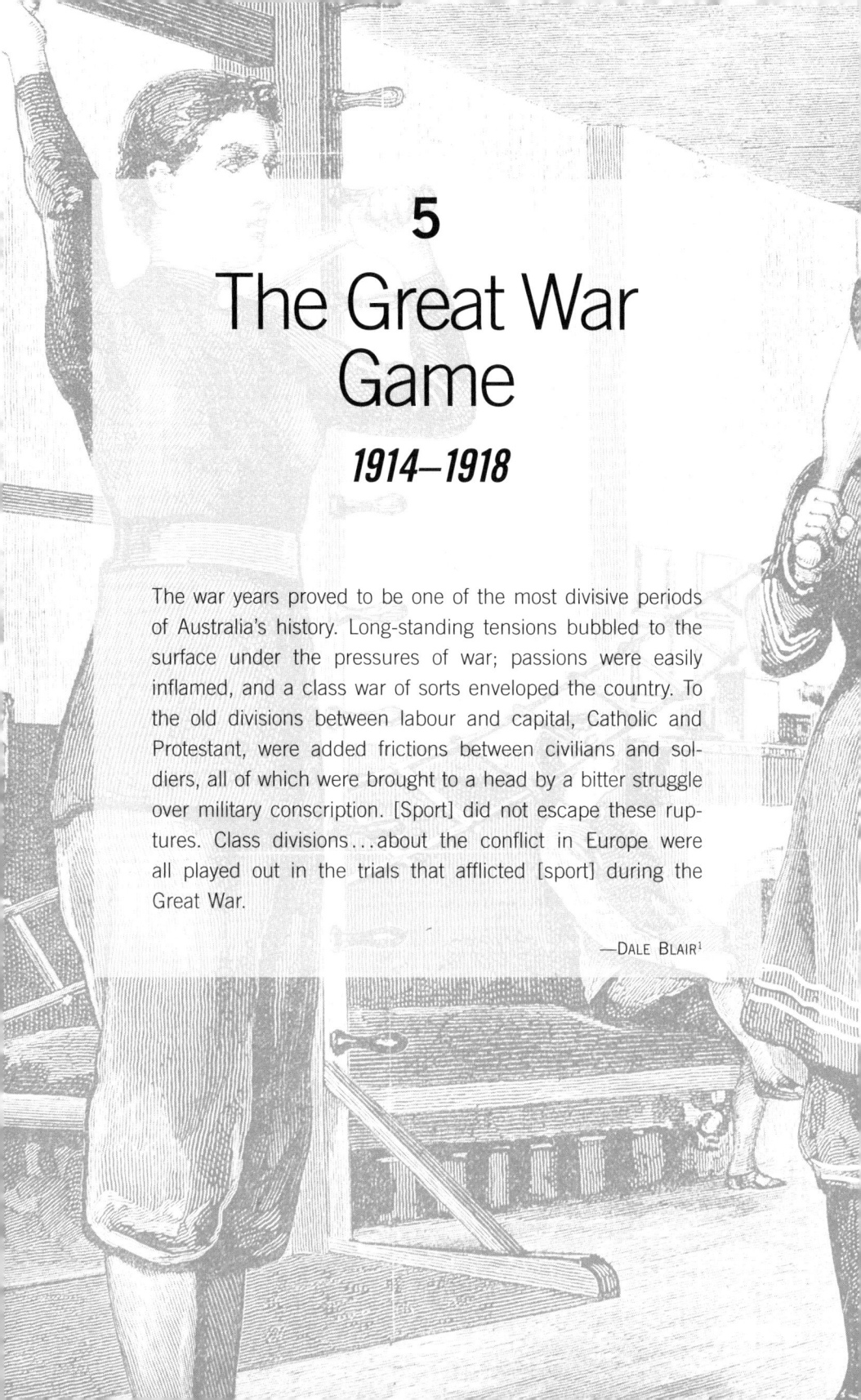

5
The Great War Game
1914–1918

The war years proved to be one of the most divisive periods of Australia's history. Long-standing tensions bubbled to the surface under the pressures of war; passions were easily inflamed, and a class war of sorts enveloped the country. To the old divisions between labour and capital, Catholic and Protestant, were added frictions between civilians and soldiers, all of which were brought to a head by a bitter struggle over military conscription. [Sport] did not escape these ruptures. Class divisions…about the conflict in Europe were all played out in the trials that afflicted [sport] during the Great War.

—DALE BLAIR[1]

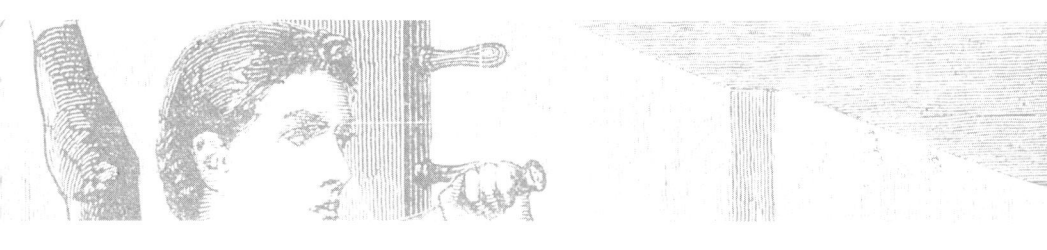

LANGUAGE AND WAR

War produces an exaggerated sense of everything. As death looms large in so many families, so life looms larger. Language swells, as do the issues it describes. Thus the famous official war correspondent and historian, C. E. W. Bean, explained the motives of the first Australian Imperial Force (AIF) on the steep cliffs of Gallipoli in Turkey:

> It lay in the mettle of the men themselves...Life was very dear, but life was not worth living unless they could be true to their idea of Australian manhood. Standing upon that alone, when help failed and hope faded, when the end loomed clear in front of them, when the whole world seemed to crumble and the heaven to fall in, they faced its ruin undismayed.[2]

One cannot help noting that intelligent grown men believe in the virtues of war. In what poet Siegfried Sassoon called the 'world's worst wound', Bean, among many others, saw the values of grit, endurance, mettle, mateship, manhood, glory, fearlessness, heroism—sporting terms indeed. The Australian war poets saw the war as positive. In his 'The Challenge', W. M. Fielding wrote, 'My sons have proved their breeding/ Upon the fields of pain'. Edward Dyson admitted that 'The guns have killed, but it is true/They bring to life things good and new'. The British war poets—Edmund Blunden, Sassoon, Isaac Rosenberg, Wilfred Owen—chose a very different vocabulary. For Sassoon, those 'doomed, conscripted ones' were 'the unheroic Dead who fed the guns', 'the dead who struggled in the slime'. In the trenches, amid the chlorine and mustard gas, Wilfred Owen heard 'the blood/Come gurgling from the froth-corrupted lungs', saw 'the incurable sores on innocent tongues' and, having done so, declared that he couldn't repeat 'The old Lie: Dulce et decorum est/Pro patria mori' [It is sweet and fitting to die for one's country].

Australia's greatest soldier, Sir John Monash, found some very strange language to describe what he saw as the unrivalled 'cool daring, courage and endurance' of the Australian soldier at Gallipoli:

> Our boys, capably led, can give the British regulars points and a beating at any part of the game, whether it be in digging a trench, or in a bayonet

assault, or in steadiness under fire, or in boiling the billy or in ambulance work, or in cheerfully suffering fatigue and privations, or in marching, or personal bravery. Our wounded are most amazing: they sing, they cheer, they smoke their cigarettes, even when so badly hit as to have to be carried on a stretcher.[3]

For Monash, the war was simply another chance to beat the Poms. But upstage them by more cheerful suffering?! The Great War game was also to be the Great Word game.

WAR AND SOCIAL DIVISIONS

In the opening quotation to this chapter Dale Blair defines the war as one of the most divisive periods in Australian history. So it was. But it is also the major font and a key source of Australian nationalism and sense of nationhood. Literally dozens of analysts talk of 'the crucible in which Australian nationhood was forged', the 'blooding and the bravery' and the inevitable 'coming of age'.[4] Time has not diminished these perceptions. On the contrary. Welcoming the NSW government's decision in 1999 to make Gallipoli compulsory history for school classes 7 to 10, the *Sydney Morning Herald* stated: 'The experience of Gallipoli helped forge Australia as a nation and the Anzac spirit that arose during that campaign immortalised the values that have come to be regarded as distinctive of Australian culture.'[5] Perhaps these were the things 'good and new' to emerge from the guns and the dead.

Britain declared war on Germany in August 1914.[6] Australians immediately and unequivocally committed themselves to the mother country. Joseph Cook, Prime Minister and leader of the Liberal Party, offered the Imperial government 20 000 Australian troops.[7] War had been hovering over Europe for years. Even before the carnage began, Andrew Fisher, leader of the Labor opposition and soon to be Prime Minister, promised that 'Australians will stand beside [Britain] to help and defend her to our last man and our last shilling'. The rush to enlist further confirmed what the Governor-General, Munro Ferguson, called the 'indescribable enthusiasm' for Britain's cause: by the end of 1914, more than 50 000 Australian men had enlisted.[8]

Duty, obligation, and allegiance to Britain only partly explain the zeal. Patriots considered the Great War an ideal opportunity to test and demonstrate Australian pluck, courage, determination, temerity and tenacity. Some joined for the adventure, or for the promise of free travel, while others simply sought to escape unemployment.[9] Not surprisingly, the fervour soon waned. More sober reflections about the realities of modern war came with reports of high death and injury tolls, descriptions of mass slaughter, first at Gallipoli in 1915 and then, the following year, in the mud-filled trenches of the Western Front in France. As the battles dragged on, apathy, weariness and opposition grew, exposing deep class and religious divisions.

Wartime economic conditions—prices rising, wages falling and living standards declining—hit the working classes hardest. As a group, Catholics—mostly Irish—bore much of the burden. Catholics comprised over 20 per cent of the population and most were working class. While they supported the war—indeed, many men in the AIF were Catholic— in general they showed a less intense commitment than Protestants. Unlike the latter, whose ideology bound them to God and King in a very public and highly visible manner, Catholics displayed a quieter loyalty to Australia and their church. They tended to take a more pragmatic view of the war, lending support primarily to win approbation and to benefit their social standing.[10]

Recruitment declined dramatically in 1916. To meet Britain's request for 16 500 Australian troops each month, Labor Prime Minister Billy 'Little Digger' Hughes argued for conscription for overseas service.[11] Hughes's proposal, which was contrary to his party's official policy, generated intense debate, heightening tensions between Protestants and Catholics. Protestant leaders supported conscription passionately. 'The Anglican synod in Melbourne passed without discussion a resolution in favour of conscription'; the war, it insisted, was a religious battle and 'the voices of the allies were being used by God to vindicate the rights of the weak and to maintain the moral order of the world'. An alternative view came from the leader of the Catholic Church in Melbourne, Archbishop Daniel Mannix. He called the conflict a 'sordid trade war' and though he prayed for an Allied victory, Australia, he said, 'had made sufficient sacrifices'. 'It was possible', the Archbishop added, for Australians to 'do their duty, and to do it nobly, without conscription'.[12]

Two bitter referendums were fought on conscription, in October 1916 and December 1917. They followed major general strikes by workers, who refused to shoulder alone the economic burden of war. These events polarised Australians further. Existing sectarian hostility increased, strong as it was following British reprisals against Catholic leaders of the Easter

JOIN TOGETHER
TRAIN TOGETHER
EMBARK TOGETHER
FIGHT TOGETHER

LIEUT JACKA V.C

Enlist in the Sportsmen's Thousand

SHOW THE ENEMY WHAT
AUSTRALIAN SPORTING MEN CAN DO.

With the failure of two referendums on conscription during the First World War, every conceivable ploy was used to recruit soldiers. The Sportsmen's Battalions was one such ploy, started in the belief that because of their training, sportsmen would be among the first to enlist, but there was a poor turnout. MURRAY PHILLIPS/AUSTRALIAN WAR MEMORIAL

Rising in Dublin in 1916. Conservatives, employers, Protestant churches and the middle classes supported conscription, while pacifists, trade unionists and Irish Catholics formed an anti-conscription bloc. Both sides claimed to represent 'real' Australians; both accused the other of betrayal. Pro-conscriptionists charged anti-conscriptionists with disloyalty to the Empire and with slighting those Australians already fighting. In a document they called 'The Anti's Creed', pro-conscriptionists insisted their opponents wanted to crush and humiliate Britain and accused them of supporting the murder of women and children. Anti-conscriptionists argued that pro-conscriptionists served the interests of imperialists and warmongers. More specifically, trade unionists condemned conscription as undemocratic: they feared it would undermine the union movement and hard-won workers' rights.[13] They saw in military conscription the seeds of industrial prescription.

The 'no' vote won both conscription referendums by narrow majorities, with voters dividing along party lines.[14] Protestants blamed Catholics for the defeat, launching vitriolic attacks and engendering further bitterness and resentment. Middle-class Protestant patriots demanded total commitment to the war: it mattered nothing to them that Catholics were well represented among volunteers. For as long as Catholic leaders and newspapers impugned the war, Protestants would inveigh against the whole Catholic population.[15]

SPORT, WAR AND CLASS

Sport became embroiled in these class and religious divisions. By 'heightening and clarifying' social conflicts, writes Michael McKernan, the Great War brought the 'meaning and purpose of sport into sharp focus'. We have seen something of the distinct views of sport held by the middle and the working classes. In general, the former believed amateur sport 'had meaning in so far as it taught the young such values as loyalty, determination, unselfishness and...team spirit'.[16] For them, in very nineteenth-century imperial language, sport was perfect training for the sternest battle of all—war. In that theatre, declared the Reverend Canon Hughes of Melbourne, sportsmen had the opportunity to demonstrate their humanitarianism by applying the 'Creator's gift of health, strength, vigour and manhood' to the defence of the nation and Empire so that 'all might have...a glorious life or grave'.[17] 'What is the good of games', asked 'Fife and Drum' in the *Pastoral Review*, 'if they do not give us men whose hands they have taught to war and their fingers to fight?' Without this purpose, the writer concluded, 'it would be better that we blotted [sport] out from our daily lives altogether, and instituted some system whereby men of war, and with them the spirit of Britons, and with the aptitude for war fostered within them, would leap at the call of bugles'.[18]

Pro-war groups never failed to draw parallels between the sportsfield and the battlefield.[19] If it was apt for General Monash, advertisers and the press were quick to appropriate his kind of language. An advertisement in the *Sydney Mail* urged readers to 'watch a struggle on the football field, when opposing teams clash in fierce contest, straining every nerve and fibre for victory' and then to imagine such men undertaking a 'bayonet rush'.

> The grim determination of the rower or sculler to win a gruelling race, the alertness and coolness of the cricketer who strives to turn the tide of an uphill game, the endurance of the long distance runner or cyclist, the self-control and pluck of the boxer who gives and takes with true sportsmanlike unconcern—all these are invaluable elements in the greatest game mankind has yet been called to play.

Sport magazine asked readers whether they considered themselves 'sportsmen'. If so, the magazine chided them, they should 'prove it by getting into khaki'. Explaining the meaning of the term 'sportsman' under the heading 'The call to arms', the editors of *Sport* explained that the phrase 'means much to honour and conscience, and something even more than that—an appeal to an almost undefinable instinct in our race that challenges a man upon his manhood and his strength, his nobility and his moral power'. Furthermore, 'no man of honour dare be deaf' to the appeal to 'Be a Sportsman!' because 'it is a supreme challenge to his quality; let him evade it, and he will know that not again will he stand the same among his people. When he is asked to "Be a Sportsman!" he knows that the full test is laid upon him—the test of the Australian. Love, patriotism, honour, unselfishness, sacrifice, duty, manly strength—all these things are summed up in that one appeal—"Be a Sportsman!"'[20]

Historically, the sporting press embodied sportsmen and sporting competitions in military parlance. Forwards playing early football in Melbourne were 'sterling, neat, efficient and dashing', defenders were 'sturdy, doggedly obstinate, staunch and showed unflinching resolution', while rucks 'laboured energetically and showed consistent excellence and cool judgement'.[21] During the Great War *Sport* magazine linked enlistment with specific sports, urging swimmers to 'make a dive', rowers to 'pull an oar', boxers to 'throw a straight lead' and 'footballers to get on the ball'.[22]

By contrast, sport for the working classes was simply recreation, entertainment and pleasure, or a way of earning a living. Sport offered 'an exciting break from the monotony of urban work'. Either way, 'sport needed no further or serious justification'.[23]

The outbreak of war brought these respective proponents into conflict. For middle-class patriots and amateur ideologues, while sport and war were coterminous in their values and virtues, there was no place for sport during international bloodletting. Their 'view of loyalty demanded that a man be so totally involved in the Empire's cause as to forgo all other concerns'.[24] They deemed sport a 'waste' of money and time and an activity that 'inhibited' recruitment and 'distracted the nation from its commitment to the Empire'. No moral person could countenance sport while men were dying. Sport, said the *Argus*, 'prevents thousands upon thousands of able-bodied men, who are looking on, from realising that their country needs them; and it is their duty to help their country when she calls; not to waste time in gazing at football matches, prize fights, or race meetings'.[25] The pro-war lobby launched scathing and vitriolic attacks on its 'enemies'. One Presbyterian minister labelled 'cold footed slackers at the stadiums and racecourses' as 'selfish, soulless degenerates'. They are unfit, he said, 'to blacken the boots of the brave men in the trenches'. The Reverend J. L. Rentoul branded any Melbourne youth who preferred football to enlistment as a 'loon, a coward and dastard'.[26] Australia's champion and 'knight-errant' of amateurism, Lawrence Adamson—headmaster of Wesley College (Melbourne) and president of the Metropolitan Amateur Football Association—called professional football treasonable: not only did it deter recruitment but 'a patriotic German could make no better gesture than to support our paid gladiators to perform in the League and Association circus'.[27] Adamson compared the miserly enlistment record of professional footballers with his noble amateurs. He proudly told his pupils that eighteen members of the South Yarra Football Club enlisted after they won the premiership.[28]

Boxers were a favourite 'soft' target: there were relatively few of them and their high profile made them easy to identify.[29] Presbyterian minister the Reverend David Brandt urged the government to prohibit the sport and to 'compel' fighters and spectators to 'train for the defence of the Empire'.[30] The Council for Civic and Moral Advancement, a Protestant interdenominational body, also took a hard line against boxing, and particularly against Australia's most prominent and admired fighter at the time.

LES DARCY

Raised by working-class Irish Catholic parents, and the second son of nine surviving children, Darcy held Australian titles in the welter-, middle- and heavyweight divisions. Many fans considered him the world middleweight champion.[31] Darcy twice attempted to enlist and on both occasions his mother lodged successful objections because he was under 21, then the age of majority. On the eve of the first conscription campaign and his twenty-first birthday, Darcy stowed away on the cargo steamer *Hattie Luckenbach*. His destination was professional boxing in the United States. Protestants deplored Darcy's action, which they said symbolised 'Catholic disloyalty to the Empire and their lack of commitment to the war'. The patriotic press vilified Darcy, with the *Bulletin* fuelling sectarian bitterness: 'Coming of a stock to which England is merely the ancient oppressor and Home Rule for Ireland a religion, it was not unnatural that [Darcy] jibbed at sacrificing a money-making career to risk his life for a "King and Empire" which meant less than nothing to him and his friends.'[32] The Censor for Military Intelligence opened Darcy's mail from America 'under regulations dealing with trafficking and corresponding with the enemy'.[33] Darcy was to be victim of both these religious crusades and of Hugh McIntosh, then owner of the sports paper the *Referee*, who had personal grudges.[34] After contracting fights in America, McIntosh successfully lobbied governors of states, no less, to cancel Darcy's matches. Darcy took American citizenship and, in an act of patriotism, enlisted (on condition he was transferred to an Australian army[35]) and was promoted to the rank of sergeant in the Signallers at the Aviation School in Memphis; his superiors gave him leave to prepare for his first American fight. Infections, pneumonia and heart complications from an earlier poisoned tooth put an end to his life before the event, on 24 May 1917. The respected journalist W. F. Corbett wrote that 'there was no cure for a broken heart. He couldn't forget the "slacker" part'.[36]

More than any other single event, Darcy's death illustrates the degree and extent of class and sectarian bitterness during this era. Well over 100 000 people viewed his body as it lay in state for two days in a funeral

The legendary Les Darcy in 1916, Australian champion in three weight divisions.
Vilified because of alleged evasion of army service, his premature death in the
United States resulted in the largest funeral for any sportsperson in Australian
history. His handwritten inscription is not correct: he was never world
middleweight champion. SMALL PICTURE FILE, MITCHELL LIBRARY

chapel in Sydney's George Street. Most were ordinary Australians; official representatives of Sydney and the state and Commonwealth governments were conspicuous by their absence. After a requiem mass in Woollahra, the body travelled to Sydney's Central Station where 'the crowd was so thick it was almost impossible to get in or out', and from there to Newcastle and then Maitland, Darcy's home town. In Maitland, 'the cortege . . . from the Darcy home to the cemetery', a distance of three miles, 'was lined with spectators. One report put the crowd at seven hundred thousand'.[37] McKernan describes the turnout as a 'demonstration . . . by those who had triumphed in the defeat of conscription but who felt, nevertheless, alienated by middle-class patriots'.[38] Professional sportsmen and working-class Catholics attended the burial *en masse* and once again shameful amateurs and notables stayed away.[39]

What the strident Adamson and other equally myopic and naive ideologues failed to recognise, as Dale Blair reminds us, was that modern warfare rendered athleticism 'impotent'.[40] Trench warfare does not require rowers' determination, cricketers' alertness, cyclists' endurance, or boxers' self-control. Anyone can mow down an enemy who stupidly and blindly rushes forward into machine-gun fire! Nor, in Murray Phillips's words, does sport prepare soldiers for 'the smell of rotting flesh, the sight of decapitated and dismembered bodies, [or the] stress caused by constant, heavy artillery fire'.[41]

Supporters countered anti-sport arguments by claiming that professional sport contributed to war funds, encouraged enlistment and gave relief from the horrors of war.[42] Murray Phillips has a crucial point to make: in terms of the total enlistment, the working classes contributed as much manpower as the middle classes and were no less patriotic. But what the working classes rejected was what McKernan calls 'the hectoring and abuse of would-be recruiters'.[43] And the working classes did not shy from expressing their feelings. In 1915 boxing fans drowned out a recruitment speech by the Labor Premier of New South Wales, W. A. Holman, at a championship boxing fight; in 1917 fans of Australian football assaulted official recruiting officers at the Fitzroy oval.[44]

THE SPORTSMEN'S BATTALIONS

Significantly, McKernan notes that supporters of professional sport would simply 'seek their enjoyment elsewhere' if denied sporting entertainment. By failing to accept that sport is just 'another form of entertainment', and by eulogising sport as some higher form, amateur ideologues, McKernan concludes, 'misunderstood its grip on the Australian people'.[45] The failure of the middle-class moralists of amateurism to secure a steady supply of fresh recruits for the front line and, more specifically, the poor turnout for the Sportsmen's Battalions give McKernan's supposition further credence.

Middle-class ideologues erroneously believed that battalions of sportsmen would lead Australia's war effort, expecting sportsmen to be among the first to enlist, not only because of 'their youth and physical condition, but also because sport had prepared them so well for the task'.[46] By mid-1915 recruiters conceded their overly ambitious expectations and began to actively encourage sportsmen to do their duty. Appeals such as that by Prime Minister Billy Hughes were common:

> Sportsmen of Australia, to you is given a great opportunity, upon you rests a heavy responsibility. As you have played the game in the past so we ask you to play the greater game now. You are wanted today in the trenches far more than you were ever needed in the football or cricket oval. When the last word is spoken in today's great [recruitment] campaign every fit man of military age in New South Wales worthy of the name of sportsman will have enrolled in the AIF. I ask you to be true to yourselves, and to prove yourselves worthy members of the great brotherhood of sport.[47]

When enlistments dropped off rapidly in 1917, sports administrators, led by officials from the NSWRU—notably H. Y. Braddon and Ernest Marks—proposed reviving the Sportsmen's Battalions, which had been first tried, without success, two years earlier.[48] The fresh initiatives achieved little; only 2247 men joined the Sportsmen's Battalions, less than 1 per cent of the men who embarked for the front line.[49]

DIVIDED SPORT

Consistent with their ideology, amateur officials cancelled their sporting competitions early in the war. Adamson's Metropolitan Amateur Football Association closed down in 1915 for the war's duration. In the same year the amateur-inclined VFA cut short its season and then suspended play until 1918. Rugby union officials in New South Wales followed suit.

By contrast, the working-class-based NSWRFL showed no inclination to abandon its competition. Phillips stresses that the continuation of

rugby league 'should not be interpreted as a failure to realise the significance of the occasion'. Indeed, he cites the League's annual report
of 1915, which 'impressed upon players...their duty to respond to the
Empire's call by enlisting'. Where that was impracticable, the report continued, then players should at least 'participate in training, in drill and
in rifle shooting, so that when the call becomes more imperative they
will step into the ranks as trained soldiers'. The senior rugby league
competition in Sydney shrank by 35 per cent and the lower grades
suffered severe depletions: 'the loss in the junior ranks, particularly
in the A division that contained youths of suitable age for military service, necessitated a temporary cancellation of the President's Cup and
a restructuring of the organisation'. In addition, league officials cancelled
interstate and international games and staged several patriotic and charity
games.[50] Similarly, Richard Stremski dismisses Lawrence Adamson's
claim that VFL players were unpatriotic. While only sixteen players from
the staunchly working-class Collingwood Football Club joined up during
the course of the war, the club nonetheless gave financial testimonials
to those who enlisted, presented the widow of one player killed in action
with £20, and 'placed its resources, including players, at the disposal of
all Local Red Cross, Soldiers' Welfare and recruiting committees'.[51]

On the other hand, the VFL presents an interesting case study of a
class-divided sport. Its competition continued throughout the war with
a reduced number of teams. After the bulk of its players joined the student battalion, the University Club disbanded at the start of the 1915
season. And midway through the year, the League considered aban-
doning the competition. Five of the nine clubs, the majority, supported
cancellation, but the motion failed because it did not gain the necessary
backing from three-quarters of the delegates. Before the 1916 season,
the middle-class clubs—Essendon, Melbourne, South Melbourne and
St Kilda—withdrew from the competition in defiance of the majority
vote. When Geelong followed, the League was left with only four
teams from inner-suburban, working-class clubs: Carlton, Collingwood,
Fitzroy and Richmond.[52] Of interest is that when the South Australian
Football League announced it would abandon the 1916 season, the Port
Adelaide League and Association clubs, both based in a solidly working-
class district, demanded the competition continue. The two clubs
subsequently amalgamated as the Port Adelaide Limited Patriotic Football Club, and the new club launched a fresh six-team competition for
the season.[53]

Consistent with the argument that working-class sporting people were just as committed to the war effort as so-called middle-class patriots, Carlton, Collingwood, Fitzroy and Richmond agreed to conduct the 1916 season according to amateur rules, that is, players would receive no payments. The logic was that 'no one could say that a player refused to enlist because he would thus suffer financially'. The clubs also agreed to raise money for patriotic funds.[54] Dale Blair argues that such stances tended to be based on 'pragmatic' rather than 'idealistic' considerations and were designed to 'placate the anti-football sentiment in some sections of the community'.[55] McKernan concurs, and suggests that the Carlton Football Club's balance sheet, for one, mocked any commitment to amateurism. Despite earning £885 in revenue, the club declared no profit for the war effort. 'In the spirit of "shamateurism"', writes McKernan, 'it appears that several entries, including £99 for losses suffered by players absent from work, £45 players' travelling expenses, and £57 for injured players, were simply "disguised match payments"'.[56]

In 1917 the VFL competition increased to six teams with the return of South Melbourne and Geelong. The crowds also returned, with 83 000 people watching the final series, 25 000 more than the previous year. The next year, 1918, Essendon and St Kilda rejoined the fold. The VFA also resumed in 1918. Led by Brunswick, the Footscray, North Melbourne, Northcote, Port Melbourne and Prahran clubs decided to resume the Association competition. Each of these clubs represented solid working-class populations. But as in the VFL, clubs in the more affluent suburbs—Brighton, Hawthorn and Williamstown—still voiced opposition.[57]

In the end, 'war weariness and the defeat of conscription' all but defeated middle-class ideologues.[58] During the May 1917 federal election campaign, Billy Hughes announced initiatives to regulate sport. But the government waited until September before making any concrete moves, which meant it didn't have to act against popular football codes. The following year all threats of control evaporated. In Sydney and Melbourne many football competitions resumed close to full strength.

WAR, WOMEN AND SPORT

Although excluded from front-line combat, women joined the war effort as cooks, signallers, dispatch riders, ambulance-drivers, stretcher-bearers, hospital orderlies and as members of charitable organisations such as the Red Cross, Soldier's Comfort Funds, and Sock Funds; abroad, 3000 women served as nurses.[59] Women also assisted recruitment efforts. In New South Wales they formed the Sportswomen's Union and in Victoria the 'One Woman, One Recruit League'. The Great War also divided women, 'thrusting them into conflicting roles'. Some opposed the war, recruiting and conscription, while others lent their full support.[60] Generally, support came from middle-class women who had long cast, and organised, themselves as the 'moral guardians of society' or, in the then popular parlance, as 'God's police'.

While the war divided women and thrust them into domestic social turmoil, Murray Phillips contends that neither pro- nor anti-war women 'challenged...traditional feminine role[s]'. On the contrary, 'motherhood and maternity were elevated' during the war to a 'mythical, heroic and quasi-religious status'.[61] Yet the war did help liberate women from the shackles of the home, and open up more opportunities and choices, and broaden their horizons. With large numbers of men fighting abroad, women moved into the labour force, where they found social and economic autonomy and increasing rights. After the war many rejected a return to passive lives as full-time carers and nurturers. These women challenged accepted traditions, demanded greater freedom to express themselves and experimented with new fashions and new social roles. Barbara Cameron identifies 'strong feelings of freedom, excitement and self-expression...amongst young women' in the decade after the war that was known as the 'roaring twenties'. So-called 'flappers'—energetic, friendly, exuberant, sporting, active young women eager to flaunt their independence and sexuality—found unprecedented social freedom and lived their lives to the full. Not everyone approved, as Dennis Phillips explains:

> By the mid-1920s...a backlash against the postwar emancipation of women was clearly evident. The media, advertising in particular, the church and other segments of society shunned the emancipated woman in favour of the 'ideal' mother whose life was guided by 'sewing, babies, fashion, diet and helpful housekeeping hints'.[62]

The same patterns occurred in sport. As women's lives and opportunities expanded, sport increasingly reflected a broadened gender base. Postwar 'women' replaced pre-war 'ladies'. They seized control of their own sports administrations, formed new clubs and associations in sports as diverse as fencing, chess, speedway racing, sailing, badminton, jujitsu, angling, skittles, skating, billiards and skiing, and staged local, regional and national sporting events. For the first time women also began to read about their own sporting achievements in the popular national press.[63] But access didn't just happen. As we show in Chapter 6, women had to fight continual battles to establish themselves in sport and to retain ground once claimed, in an environment that grew increasingly hostile from the late 1920s. In 1938, for example, the *Sydney Morning Herald* reported that sportswomen

> regard it as inevitable that after any meeting they hold in any sport they will be immediately subjected to a series of denunciations from a section of the community. Their performances are compared unfavourably with those of men in similar sports, their dress and uniform are criticised, their appearance bewailed. Indeed, sportswomen are considered fair targets because they do not live up to some individuals' idea of what women should do—principally stop at home. This attitude is quite in keeping with the supreme ego of the male. The idea that a woman might do something for her own enjoyment is incredible to him.[64]

Large retail stores and manufacturing industries were among the most progressive institutions in this era. They hired large numbers of women, and many employed welfare superintendents to look after the interests of women workers. Some organised sporting teams. Thus in 1919 Farmer & Co. (Sydney) appointed Eleanor Hinder as a welfare superintendent and, together with Jean Stevenson from the Young Women's Christian Association, they formed the City Girls Amateur Sports Association. Young women from around Sydney joined the Association, including workers from Farmers, David Jones, Anthony Horderns, Harrington's and the Wills Tobacco Factory. By 1926 the Association sponsored 30 basketball teams, nine hockey teams, 21 tennis clubs, a swimming school and physical culture classes. In 1926 the Association organised several camps, weekend walks, and bought a house at Narrabeen.[65]

A MIDDLEWEIGHT OF ANOTHER COLOUR

Despite the closure of successful entrepreneurial missions like Coranderrk in Victoria, despite their increasing segregation in remote Australia, despite exclusion from the ordinary systems of politics, law, economics, education and social service benefits, and notwithstanding their military service exemption, at least 289 Aborigines went overseas with the AIF.

There may well have been many more: the Australian War Memorial exhibition says there were over 400.[66] In 1916 the *Bulletin* cartoonist B. E. Minns showed a white gentleman asking 'Jacky' if he'd enlisted, to which came the reply, 'No, too plurry [bloody] dark for the Light Horse'. Many posed as Maori in order to hide their origins (and their 'exemption'). They had a high casualty rate: 36 per cent, 44 dying for what they saw as their country, even if their country never saw them, and 59 wounded. Medals abounded.[67] Herein lay a remarkable loyalty in the face of very real double adversity, perhaps a quadruple one in that they were black, couldn't legally enlist, fought in the front lines, and only one was allowed to claim some land in the postwar soldier resettlement scheme.

Two of the Coe brothers from Erambie Mission in Cowra, New South Wales, went missing in action. Despite having family, remaining brothers Paul Joseph and Leo Coe were defined as orphans and sent to Mittagong, and from there to one of the 'assimilation homes' for removed children, Bomaderry in New South Wales. Paul was then 'stationed out', that is, sent to work on cattle properties in return for rations. Known later in life as Jimmy Callaghan, he became a renowned roughrider, very much a working-class sport; remarkably, he moved on to the silvertail arena of equestrianism and showring riding in the 1920s. He won literally dozens of pairs events with the legendary Rowley Doctor, said to be Maori but more than likely of Aboriginal descent. Brother Leo also rode successfully.

Apart from the Coe family, the only other Aboriginal connection in the Great War era was, coincidentally, another middleweight of great fame, Jerry Jerome, from Jimbour Station, near Dalby in Queensland.[68] At the turn of the century he spent much time at Warra breaking in horses for use by the army in the Boer War. In 1912 *Snowy Baker's Magazine* wrote that 'he was known right from Toowoomba out west to Charleville as one of the smartest stockmen who ever sat astride a pigskin'. A professional runner of note, an excellent rifle shot, he took to boxing, somewhat reluctantly, at the age of 34. At close on 40, in September 1912, he won the Australian middleweight championship, the first of dozens upon dozens of professional and amateur titles won by Aborigines. Exempt from army service, he had several fights at the Sydney Stadium. C. P. Jeffries, esteemed author of *Famous Fights at the Stadium*, included several of his fights in his book, often referring to Jerome fondly as 'The Book of Lamentations'.

Jerry Jerome

A professional runner, expert rifleman and renowned stockman, Jerry Jerome began his boxing career at the late age of 34. He was the first of many Aboriginal national champions, winning the Australian middleweight title in 1912. His remarkably varied athletic career was facilitated by his not being under the control of the special legislation for the protection of Aborigines, enacted in 1897. He was a thorn in the side of the Chief Protector, J. W. Bleakley. J. C. DAVIS COLLECTION, MITCHELL LIBRARY

According to the Chief Protector, J. W. Bleakley, Jerome led a strike at Taroom Aboriginal Settlement in 1916. He refused to work and incited 'all others to refuse to work unless paid cash'. Bleakley regarded him as 'a pernicious and retarding influence', his behaviour immoral. Jerome and his family, he argued, would best be dealt with on the segregated reserve (Cherbourg): 'his position as a moneyed gentleman gives him privileges which he abuses and takes a mean advantage of to obstruct discipline and defy authority'. The 'Prophet' died, squalidly yet nobly, at Cherbourg in 1943, his earnings poached by the Aboriginal authority and the hangers-on. There are two public testimonials to this fine man: the first street in Cherbourg and a main street in Dalby bear his name. Incidentally, he never fought Les Darcy, but they shared several opponents.

The Great War was a particularly bitter period in Australian history. But it also marked the beginning of a new era of conscious nation-building and raised fresh questions about Australia's independence and reliance on Britain. Once again, sport illustrates the issues and debates. While amateurs resisted change and attempted to preserve British sporting traditions within the framework of the British Empire, professional players and entrepreneurial interests saw sport in more pragmatic terms. They continued to develop sport as an entertainment industry which happily nurtured and exploited jingoistic nationalist sentiments.

6

Empire First, Australia Second, Aborigines… Last

1919–1939

A culture should be identified not so much by any sense of shared values, which may often be artificially induced, as by the means it develops to reconcile, or at least accommodate the dissonant forces within it. The characteristic feature of Australian society between the wars was the extent to which it institutionalised the cultural accommodations which had been reached. So Catholic and Protestant were joined together by a regulated code of mutual hostility; men and women married and raised families yet lived much of their lives in separate cultural spheres; employers and trade unions ritualised their no longer new conflict in the workplace and courtroom; middle class and working class shared the same cities while respecting each other's territorial limits…

—John Rickard[1]

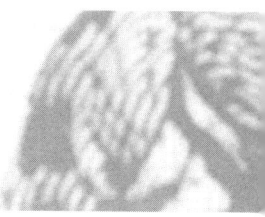

Richard White contends that Australian identity from the late nineteenth century became something of a 'tug-of-war between Australianness and Britishness, between the impulse to be distinctively Australian and the lingering sense of a British heritage'.[2] The late Don Dunstan, former Premier of South Australia, nicely summed up the British–Australian relationship in these terms:

> On the one hand, Australians were belligerently proud of their country. On the other, they were taught that their heritage was British. England was commonly referred to as 'Home'. English history, and English literature, were taught in schools and Henry Lawson's 'Wattle and Waratah' came a bad second to Wordsworth's daffodils. Australian children learned of their glorious heritage, but it was British not Australian.[3]

Sport confirms Dunstan's thesis. Very few sportspeople looked beyond the Empire for their identity. Not even the more conspicuously international olympic movement seriously challenged a sporting tradition firmly wedded to the British tradition and 'international' competition within Empire. Only in the 1930s did new commercial interests, driven in large part by new technologies of mass communication, begin to alter the structure of Australian sport significantly. For the first half of the twentieth century, Australia remained a comfortable sporting dominion.

AUSTRALIA AND THE BRITISH EMPIRE

Cricket was the yardstick of the British–Australian relationship in the second half of the nineteenth century.[4] The 'Australian Eleven' touring England in 1878, wrote the *Australasian*, wished 'to show John Bull that we can play cricket here as well as the old folks at home'. 'By their very presence', Ken Inglis notes, they helped educate the English: on railway stations and at hotels [the Australians] noticed that people 'looked steadfastly at them, surprised to find them fashioned as they were, and their habits and customs the same'. The Australians beat 'the greatest and most powerful club in the world', as *The Times* described the Marylebone Cricket Club, in the second match of the tour. The English press praised the winning team as 'all of our own flesh and blood'. The colonials, moreover, were 'proof that the old stock is not degenerating in those far off lands'. In 1880 Lord Harris, the aristocratic patron and captain of the English team which toured Australia in 1878–79, boasted that 'cricket had done more to draw the Mother Country and the Colonies together than years of beneficial legislation'.[5]

Most commentators interpreted Australia's determination to thrash Britain as evidence of strong anti-imperial nationalism. 'This ruthless rout of English cricket', wrote the *Bulletin* after Australia beat England decisively in 1897–98, 'will do—and has done—more to enhance the cause of Australian nationality than could ever be achieved by miles of erudite essays and impassioned appeal'.[6] Inglis offers another interpretation. 'Intense...devotion to the most English of games', he suggests, indicates 'how spontaneously and profoundly Australians embraced the culture of the motherland', while real 'anti-imperial nationalism might have disposed Australians not to play cricket at all'.[7]

Analyses of Australian sport in the late nineteenth and early twentieth centuries, and particularly the concerns and debates over olympism, support Inglis. Even as the olympic movement matured in the inter-war years, British sporting bonds remained firm. Australians showed little desire to express themselves as a truly independent state in the comity of nations.

AUSTRALASIA, CUFF AND COOMBES

In the late nineteenth century the settler populations of Australia's eastern colonies and New Zealand shared close ties based on a similar heritage and common experience. Rickard attributes the 'cultural divergence' between them to the 'artificial creation of separate national identities in 1901'.[8] At the turn of the twentieth century, many thought New Zealand would join the Australian federation. In sport, New Zealand and Australia formed the Australasian Lawn Tennis Association in 1904 to enter a team in the international Davis Cup. The first team comprised two New Zealanders, Alfred Dunlop and Anthony Wilding, and one Australian, Norman Brookes. An Australasian rather than an Australian team went to the 1908 and 1912 olympic games. At Stockholm they shared gold when the Kiwi swimmer Malcolm Champion joined three Australians in the winning 4 x 200m freestyle swimming relay team, and Australasia added a bronze to its official records when

THE SYDNEY MAIL, WEDNESDAY, SEPTEMBER 9, 1908.

THE OLYMPIC GAMES.

Australasian athletes at the olympic games in London, 1908. There were 25 Australians and four New Zealanders in the combined team: the Wallabies won the rugby gold; R. L. (Snowy) Baker took silver in the middleweight boxing; Frank Beaurepaire won silver in the 400m freestyle and bronze in the 1500m. SYDNEY MAIL, 9 SEPTEMBER 1908

Anthony Wilding came third in the men's singles tennis. New Zealand did not leave the Olympic Federation of Australia and New Zealand until 1919, it entered its own team in the Davis Cup only in 1924, and it stayed in the Amateur Athletic Union of Australasia until 1927. New Zealanders played Australian football and New Zealand teams competed in a Melbourne football carnival in the first decade of this century.

Leonard Cuff, a Christchurch cricketer and track and field athlete, provided Australasia's official entry into the olympic movement. A founder of the New Zealand Amateur Athletic Association (NZAAA) in 1887, he helped organise New Zealand's first national track and field meeting held in Dunedin in 1889. There Cuff met the 'father' of Australian athletics, Richard Coombes. Several months before Cuff founded NZAAA, Coombes launched the Amateur Athletic Association of New South Wales. Coombes also managed the Australian team at the meeting in Dunedin. Impressed by the organisation of that event, Coombes invited the Kiwis to the New South Wales championships in 1890 and the first Australasian championships in Melbourne in 1892.[9]

New Zealand success at the New South Wales championships—Kiwis won seven of the eleven events—provides early evidence of trans-Tasman rivalry. New Zealanders greeted the victories 'with huge, at times even extravagant, enthusiasm. At the Auckland opera house, the leading lady came to the curtain to announce R. D. Lusk's victory over the Australians in the hurdles, to great applause'.[10] Following the 1892 Australasian championships, Cuff took a team of New Zealand athletes on a European tour, during which he met Pierre de Coubertin. It was a fortuitous meeting: Cuff was the Baron's only contact in Australasia and he invited the New Zealander to an international conference of athletics officials in Paris. Ostensibly a conference to study amateurism in sport, the occasion was used by de Coubertin to establish the IOC and to revive the ancient olympic games.[11] Cuff wrote a letter of support to de Coubertin and forwarded details of the conference to Coombes and Basil Parkinson, chairman of the Victorian Amateur Athletics Association. Although none of these men attended the conference—Charles Herbert, secretary of the Amateur Athletic Association of England, represented Australia and New Zealand—de Coubertin invited Cuff to join the IOC. Cuff officially represented the IOC in Australia and New Zealand until 1905.[12]

Ironically, New Zealand rather than Australian officials led the push for national representation in the olympic movement. Coombes, whom Harry Gordon describes as 'the engine' of the olympic movement in Australia, continued to advocate Australasian representation in international competition for some time after New Zealand abandoned the idea.[13] A former English public schoolboy, champion walker and cross-country athlete, Coombes emigrated to Australia in 1886. He became a journalist, editor of the Sydney-based sporting paper the *Referee*, and helped organise state and national athletics federations and olympic councils. He served as president of the NSW Amateur Athletics Association, the Amateur Athletic Union of Australia and the Australian Olympic Federation. The latter comprised representatives of athletics, rowing, swimming and tennis. After replacing Cuff as the IOC's member in Australasia, Coombes attempted to unite the Sydney, Melbourne, Hobart and Wellington olympic councils, in large part to coordinate the selection of representative Australasian teams.

At a conference of olympic councils in Wellington in 1912, Coombes proposed the formation of an official Australasian Olympic Council. But it was another two years before representatives of the regional councils, which by then included Queensland and South Australia, agreed to form the Olympic Federation of Australia and New Zealand. It was, in Gordon's words, 'born in disharmony and rendered lame by the outbreak of war. Despite the fraternal, trans-Tasman embrace of its title, New Zealand wanted nothing to do with it'.

Most historians contend that Coombes attempted to juggle the irreconcilable notions of Australian nationalism, olympic idealism and 'loyalty and devotion to Great Britain and the Empire'.[14] But in the final analysis, Coombes was an unabashed Anglophile; he supported Australian nationalist sentiments only when they didn't undermine his devotion to Empire.[15] Coombes's support for a Pan-Britannic festival, his management of the Australian team at the 1911 Festival of the Empire and his proposal—in the face of considerable opposition—that the Empire compete as a single team at the olympic games, all testify to his unswerving allegiance to an Empire on which, it was believed by all and sundry, the sun would never set.

THE PAN-BRITANNIA AND OLYMPIC GAMES

In the late nineteenth century many Britons expressed concern about the physical degeneration of the Anglo 'race' and the long-term future of their Empire.[16] (There was, and is, no such thing as the British, or French or Swiss 'race'—merely imagined and mythical ideas about nationalistic races.) In these contexts, John Astley Cooper suggested to the British press a Pan-Britannic festival to 'celebrate the industrial, cultural and athletic prowess of the Anglo-Saxon race'.[17] This idea appealed to Coombes, a regular pontificator on the value of the Pan-Britannic Festival to the Empire generally and to the still unfederated colonies. Judged by the less than favourable reaction to news of the olympic revival, it was clear that Coombes's view held sway in the broader press. A columnist in the *Australasian* hoped that 'Mr Cuff will decline the proposed honour [to send a team to Athens] until it is shown whether and why this scheme is intended to supersede that of Mr Astley Cooper'.[18] While preparations for the second Australasian athletic championships preoccupied Coombes, the fact that neither he nor Cuff organised a team to compete at the first modern olympic games in 1896 suggests the low priority they afforded the Baron's project. The sentiment of Empire unity prevailed in the Australian press, which struggled to find merit in the olympics. According to the *Sydney Morning Herald*, a few Englishmen, an Australian and some Yankee amateurs opposed the Greek amateur productions, and some French men were there on the scene...As an athletic festival the whole affair is a farce, except that, like the tower of Babel, it has brought a lot of different nationalities together. The French, who thought up the whole affair, do not appear to have done very much.

The paper also reprinted the damning judgement made by the London *Spectator*:

The probability is that Olympic Games...will have the effect of games, merely, that is, of distractions, innocent and otherwise, according to circumstances, from the peremptory work of the world. They are not worse than other amusements, and, being enjoyed in the open air and under thousands of eyes, they are probably better than some of them. Rather a population of football-players than a population devoted, like the Chinese, to cards, or, like the Bengalese, to gossip; but that is about as much as it is yet justifiable to say.

Melbourne's chauvinistic *Argus* considered the olympics inferior to local sport:

[The] average Victorian football team, in good condition, could outrun, outjump, outkick, and outlast an equal number of athletes from the age of Phidias and Pericles...When Melbourne and Essendon or Geelong and South contend together, the green turf of the MCC or the SMCC will witness feats of skill and speed and endurance equal to anything ever seen under the shadow of Mount Olympus or on the banks of the sacred Alphaeus.

Cosmic, indeed, has been the change in values over a century. Olympism, then 'not worse than any other amusements', has been transformed into a global godhead, into an international 'philosophy' and ideology, at once haloed, enshrined and sacralised—despite the tarnish that began with the works of Paul Hoch and Jean-Marie Brohm in the 1970s, Alan Tomlinson and Gary Whannel in the 1980s, and Vyv Simpson and Andrew Jennings more recently.[19] The IOC is the world's foremost non-accountable statutory body, one considered blasphemous to criticise or condemn. When Andrew Thomson, former federal Minister for Sport in the first Howard Coalition government (until the October 1998 election), suggested that Athens in 2004 be the last games because corruption has virtually eroded and corroded all of its original principles, sports officials, politicians and the press vilified him; Australia's two IOC members, Kevan Gosper and Phil Coles, urged the Prime Minister 'to deal with him'.[20]

THE FESTIVAL OF EMPIRE AND EMPIRE UNITY

Despite Coombes's advocacy, the Pan-Britannia Games never eventuated. Historians generally regard Cooper's proposal as planting the seeds for the later Empire Games. But they were still three decades away. The closest event to a Pan-Britannia games was the modest sports program associated with the 1911 Festival of the Empire, staged to celebrate the coronation of George V. Organisers invited the white dominions of Canada, South Africa and Australasia, and the last sent a seven-man team to Crystal Palace, with Coombes serving as manager.[21] Canada won the Lord Lonsdale trophy for the winning team. Even Aborigines were there for George. Champion roughriders Billy Waite and Billy Jonas were part of Lance Skuthorpe's troupe for the 'Coronation Rodeo' in 1911.

In London, Coombes's fidelity to the Empire resurfaced. A proposal, put forward jointly with James Merrick, manager of the Canadian team, was that athletes from Canada, Australasia, South Africa and Great Britain compete as a single British Empire team at the next olympic games. Although the olympics barely survived as appendages to world fairs in 1900 (Paris) and 1904 (St Louis), they showed signs of prosperity in London in 1908.[22] Coombes and Merrick suggested the dominions send their best athletes to London in 1912, one week before departing for Stockholm. The athletes would train together as an Empire team and travel as a unit. This, Coombes wrote in militaristic language under the name 'Prodigal' in the *Referee*, 'is surely the very ideal of Empire—the forces of the Mother Country and her children, and Colonies, congregating on the shores of Britain to concentrate the forces of Empire, and then voyaging to the battle-ground of Stockholm to challenge in friendly warfare the best of the world's athletes'.[23] *The Times* of London agreed: 'It would be vastly better to be associated with a powerful Empire team, the flag of which everybody at the Games knows and respects and to help keep that Empire in its place at the head of nations.'

Not everyone embraced the sentiments. As the *Sydney Morning Herald* pointed out, an Empire team would sacrifice national identity:

> At present any competitor sent from Australia competes in the Games as an Australian, and any victory credited to him is recognised by the hoisting of an Australian flag. Apart from all questions of loyalty to the Empire, there is a narrower local patriotism for Australia, which is certainly gratified by the present system, which is also a tremendous advertisement to this continent.

Even so, the *Herald*'s wording of 'narrower local patriotism' suggests that national sentiment remained subordinate to the supreme British Empire.

The IOC squashed the proposal for an Empire-based sporting entity. In 1913 it ruled that the dominions must compete separately. Coombes clung to the idea of British unity. He lent support to a proposal put forward in 1923 by General Kentish, honorary secretary of the British Olympic Association, that Great Britain and her dominions share accommodation and parade together. Coombes also approved of contests between teams from the Empire and the United States at the conclusion of each olympic games. They were 'an ideal opportunity for the Britisher to show his worth'.[24] This popular United States versus Empire athletics contest, a vehicle for several world records, began in the 1920s and ended in 1952.

BRITAIN, AUSTRALIA AND THE WORLD

Despite federation, Britain held great political and economic power in Australia. Britain provided Australia's naval defence, nearly all foreign investment capital, and was the principal foreign economic market. In 1907 Britain recognised Australia's special status and that of Canada, New Zealand and South Africa by designating them 'dominions'. Regular Imperial conferences helped cement relations between Britain and her four reasonably independent daughters.

The Great War and its aftermath produced the first signs of political restructuring within the Empire. During the slaughter, Britain unintentionally highlighted the political autonomy and independence of Australia, and the other dominions, by granting them places in the Imperial cabinet. After the war, the dominions affirmed their independence by taking seats at the newly created international organisation the

League of Nations. At the same time the League effectively diminished Britain's position as the world power. Britain's economic power also waned in the 1920s as Europe opened its markets to the expanding economies of America and Asia. Rising nationalist sentiments, particularly in Canada and South Africa, forced Britain to clarify dominion status. At the Imperial conference in 1926 the Balfour Report formally defined the dominions as 'autonomous communities within the British Empire', with 'equal status' in 'all aspects of their domestic [and] external affairs', and 'united by a common allegiance to the Crown'. In 1931 the Statute of Westminster gave full expression to the Balfour Report. Under the Statute, no law passed by the British parliament would ever again apply to any dominion, unless they so consented.

For the most part, Australians remained ambivalent about these shifts. Imperial loyalty, material progress and preservation of the white race were 'national preoccupations'.[25] Australia took eleven years to adopt the Statute of Westminster. 'Labor was the party of Australian nationalist sentiment' in the inter-war years[26] but it held power at the federal level only between 1929 and 1931. Liberals and conservatives governed between the Great War and the Second World War. Some measure of their favourable disposition to Britain and acceptance of Australia's dominion status can be gained from their consternation when the Labor Prime Minister, James Scullin, nominated Isaac Isaacs, a Jew, as Australia's first native-born Governor-General. It was his Australianness rather than his Jewishness that caused upset.

The Scullin Labor government coincided with the onset of the Great Depression, an economic catastrophe that focused sharp attention on Australian–British relations. As Australian commodity prices fell, Britain withdraw large amounts of capital. By 1933 nearly one-third of bread-winners were unemployed. In 1930 Scullin invited Sir Otto Niemeyer, chairman of the Bank of England, to meet the state premiers. Niemeyer's solution, less borrowing and balanced budgets, worsened the plight of the working and middle classes. While Scullin acquiesced, Jack Lang, the Labor Premier of New South Wales, cast Niemeyer as 'a malevolent tool of the English bondholders who were determined to squeeze the last penny out of simple-minded, hard-working Australians'. He depicted 'the Englishman...as sinister, complex, and corrupting'.[27] But after the Lang government repeatedly defaulted on loan payments to Britain, the Governor of New South Wales, Sir Philip Game, intervened and dismissed it.

Phar Lap, a national celebrity. From the time of his victory in the Rosehill Guineas as a three-year-old, he won 36 of his 41 starts. His hide, mounted by an American taxidermist, is the most popular exhibit at the Victoria Museum in Melbourne. REFEREE, 13 APRIL 1932

Sporting relations with Britain in the inter-war years followed this general political climate of complacency, occasionally interrupted by political tensions. On the one hand, enthusiasm for the Empire games,[28] and the nonchalance towards the intense international debate over participation in the 1936 olympic games in Berlin, illustrate the high degree of self-satisfaction Australians felt for traditional sporting relationships. On the other hand, the tensions arising during the 1932–33 England cricket tour of Australia, the so-called bodyline tour, proved that even traditional relations required continued hard work and were not immune to stress and strain.

In passing, we note that in the inter-war years sporting relations with the United States were grim. In 1932 the great horse Phar Lap travelled to Mexico and the States. At Agua Caliente he won his first race in magnificent style. Two weeks later, at a stable outside San Francisco, he died. This 'mountain of a horse', as the famous writer Bert Wolfe described him, was 'gentle and kind', his 'intelligence such that he could be taught almost anything', with a heart 'almost double the size of an ordinary horse's'. Wolfe interviewed an Australian vet who had attended the autopsy. Poison, was his verdict. Quite unreasonably, Harry Gordon argues, 'Phar Lap's demise was linked with Les Darcy's fifteen years earlier—and vaguely, "the Yanks" were accused of two killings'.[29]

CULTURAL BONDING: THE EMPIRE AND THE OLYMPIC GAMES

Cooper's proposal for a Pan-Britannic sporting festival finally came to fruition in 1930 with the first British Empire games in Hamilton, Canada. At the olympic games in Amsterdam two years earlier, Canadian officials had presented concrete proposals for an Empire-based multi-sport festival. They were particularly concerned about American domination of the olympics and their alleged violations of amateur competition, concluding that only members of the 'British race' fully understood the true spirit of amateurism.[30] Coincidentally, Canadian and South African support for the games—as a means of enhancing cultural bonds with the Empire—came precisely as these two dominions demanded more political independence from Britain.

Although Australian sports officials and politicians would repeatedly voice support for the Empire games as a way to preserve traditional sporting values, lack of funds amid economic depression nearly scuttled Australia's attendance at Hamilton. Only when the Canadians offered subsidised travel and accommodation did Australian officials accept the invitation. Disillusioned by what he considered extreme nationalism and professionalism at the 1936 olympic games, Harry Alderson, general manager of Australia's team in Berlin, recommended that Australia withdraw from the olympics and concentrate on the Empire games. His comments about the olympics, at least, were perceptive, with insights that later sports officials, including those of the 1990s, failed to see:

> Instead of the Olympic Games developing international amity and goodwill, as was the intention . . . , the Games now caused international strife, ill-will and bitterness. There are no longer Olympic Games, but international contests in which the different nations regard the results and

Australian British Empire Games Team,
LONDON, 1934.

D. Gray, R. Clark, L. Cook, N Dempsey, Miss C. Dennis, H. Yates, F. Woodhouse, A. Higginson, J. Metcalfe.
H. Pethybridge, J. Knight, H. K. Maxwell, Mrs. M. Watson, R. Garrard, Miss L. Thompson, N. Ryan.
(Hon. Manager)   (Chaperone)

The 1934 team of 28 members won eight gold medals: J. P. Metcalfe, C. Dennis, N. P. Ryan (2), E. L. Gray, R. E. Garrard, J. L. Knight and L. Cook. Clare Dennis won the 220 yards breaststroke; earlier she had won the 200m breaststroke at the 1932 Los Angeles olympics. The Empire games were first mooted as a Pan-Britannic festival to 'celebrate the industrial, cultural and athletic prowess of the Anglo-Saxon race', partly as a British answer to Baron de Coubertin's international olympic games. MITCHELL LIBRARY

conduct of contestants as a serious national matter. It is only in the British Empire Games that the amateur status of the Olympic Games is genuinely recognised. In most of the other teams, the semblance of amateurism is scarcely maintained.[31]

Similarly, at the close of the 1938 Empire games in Sydney, staged as part of Australia's 150th anniversary celebrations, the NSW Minister for Labour and Industry, J. M. Dunningham, 'prophesied that the Olympic Games would bring about the ultimate degradation of sport because they had become commercialised, whereas the Empire Games could do something of lasting benefit to the Empire'. Countries like Germany and Japan, Dunningham continued, 'were betraying the sporting ideal by subsidising athletes, while the British Empire upheld that older sporting ideal in which sport was a world of its own, far removed from politics'.[32] The fact that the Empire games were equally political seemed to escape Alderson and Dunningham and, for that matter, most Australians. When Australian sportsmen and women swore the oath of allegiance to His Majesty the King, and promised to participate in 'the spirit of true sportsmanship...for the honour of our Empire and for the glory of sport', they were very much playing politics. Whereas the politics of the Empire games subordinated Australia to the British Empire, olympic politics in the 1930s increasingly emphasised the primacy of the nation. Dennis Phillips identifies the 1932 olympic games in Los Angeles as the turning point in 'sharpening the focus on national performance, particularly by introducing the modern victory ceremony complete with the playing of national anthems and the unfurling of national flags'.[33]

Australians seemed to take comfort in their isolation from international affairs and politics. In the inter-war years, sport offered Australians a preferred means for dealing with the world. As war loomed in Europe, 'cricket and politics jostled for headlines'. 'It was', writes Brian Stoddart,

> as if an Australian tour of England was an assurance of normality, not merely for the nations directly involved, but for cricket lovers throughout the empire. While Bradman flayed the Worcestershire attack it was perhaps easier to ignore Oswald Mosley's fascists demonstrating in London and to forget that in Germany Gottfried von Cramm, the great German Davis Cup tennis player, was in gaol. News that Bradman had reached his thousand in May was perhaps some antidote to reports of Japanese air raids in southern China and tension over Hitler's attitudes towards Czechoslovakia. While [Bradman] was making his match winning century at Headingley, at Villers-Bretonneux in France King George VI was unveiling a memorial to the AIF who had fallen on the Western Front during the Great War. As the Australian team set off for home riots were flaring in Sudetenland, General Franco was preparing his final victories in Spain and Neville Chamberlain was in Munich on his peace mission. In summing up the tour the Melbourne *Argus* was as much seeking reassurance as stating fact when it declared cricket 'a power, a bond with England'.[34]

There was nothing exceptional about the 1938 Ashes tour. Australians had also stayed well away from the bitter and acrimonious international debates leading up to the 1936 olympic games. Those who recognised the inseparability of politics and sport wanted to boycott Berlin in protest at German antisemitism. The anti-boycott forces, led by the unlamented American Avery Brundage, ensured that the games went ahead. In doing so, the world handed the Nazis a spectacular propaganda coup.[35] The Australian press published frequent reports about Nazi repression of Jews and the opposition of the United States (as well as Holland and Czechoslovakia) to the olympic games. But 'there was little public reaction locally to the global debate; it was as if it did not concern Australia. The boycott issue failed to arouse any discernible interest among editorial writers or politicians; for Australians generally, the significant olympic questions seemed to relate to matters of teams selection, performance and cost'.[36] One Australian did stay away from Berlin on political grounds—the young Jewish bantamweight boxer Harry Cohen. 'I did not accept the invitation' to attend the games, he said, 'because I feared that I might become involved in some trouble over Hitler's persecution of the Jews, and I am of Jewish faith. In fact, I told the Olympic authorities not to select me.'[37] Morality and ethics have not been a notable or even observable feature of Australian sport.

This Australian political myopia and/or amnesia remains. The exhibit at the Australian Gallery of Sport and Olympic Museum—established in 1986—depicts Australia's participation in each olympics to date. The 1936 exhibit is so sanitised that no viewer can associate a single facet of Nazism with that event. There is only one tiny clue: the official book of the games, encased in glass, carries a foreward and official greeting by Field Marshal Hermann Göring, second in power only to Hitler. His photo, opposite the text, shows him in full military regalia.

POLITICAL TENSIONS AND THE BODYLINE TOUR

While Australians measured progress by 'success in British terms against British standards maintained in British institutions',[38] this didn't always equate to harmonious relationships. Even in cricket, that most archetypal of British institutions, trouble sometimes developed. In one infamous incident at the SCG in 1879, on the second day of play between England (led by Lord Harris) and New South Wales, some 2000 spectators rushed onto the ground after the umpire gave a 'run-out' decision against William Murdoch:

> A large number of larrikins, sitting at the bottom of the terrace and within the boundary fence, made a rush for the centre of the ground . . . and were

quickly followed by hundreds of roughs who took possession of the wickets. The English team soon found itself in the centre of a surging, gesticulating, and shouting mob...One person tried to strike [umpire] Coulthard but was floored. Harris was struck across the body with a whip or a stick by a rough. Another English player, Hornby, promptly tackled his captain's assailant and with the assistance of some gentlemen and members dragged the person to the pavilion. This was no easy task as some of the roughs made unsuccessful attempts to snatch their cohort from the clutches of Hornby. Hornby had his clothes torn, and was struck on the face, and a few others had scratches. Harris...even landed a few blows himself...The melee lasted 30 minutes and throughout it the pavilion bell was rung, rather optimistically it seems, with the vigour of a fire alarm to encourage spectators to clear the ground.[39]

Apparently two English players provoked the pitch invasion by loudly referring to the crowd as 'sons of convicts'.[40] Groups of spectators ran onto the ground twice more that afternoon before officials cancelled play for the day. The match resumed two days later without further trouble. But Lord Harris didn't forget the invasion. When Murdoch's Australian XI arrived in England the following year, they could find no credible opponents. Only late in the tour did Harris relent and allow the Australians to play one match against England.[41]

Trouble strained relationships 50 years later. England's tour captain in 1932–33, Douglas Jardine, instructed Harold Larwood to bowl fast 'on the line of the body' throughout the Test series as a tactic to contain Australian batsmen, especially Don Bradman. The press vehemently criticised England's tactics and, with the series levelled after the first two Tests, interest in the third Test in Adelaide was very high. The hostility of the Adelaide crowd warranted the stationing of 440 police at the ground. Angry shouting, jeering and barracking marked the match, especially after short-pitched deliveries hit William Woodfull over the heart and William Oldfield in the face. Had these incidents occurred in Sydney and Melbourne, instead of 'conservative Adelaide...there might have been a reoccurrence of the 1879 riot'.[42]

During the Adelaide Test, the Australian Board of Control sent a telegram to the Marylebone Cricket Club (MCC):

Bodyline bowling assumed such proportions as to menace best interests of game, making protection of body by batsmen the main consideration and causing intensely bitter feelings between players, as well as injury. In our opinion it is unsportsmanlike, and unless stopped at once is likely to upset the friendly relations existing between Australia and England.[43]

While the allegation of unsportsmanlike behaviour 'challenged the imperial tradition that Britain set the standards for civilised social behaviour', Stoddart contends that the members of the Australian Board of Control 'identified solidly with the British and imperial traditions of cricket'. In this sense, they were as much issuing 'a plea as a demand for protection of the game and all that it had come to represent socially for them'.[44]

The charge of unsportsmanlike behaviour outraged the British establishment. They considered sportsmanship and fair play the essence of Englishness. *The Times* of London wrote that 'it is inconceivable that a cricketer of Jardine's standing, chosen by the MCC to captain an English side, would ever dream of allowing or ordering the bowlers under his command to practise any system of cricket that, in the time-honoured English phrase, is not cricket.' The Marylebone Cricket Club took a similar line:

> We...deplore your cable message and deprecate the opinion that there has been unsportsmanlike play. We hope that the situation is not now as serious as your cable appears to indicate, but if it is such as to jeopardise the good relations between England and Australian cricketers, and you consider it desirable to cancel the remainder of the programme, we would consent with great reluctance.

Yet even 'Gubby' Allen, a member of the team, would write to his father, Sir Walter Allen, saying 'Jardine is a perfect swine'.[45]

Australians clearly overreacted to England's tactics, which were hardly new.[46] Stan McCabe scored 187 not out in the first Test, and Australia had won the second Test, with Larwood taking only two wickets in each innings and Bradman scoring 103. But the bodyline tour provided one of the first examples of sport helping to nationalise Australians in the face of an aggressive 'other'. It also signalled, perhaps, the beginnings of a sense of Australian sport taking defeat none too well. Lloyd Dumas, editor of the Adelaide *Advertiser,* 'was asked to use his influence to stop the English commentators from using reports accusing the Australian team of being "squealers"'.[47] From this period on, it can be argued, Australian sport generally showed an inability to win and lose with grace. Playing hard or 'hardball' is not quite the same thing as showing grace, or ease, in victory and defeat. By the 1970s, Australian sportsmen and women had developed a sense of expectation about winning every time. By the 1980s this was not so much replaced as added to by a sense of 'right' and entitlement that Australians *should* win, especially in the sports where we have repute, like cricket.

The real potency of the bodyline event stemmed from its timing— at the height of economic depression. 'Diplomatic' exchanges, involving the Australian Prime Minister Joseph Lyons and Australia's representative in London, followed the telegram as the English demanded that the Australian Board of Control unconditionally remove the word 'unsportsmanlike'. The fourth Test in Brisbane remained in doubt, with the England team demanding that the Australian Board of Control withdraw the offending word. But the players were equally aware that to withdraw from the tour would have been popularly interpreted as a slur on their character. In the end, the Board offered an honourable compromise: 'We do not regard the sportsmanship of your team as being in question. We join heartily with you in hoping that the remaining Tests will be played with traditional good feeling.'[48] In the 1930s liberal and conservative sports officials saw greater merit in the British Empire than in the Australian nation.

COMMERCIAL FORCES

Not every aspect of sport proved so durable. In the late nineteenth and early twentieth centuries, commercial, mass entertainment forms began increasingly to replace the older, class-based amateur foundations of sport. Commercial interests intervened at every level. Robin Grow explains graphically the effects on sporting relationships of entrance fees for spectators at Melbourne football grounds:

> With revenue flowing into club coffers, the relationships between the VFA, the clubs, players, ground managers, crowds and commercial interests such as the press all had to be redefined. In football's early years, club revenue had been derived from members' subscriptions and donations, and the prevailing ethos was that these sources should fully fund the game. From these amounts clubs had to purchase balls, stockings, liniment and equipment, maintain their buildings, pay for advertising and defray the costs of travel to away games. Many features of the game were changed in order to provide benefits for the paying customer—match-day controls

were tightened, the number of matches was increased, and efforts were made to improve the game as a spectacle...The trend towards playing more matches...had the effect of shortening the cricket season, and footballers and cricketers...clashed over the use of the grounds. At some grounds the footballers would simply chase the cricketers off.[49]

Underpinning the growth of sport as a form of mass entertainment was the rapidly expanding sporting press. New printing technologies produced cheap, mass circulation newspapers. Sporting stories and gossip helped fill these papers. Sport made good action copy and allowed for appealing, even riveting, photographs; regular press coverage turned champion athletes and star players into household names; and constant public exposure, in turn, made the best sportspeople attractive to commercial enterprises who courted them to promote and endorse every conceivable type of product in their pages.[50]

Commercialism intensified in the inter-war years with the introduction of new forms of mass communication, notably the radio (1923) and 'talking pictures' (1928). Radio broadcast descriptions of cricket and Australian football began in 1925. Radio broadcasting often demanded creativity. The ABC used 'coded messages and studio sound effects' to 'simulate direct broadcasts of [Test cricket] matches being played in England' in 1934: 'the nation sat up through the early hours of the morning, enthralled by the sound of the commentator's pencil "batting" to a background of recorded crowd noises.'[51]

Even economic depression couldn't deflate the popularity of sport. Record crowds watched cricket and Australian football in the early 1930s. Historians acknowledge that sport provided an emotional outlet for Australians struggling with economic depression, but they also stress the profound influence of Hollywood on the popularity of sport. Hollywood directed attention to the hero status of leading sportspeople:

The movies had placed individual stars on a pedestal and at a local level the same sort of adulation was directed toward footballers, cricketers and even horses (notably Phar Lap). [Australian footballer] Haydn Bunton was a good example. Handsome and fastidious about his appearance—it was said that he even washed and ironed his bootlaces before a game—Bunton was every inch a star. There is a photograph of him in a fashionable cream trench coat that could easily have been produced by Hollywood's publicity machine.[52]

Dennis Phillips pursues the Hollywood-and-sport theme in his description of the American press reporting of the 1932 Los Angeles olympics: 'they informed the world of the intimate lives of Olympic "stars" and "starlets". The best looking and the most popular female Olympians were asked to share their special diets and beauty secrets.'[53]

Major sports produced major stars. Davis Cup tennis players—John Bromwich, Adrian Quist, Len Schwarz and Harry Hopman—were household names, and crowds 12 000 strong watched them play at Kooyong in Melbourne and White City in Sydney. Cyclist Hubert Opperman, who captained Australia's Tour de France team four times, won the world's longest non-stop road race (Paris–Brest–Paris), and was crowned sportsman of the year by the French newspaper *Auto*. Australian footballers—Carlton's 'Soapy' Vallence, Collingwood's Coventry brothers, Richmond's Jack Dyer and South Melbourne's Bob Pratt—were 'larger-than-life figures'.[54]

The star of stars was Donald Bradman. He 'towered above his contemporaries like a colossus', with a batting average of 99.94, a century every three innings, the most double centuries, the only person to score two triple centuries, and the only person to twice score 1000 runs in English first-class cricket before the end of May.[55] (The ABC has the same post office address in every city and major town: PO Box 9994. This is in honour of Bradman's Test average. Like Pilita Clark, we wonder whether the BBC, or any national broadcaster anywhere for that matter, could arrive at such a decision.[56]) In a tribute after Bradman's final match, former Test slow bowler, cartoonist and writer Arthur Mailey wrote that the man 'is an enigma, a paradox; and idol of millions of people, yet, with a few, the most unpopular cricketer I have ever met'.[57]

More important than these statistics, Bradman demonstrated how to turn sport into commercial success. In the process he prised open widening cracks in the amateur foundations of Australian cricket. During the Australian tour of England in 1930, Bradman contravened Australian Board of Control rules by writing a book, which the press serialised. The Board censured him and fined him £50, one-third of his tour bonus. Returning to Australia at the conclusion of the 1930 tour, Bradman left the rest of the team in Perth and made a triumphal overland journey. In 1931 he again violated Board rules by signing a joint contract with a newspaper, a radio station and a sports goods organisation. The Board initially threatened to sack him but retreated after Bradman 'emphatically protested' against what he called the cricket authority's 'interference

TWO AUSTRALIAN CHAMPIONS

DON BRADMAN

and

PETERS

ICE CREAM

*Don Bradman demonstrated how to turn sport into a
commercial success. The Australian Board of Control
censured and fined him for writing a book serialised in
the press. When they threatened to sack him for signing
a contract with a newspaper, a radio station and a sports
goods organisation, he protested against what he called
'interference with the permanent occupation of a player'.*
SMALL PICTURE FILE, MITCHELL LIBRARY

with the permanent occupation of a player'. In Bradman's words, 'the
Board was never meant to have powers directing the business interests
of players'.[58] Mailey, however, said 'he is a law within himself'.

Over the following decades, these commercial interests would gather
steam and ultimately gush forth in the 1970s to totally reconstruct
Australian sporting culture. Neither geographic isolation nor the protes-
tations and conscious strivings of sporting ideologues and polemicists
could preserve the past, most of which rested on idealised, fictionalised
and romanticised images.

EXCLUDED WOMEN

Women made significant advances in political, economic and social life after the Great War, but their sport made little progress. The potential begun by Fanny Durack and Mina Wylie before 1914 didn't blossom. The reason was simple: men maintained their basic prejudice against vigorous female activity and 'closed the doors to women'. After the Great War, male sports officials did little to encourage sportswomen. Lily Beaurepaire was the sole female representative at the Antwerp olympics in 1920; selectors ignored women completely four years later in Paris; three women swimmers (Edna Davey, Philomena 'Bonnie' Mealing, Doris Thompson) and one athlete (Edie Robinson) competed in Amsterdam in 1928; four women went to Los Angeles (Frances Bult, Clare Dennis, 'Bonnie' Mealing, Eileen Wearne); and again four travelled to Berlin (Doris Carter, Evelyn de Lacy, Kitty Mackay, Patricia Norton). Canadian organisers excluded women's athletics from the 1930 Empire games and Australia sent no women swimmers; two Australian female swimmers (Clare Dennis, Lesley Thompson), but no women athletes, made the trip to London four years later.[59] (Things changed in Sydney in 1938: the Australian team included fourteen female athletes and sixteen female swimmers.)

Women educated at private schools and universities and employed outside the home refused to passively accept sporting crumbs. In the late 1920s and early 1930s they formed separate associations 'either because they felt they were better off on their own or because the men's association would not allow clubs with women athletes to affiliate'.[60] Sometimes they successfully negotiated and won new deals. In 1928 the City Girls Amateur Sports Association, established by Eleanor Hinder and Jean Stevenson, entered negotiations with the NSW Minister for Lands for eleven acres of recreational and sporting land in Maroubra. Finance for the site came from the subdivision and sale of adjoining crown land. Not all negotiations went so smoothly. During the Depression, women cricketers in Sydney lobbied the Annandale council to provide them with a concrete wicket in a local park. After the council built the pitch, male cricketers took control. The mother of the captain of the women's team responded by threatening to withdraw the allocation of food coupons to the male cricketers concerned. The men returned the wicket.[61]

In the expanding global sports arena, men couldn't afford to ignore women totally. As Doris Magee, who founded the Australian Women's

Amateur Athletics Union in 1932, reminded male colleagues, the depth of talent and potential among women athletes presented a real opportunity to win national prestige and status abroad. Male selectors had no reply to this impeccable logic and selected fourteen women athletes in track and field events at Sydney's Empire games in 1938.[62] Of the 30 women in the 1938 team, fourteen won medals, including Decima Norman who won five gold. Praising what it called a 'marvellous performance', the *Sydney Morning Herald* publicly identified the national significance of this success when it said that 'overseas managers might well ask why they had not heard more of the Australian women athletes'.[63]

Not even national pride could totally override men's concerns and they implemented new strategies to keep women in their place. Women could compete, provided they demonstrated feminine charms—obedience, grace, beauty and modesty. Clare Dennis, who won gold in the 200m breaststroke at the 1932 olympic games, was an early example of the acceptable Australian sportswoman. Her delightful manner countered the 'masculine' appearance and aggressive 'pushy' style of American athletes like Mildred 'Babe' Didrikson [later Babe Zaharias]. Australian sportswomen 'really were the best in the world because...they were women first and athletes second'.[64]

Many women accepted this feminine ideology. Prior to the 1938 Empire games, at which she won gold in the 110 yards freestyle, swimmer Evelyn de Lacy revealed her feelings to the *Women's Weekly*:

> Five years of championship swimming is enough for any girl. The years of striving to reach championship standard are a tremendous thrill. Though I prefer an outdoors life and am not very fond of dancing, at the same time I can't help being a bit envious of girls who have a good time, go to parties, and wear pretty clothes. A champion swimmer has not much time for pretty clothes or opportunity for wearing them. Yes, I know we all look very fit and healthy, but we cannot do much about the care of our complexions or about keeping our hair really nice. Now that I have had my swimming career, I want a really feminine, glamorous job. So I am planning to study beauty culture.[65]

Increased commercial activity and greater participation by women in the inter-war years laid the seeds of change for sport. But the full expression of these embryonic trends was still five decades away.

EXCLUDED BLACKS[66]

For native Australians, the inter-war years were grim. On Australia Day 1938, the 150th anniversary of settlement, John Patten and Bill Ferguson organised a 'Day of Mourning and Protest' in Sydney's Elizabeth Street. Amid 'your rejoicings', they asked white Australians, can you find a clear conscience?

> You have almost exterminated our people, but there are enough of us remaining to expose the humbug of your claim, as white Australians, to be a civilised, progressive, kindly and humane nation...We do not ask for your charity; we do not ask you to study us as scientific freaks. Above all, we do not ask for your 'protection'...We ask only for justice, decency and fair play.[67]

This was the era of race theorists, the vogue years of eugenics and race purity. Race scientists predicted that 'full-bloods' would die out and that interbreeding would eliminate 'half-castes'. But governments refused to wait and busied themselves removing children, often forcibly, from 'over-influential' parents. In all states and the Northern Territory, special legislation confined Aborigines to reserves. Only a few received 'exemption certificates', documents that allowed them to live in white Australia. Authorities were no more receptive to 'moneyed gentlemen' who 'defied discipline' in this period than they were in the age of Jerry Jerome. Only their sporting prowess enabled Aborigines to surmount the prevailing racism. But their numbers were small: perhaps only a dozen and a half men and two women made careers in sport during the inter-war years.[68]

After the Great War, Aborigines entered competitions often in the guise of Maoris, West Indians, Filipinos and American–Indians: as with war service, this made access easier. In the land of the 'fair go', talented Aborigines learned that evasion of origin provided the easiest path to a sports career. In the 1920s Leo Appo, an axeman from Tweed Heads, New South Wales, overcame difficulties in entering contests by calling himself a 'New Zealander'. Only after winning the Commonwealth title at the 1928 Sydney Royal Easter Show did he announce his Aboriginal ancestry. Similarly, for 27 years champion jockey Frankie Reys—winner of the Melbourne Cup on Gala Supreme in 1973—believed that senior horse-racing was a difficult enough profession without, as he saw it, the added handicap of being a black Australian. In retrospect, his large family is now happy to avow his mother's membership of the Jirrbal (Dijbalangan) tribe of north Queensland. Sadly, some prominent sportsmen and women still refuse to speak about their Aboriginal ancestry.

Early on, the man who was to become Pastor Sir Douglas Nicholls, KCVO, OBE, KStJ, Governor of South Australia in 1976, discovered a principle: the only way 'to crack the white world' was to do something better than the white man. In 1929 he won the Nyah Gift and then the Warracknabeal, which was second only to the Stawell Gift in importance. In the Warracknabeal, Nicholls won 100 guineas (£105 or $210) for running 120 yards in a fraction over 12 seconds. Some idea of the scale of this 12-second win can be gained by comparing it to the total income for Cummera in 1928: £582 (or $1164) earned by 140 people working 48-hour weeks in grain, stock, wool, agistment and leasing! Doug was not a descendant of West African slaves; he didn't have special muscle twitch-fibres, different calf muscles, peripheral vision or any of the other physical features that some scientists and journalists attribute to black athletes. He was simply hungry. He experienced rejection trying out for Carlton Football Club. They said that because of his colour he must smell and this would offend the other players. He went to North-cote and played in the VFA for five years before beginning a memorable career with Fitzroy in 1932.

Racism stifled and stultified many. The Eddie Gilbert story is a shocking indictment of Australia in the 1930s. Gilbert was 'a dynamic Aboriginal fast bowler who at his prime ranked second only to Bradman among Queensland fans'. From a run of only four or five paces, he bowled Bradman for a duck in December 1931, after a five-ball spell which Sir Donald later called 'the fastest bowling I can remember...one delivery knocked the bat out of my hand and I unhesitatingly class this short burst faster than anything seen from Larwood or anyone else'.[69] The Aboriginal Protector wouldn't pay his expenses for these matches, but gave his permission for Gilbert to travel and to play—with a chaperone. Gilbert's career ended in 1936 with a remarkable letter from the secretary of the Queensland Cricket Association to the Chief Protector. It asked the official to tell Eddie that his services were no longer required and in the next sentence stated: 'With regard to the cricketing clothes bought for Gilbert, it is asked that arrangements be made for these to be laundered at the Association's expense, and delivery of the laundered clothes to be made to this Office.' Alcoholism and brain disease placed Gilbert in a mental institution for 23 years, until his death.

A Cherbourg kinsman and contemporary of Eddie Gilbert, Frankie 'Big Shot' Fisher, also suffered cruelty. Gus Risman, the visiting English rugby league captain in 1932 and 1936, wrote to Fisher saying he was the best player they'd met in Australia and invited him to play in the United Kingdom. As a 'controlled Aborigine', he had to get permission from the Queensland Aboriginal authority to even apply for a passport. They refused, stating that 'one star from Cherbourg [Gilbert] was enough'! Fisher was Cathy Freeman's paternal grandfather. His story, well known to her, explains some of her sharp political awareness.[70]

Most boxers are exploited; Aboriginal boxers are more exploited than most. Most boxing careers end sadly; Aboriginal boxers tend to be even sadder. Few dispute the view that Ron Richards was the best of many Aboriginal boxers. He was national champion in three divisions and Empire middleweight champion. Had opportunity come his way, he would have been world champion. His hardest battle, wrote Peter Corris, 'was for full, dignified human status within a prejudiced community'. His life was a disaster. The early death of his Aboriginal wife, poor management coupled with commercial exploitation, police harassment, and alcohol concluded with Sydney larrikins in the Haymarket beating him up for the glory of saying 'I KO'd Ron Richards'. The authorities sent him off to Woorabinda (Queensland) for three years. The final humiliation came after another arrest for vagrancy in Sydney: sent to the notorious and remote Palm Island penal settlement off the coast of Townsville where he grew vegetables until his penniless death in 1967.

One Aborigine did succeed in racist inter-war Australia. Lynch Cooper won the World Sprint Championship in Melbourne in April 1929. Born in 1906 at Moira Lake, very close to Cummera, Cooper won the Warracknabeal Gift in 1926. Twice, once in 1926 and again in 1927, he failed in the Stawell Gift, the world's oldest and richest professional race. In 1928 he sold his fishing boat and then, unemployed, he risked his remaining £20 on himself at 60 to 1 at Stawell. Cooper won by a narrow margin. His talents enabled him to sustain himself and his family with dignity through the Depression years—something virtually no other Victorian Aborigine could do.

Queensland, ironically, had the highest number of 'uncontrolled' Aborigines—those exempt from the special legislation. The least known and most unsung story is that of two Queensland women in the 1930s. Queensland women did not formally organise cricket in their state until 1929, and even then it was the domain of private girls' schools. Yet two first cousins, Edna Crouch and Mabel Campbell, both from state schools, gained selection for the state side against the visiting English women in 1934–35. Edna's brother, Glen 'Paddy' Crouch, also achieved a notable first: he was the first black man to represent Queensland in rugby league, in a team touring New Zealand in 1925. It is likely that the general acceptance of the talented Crouch family was due to their level of education. It is a bitter irony to reflect that had Richards (and Jerry Jerome before him, and later Jack Hassen, Elley Bennett and Georgie Bracken) not been exempted from the special Queensland laws, neither he nor they would have had boxing careers of any kind.

The organisers of the 'Day of Mourning and Protest' in 1938 had little to celebrate. Whatever headway Aborigines made in the 1930s was achieved by politics, not sport—with Pastor Doug the possible exception. The Aboriginal and Islander response to the 1988 Bicentennial was also a moment of mourning, an occasion on which tens of thousands said they had nothing to celebrate. Yet by then—in contrast to 50 years earlier—sport for Aborigines and Islanders had become a major avenue to *some* social status and social mobility.

7
Prosperity and Turbulence

1945–1972

[Australia] is a country in the grip of change: it is impossible to understand Australia unless one realises that almost everything is in the process of becoming something else. The process of change is obvious enough. But because the transition from the old society to the new is not yet complete Australia [in the mid-1960s] presents a jumble of contradictions and dissonances, tensions and conflicts which many Australians are unwilling to recognise but which are inexorably changing the way they live: mateship being eroded by successship, status snobbery competing with the old egalitarian tradition, sociability giving way to exclusiveness, materialism v. collectivism, even surfies v. rockers (new affluence v. old resentments)...the old puritanism giving way to a forthright hedonism, the cult of masculinity v. the cult of sexuality, art v. philistinism, the growth of bohemianism and dissent in what has been an overpoweringly conformist community, [and] the displacement of old people and ideas by the young (40 per cent of the Australian population is under 21 years old).

—CRAIG McGREGOR [1]

AN ERA OF GOLD

The period after the Second World War was golden. The forties, fifties and sixties saw unparalleled economic prosperity. Prices soared for Australian commodities, especially wool. Expanding industrial manufacturing industries, technological advances in production and communication, cheap energy, new mining ventures and explorations and innovative welfare programs gave Australians a level of affluence and standard of living comparable with North Americans. 'It seemed', wrote Manning Clark, 'as though the whole continent was to be brought under the influence of bourgeois civilisation'.[2]

For sport, the 1950s and early 1960s were glory years. New champions emerged in tennis (Frank Sedgman, Lew Hoad, Ken Rosewall, Rod Laver), swimming (Dawn Fraser, Lorraine Crapp, John Devitt, Murray Rose, Jon Hendricks, John and Ilsa Konrads), women's track (Marjorie Jackson, Shirley Strickland, Betty Cuthbert), men's distance running (Herb Elliot, John Landy, Ron Clarke), cricket (Richie Benaud, Alan Davidson, Neil Harvey, Wally Grout, Norman O'Neill), Formula One motor-racing (Jack Brabham), golf (Peter Thomson), cycling (Russell Mockridge), surfing ('Midget' Farrelly), and equestrianism (Bill Roycroft).[3] Australia dominated world tennis: between 1950 and 1968 Australia won fifteen Davis Cup titles, eleven Wimbledon singles titles, thirteen Wimbledon doubles titles, nine French and thirteen American titles. Melbourne hosted the 1956 olympic games, the first in the southern hemisphere, and Australians won an unprecedented and unequalled thirteen gold medals to finish third in the medal count. As the American magazine *Sports Illustrated* commented, 'when you consider what the Australians have managed to do in the intensely competitive field of international sport against nations with huge populations, it simply staggers your comprehension'.[4]

Victories, of course, tend to blur or blunt the failures. Not all was glory. Australia lost the Ashes in 1953 and only regained them in 1958–59; the Kangaroos shared the rugby league honours with Great Britain and even lost to France in 1951; and England beat the Australian soccer team 17–0 at the SCG. The sporting world was very much smaller and competition less intense in the 1950s: only 67 nations sent teams to the Melbourne olympics. There were also conspicuous gaps: apart from Herb Elliot, Australia performed poorly in men's track events, the most prestigious and competitive of olympic sports, and in soccer, the world's most popular game. Australia's sporting reputation didn't stop the international press from criticising our sports officials and civic leaders prior to the 1956 olympics. 'Originally there was quite a number of positive considerations in favour of choosing Australia', observed one correspondent to the German newspaper *Taegliche Rundschau*, but it soon 'became evident that everything was built on sand'.[5] Indeed, such was the organising committee's ineptitude that the president of the IOC, Avery Brundage, threatened to transfer the games from Melbourne:

> A group of pretty smart Melbourne citizens attended the Rome meeting [of the IOC] six years ago at which the Games were awarded to Melbourne. I don't know how they did it. There were a dozen cities after the Games. Some were prepared to spend up to $20 million to stage the Games, but your delegation was successful. For six years we have had nothing but squabbling, changes of management and bickering. Melbourne has a deplorable record in its preparations for the Games— promises and promises.

Publicly aired disputes over finances, the main stadium and other venues, and industrial action tarnished Australia's reputation. It took a three-day summit, arranged by the Victorian Premier John Cain senior, and attended by Prime Minister Robert Menzies, the deputy leader of the opposition, Arthur Calwell, state premiers, the Lord Mayor of Melbourne, William Brens, and the trustees and officials of the MCG, to resolve the venues wrangle.

THE COACHING FACTOR

Shortfalls, hiccoughs and a few blemishes notwithstanding, Australia's sporting achievements after the war warrant explanation. Sports historians have traditionally attributed success to 'favourable climate', 'superior diet' and 'natural sporting prowess'. These supposedly gave Australians an advantage over Europeans 'physically and emotionally devastated' by the Second World War.[6] But this would leave unexplained European domination of track and field events at the 1948 and 1952 olympics.[7] While these factors are no doubt part of the explanation, the role of coaches—

including Harry Hopman (tennis), Percy Cerutty and Franz Stampfl (athletics) and Forbes Carlile, Harry Gallagher, Sam Heford, Don Talbot and Frank Guthrie (swimming)—requires attention. Harry Gordon argues that these coaches, more than any other factor, explain the achievements in the 1950s.[8] Moreover, the peculiar methods they adopted may have also contributed to Australian sport faltering in the 1970s.

After the Great War, 'Australia maintained a fanatical and self-congratulatory commitment to...amateurism'. Athletes, coaches and officials subscribed to an amateur ideology where success was 'presumed to emerge magically from the bosom of a sun-drenched country'. Even as our performances declined relative to others, 'Australia continued to congratulate itself for being the only genuinely "amateur" nation left in the Olympic movement'.[9] When triple-jumper Jack Metcalf returned from the 1936 olympic games in Berlin with Australia's sole medal, a lowly bronze, his lonely success exposed the primitive state and uncompetitiveness of this country's sport:

> Most of the track and field team had never even *seen* cinder tracks before they reached Berlin, and because of the absence of heated pools, the swimmers had been denied an opportunity to train during the critical months after summer. The rowing eight had been allowed to make the trip not because it was the best in the land, but because its club could afford to pay its fare. Specialist coaches were almost nonexistent; [Fred] Woodhouse had learned his pole-vaulting techniques from a four-and-sixpenny manual, using a clothes-prop as his pole, and Doris Carter had rigged up makeshift high-jump equipment in the backyard, with the aid of a carpenter's trestle and some wooden stakes. Before Berlin it had been possible for some Australians to do well at the Olympics on the strength of just natural ability—but not any more.[10]

After the Second World War, these renowned coaches helped turn Australian performances around. Their methods involved massive amounts of preconditioning and punishing workloads in and out of the pool and on and off the track or court. Iron-fisted discipline, which included manipulating and exploiting their charges' fears and vulnerabilities, complemented gruelling training. The coaches claimed their techniques as 'scientific'; some, notably Forbes Carlile, who coached the Australian swimming team at the 1948 and 1956 olympic games, worked with exercise physiologists, including Sydney University's Professor Frank Cotton. While the science label gave these methods credibility, Bill Berge Phillips—

secretary of the Australian Swimming Union (ASU), swimming's representative on the Australian Olympic Federation and later president of the Fédération Internationale de Natation Amateur—dismisses any notion that science gave swimmers the 'winning edge'.[11] According to him, Carlile simply applied the training techniques of Bob Kiphuth, head swimming coach at Yale University, as described in his *Kiphuth on Swimming*. Carlile did make one crucial change: 'Where [Kiphuth] advised doing 25 push-ups, we'd make it 250. Whatever exercise [Kiphuth] recommended, we multiplied by ten. It worked, too.'[12] Carlile was not alone. Harry Hopman, non-playing captain of the world-conquering Davis Cup team from 1950 to 1969—and variously known as 'Svengali', 'Forty-love's Little Caesar', and 'Tennis's Captain Bligh'—'forced his charges to run mile after mile before breakfast, to keep hours as rigid as boarding school girls, and for misdemeanours he would fine them with all the discipline of a Prussian headmaster'.[13] Percy Cerutty, who coached Herb Elliot (and John Landy for a short time), believed that 'the human body thrives best on heat and cold, love and hate, plus punishing effort'. His formula for success was 'blood, tears, sweat and suffering'. 'For any achievement highly valued by knowledgeable man', the philosopher coach declared, 'sweat, tears, often blood is the normal concomitant'.[14]

Australian football coaches applied identical approaches. John Kennedy coached Hawthorn to its first VFL premiership. In 1961 he designed a torturous system of training based on circuit training, resistance work and long-distance running; his players began training for the season two months before any other team. Similarly, Norm Smith 'wielded the whip' to win Melbourne four grand finals. He even sent home players who dared venture to training with anything resembling a beard.[15] But in a rapidly changing society, authoritarian coaches had a limited life.

CHANGING TIDES

Amid the years of economic prosperity and sporting plenty lay the seeds of change that would fundamentally transform the Australian social fabric, and its sporting culture, in the late 1960s and 1970s. Prosperous economies need large supplies of labour and a highly skilled workforce. Underpopulated Australia lacked both. Successive governments recruited labour from abroad and built a system of mass education, naively assuming that they could fully control both processes.

Immigration

Australia's postwar 'bourgeois civilisation', based on a suburban house overflowing with creature comforts and electronic gadgetry, a private motor vehicle, a 35-hour working week and 'never-ending titillations on the television screen',[16] needed a large workforce and eager consumers. Mass immigration seemed the answer. It would confer economic advantages and it seemed a sure way to bolster national security and assuage fears of foreign invasion. Most importantly, government ministers and policy-makers assured Australians that mass immigration posed no threat to the cherished century-old white Australia policy. 'New Australians', as the 2.5 million immigrants living in Australia in 1971 were dubbed,[17] would assimilate, that is, meld into the pre-existing society and adopt its language, beliefs and customs. Announcing the initial program in 1947, Labor's Minister of Immigration Arthur Calwell promised that all arrivals would be 'Caucasian'; he predicted that 90 per cent would come from Britain. When a shortage of Britons forced the Chifley Labor government to recruit displaced people from eastern and central Europe, Calwell cheerily noted that many were either 'red-headed and blue-eyed' or 'natural platinum blondes'.[18] He initially allowed 2000 Jews to come on humanitarian grounds, but the scheme lasted only two years, whereafter the government introduced quotas for Jews.[19] When, in the mid-1960s, Robert Menzies' Liberal–Country Party Coalition government extended assisted passage to Turks, Greeks, Italians, Spaniards and Portuguese, Minister of Immigration Billy Snedden swore that Australia was, and would remain, 'a monoculture, with everyone living in the same way, understanding each other, and choosing the same aspirations'. It was a classic denial of Australia's cultural revolution and proved that Anglo-Australians wanted the benefits of immigration without foreigners and that they wanted population growth without social or cultural diversity.[20] Aboriginal policy was little different. The Minister for Territories, Paul Hasluck, announced a national policy whereby 'all Aborigines…will attain the same manner of living as other Australians and live as members of a single Australian community…observing the same customs and influenced by the same beliefs, hopes and loyalties as other Australians'.[21] The 'other' Australians, of course, included the 2.5 million immigrants who, in theory (only), 'lived as members of a single community'.

Few policies have sat more at odds with human social organisation. Not surprisingly, assimilation failed in both mainstream and Aboriginal

Australia. Patterns of settlement initially helped disguise the effects of immigration. Migrants seeking the fruits of prosperity and the trappings of success located themselves in the expanding web of suburbia and appeared to 'blend'. But few could afford this option. Most needed cheap accommodation close to places of work, and this meant living in inner-city suburbs. It also meant ethnic enclaves. By 1971 sizeable European minorities, including some 130 000 Yugoslavs, 300 000 Italians and over 160 000 Greeks,[22] virtually occupied entire suburbs where they created, and recreated, their own social and cultural institutions.[23] Professor F. Lancaster Jones's study of the demographics of Melbourne suggested it was the most ghettoised city in the world. Spatial segregation was an economic strategy and a social strategy to deal with Australian xenophobia and to maintain a sense of connectedness. It also perpetuated disconnectedness: Anglo-Australians showed little willingness to accommodate 'new Australians' who would not discard the very cultural institutions—religion, language, customs, folklore—which bound them together in a cold social environment but which also differentiated them.

Soccer illustrates the process of disconnection between the two Australias in the 1960s. Anglo-Australians controlled soccer, and initially soccer administrators 'enthused about the arrival of boats crammed with new Australians'. But 'goodwill dissipated very rapidly' when the new arrivals refused to play the British way. At issue were 'vastly different concepts of manliness and method, aggression and authority'. Australians played a physical game based on hard running and body contact; Europeans played at a slower pace, emphasising skills and the 'deft touch'. Australians unquestioningly accepted the referee's decision and they did not pull shirts or spit; immigrants 'voiced dissent' and sought 'retribution for perceived injustices on the field'. District identities provided the foundations of Australian soccer, while ethnic identities—which manifested in 'foreign' flags, tunes and chants—underpinned the immigrants' soccer clubs. The latter also invested more in the financial and social structures of individual clubs rather than the code.[24]

Soccer, writes Phillip Mosely, 'was an exceptional forum in which immigrants felt they stood equal with, if not superior to, host Australians'; European-style football had already surpassed the British style and immigrants knew they were good.[25] In the late 1950s, first in New South Wales and then in other states, immigrants defected from ruling state federations. In 1963 the Australian Soccer Federation replaced Australian Soccer Football. Immigrants now controlled the game's chief organising associations and ethnic clubs dominated the top competitions. In the 1950s and early 1960s, Italians and Greeks were the most numerous, joined later that decade by those national groups comprising the former Yugoslavia. Jews, Hungarians, Czechs, Ukrainians, Poles, Germans, Dutch and Maltese also wielded influence.

Anglo-Australians generally dismissed soccer as a 'wog's' game, but the major codes considered it a threat. In 1952 the VFL directed suburban affiliates to 'secure all available public sporting space in Melbourne in order to stifle the burgeoning threat posed by soccer's migrant-inspired growth'.[26] In 1965 Melbourne youths daubed anti-soccer slogans over Middle Park, chopped down the goalposts and tried to set fire to the grandstand.[27]

Australian football, rugby league and even cricket attracted numbers of immigrants, some of whom became stars. Players from non-English-speaking backgrounds who made names for themselves in Australian football include John Benetti, Sergio Silvagni, Tony Ongarello, Sam Kekovich, Renato Serafini, Peter Daicos, Robert DiPierdomenico, Ang Christou and Anthony Koutoufides. More often than not, they participated despite rather than because of assimilation policies. Of Maltese origin, rugby league player Mario Fenech describes being called a 'wog' and being made to 'feel different'. He 'thrust his hand up to play rugby league at school as much because his Australian peers did as for any other reason'.[28] Similarly, taunts of 'wop' and 'dago' followed Alex Jesaulenko, born to Russian and Ukrainian parents, before he became the mighty 'Jezza' of Australian football fame.[29]

Immigrants were not the only ones to contribute to Australia's postwar population growth. Such was the upsurge of births among 'native-born' Australians after the Second World War that demographers referred to a 'baby boom'. Between 1947 and 1966, the under-20 age cohort grew by 5.7 per cent, from 32.7 per cent to 38.4 per cent of the total population.[30] But the impact of youth on Australian society far exceeded these raw numbers.

Youth, authoritarianism, alternative sport

Hogan may well have been right in 1880 about the 'disinclination' of youth to listen to their parents, but after the war youth rebelled rather than disinclined. Unencumbered by memories of the hardships of the

Depression, these 'overstimulated over-consumers'[31] were the first generation freed from the responsibilities of young adulthood. They benefited from an expanding education system that underwent a liberal transformation—in part a consequence of the technological requirements of advanced industrial production—which encouraged self-expression and self-actualisation.[32] In 1960 the principal of Sydney's Pymble Ladies College painted the ideal young person as 'reasonably rebellious, reasonably questioning, warmly impulsive and wilful within limits'. These, said Dorothy Knox, were the foundations of 'valuable adult qualities'.[33]

But who defined the limits? When 'new social impulses are set free they are impossible to fully contain',[34] and by the late 1960s it was clear that Australian youth were determined to restructure the entire society. Paradoxically, the political consciousness of this generation, which derived in large part from the liberalised education system that previous governments hoped would preserve and develop bourgeois civilisation, encouraged youth to probe, question and challenge what it believed disagreeable and dissatisfying. The new generation found much reason for discontent: nuclear armaments, environmental rape, social alienation, suburban affluence, sexual puritanism, bureaucratic careerism, even the treatment of Aborigines. ABSCHOL, a nationwide student movement, not only sought funds to help Aborigines through high school and university, but also lobbied on a wide range of social policy, legal and political issues. In other words, Australian youth in the 1960s and 1970s would challenge every major economic and social institution, including sport, and every traditional authority relationship, including sports coaches.

Lorraine Crapp, a dual gold medallist at Melbourne in 1956, is a good example of the new generation of athletes who grew up in the postwar period. By 1958, at just 20 years of age, she felt the fun being 'remorselessly filtered out' of swimming: non-stop travel, exhibition swims, a prying media, stultifying repetition, constant orders, and demands for 'more records, more medals, more hype for Australia' took their toll. She made one more supreme effort to make the Australian team for the 1960 olympics in Rome and then retired.[35] Crapp wasn't alone in disenchantment. A member of the team at Tokyo in 1964 described the 'little dictators' and 'absolute autocrats' who ran swimming: 'as soon as you were on the team they acted like you were their toys, their puppets.' Herb Elliot agrees:

There is no doubt that during the time of my athletic career there was an unhappy blend of bureaucracy/autocracy in athletics officials... Many...had been relatively unsuccessful in other walks of life, and had not learnt to deal with power. When they obtained power, they misused it...Perhaps because sport was amateur and the vast majority of the population were not prepared to spend the hours in mundane tasks...you ended up with relatively small people getting to the top in many circumstances.

The treatment meted to Nan Duncan, Linda McGill and Dawn Fraser at the Tokyo olympic games by Bill Slade, the manager of the swimming team, illustrates swimming officials' small-mindedness. After the Swimming Union banned swimmers competing in the first three days from participating in the opening ceremony, Slade discovered Duncan and McGill on the bus taking the team to the march. According to Fraser, who was hiding on the same bus, Slade ordered them off and addressed them 'like a pair of guilty schoolgirls. Nan's face was quivering, and it was apparent that she was ready to burst into tears. Linda kept saying, "Mr Slade...I promise you I'll swim so well. Please let me march". "You know the rules, you're causing a lot of trouble", Slade retorted.' Ostensibly in good faith, the Union introduced the ban to keep the swimmers fresh for competition. But as Fraser points out, the opening ceremony is a highlight of the olympic games and participation offers 'inspiration' and 'incentive'; 'what it amounts to is a hike around the main stadium, an hour of standing easy...and about a quarter of an hour standing at attention. If you can't take that...after months of training...you...should pack up and go home'.[36]

Fraser defied officials and participated in the opening ceremony. In 1965, after considering reports by Slade and Anne Hatton, the team chaperone, the ASU suspended Fraser for ten years, later reduced to four years, McGill for four, and Duncan and Marlene Dayman for three. Officials never made public the precise reasons for the suspensions, and they allowed no appeal. In Fraser's case, it is not clear whether officials terminated her swimming career because she marched in the opening ceremony, because she wore a non-regulation swimsuit or because she tried to take a Japanese flag as a souvenir. Judy Joy Davies, twice an olympic representative and later a journalist, reported the chairman of the Japanese organising committee as saying: 'We, in Japan, do not recall any incident in which the Australian swimmers were involved which could have led to such drastic action.'[37] The evidence points to malice and spite. As the Premier of New South Wales John Renshaw said at the time, 'these disqualifications seem savage in the extreme. They appear to have all the elements of hate rather than a reasonable or rational approach'.[38] Whatever the reason, no one will ever know: the official report lies buried deep in the Australian olympic archives, mutilated by scissors, with all reference to Fraser's behaviour removed![39]

In the early 1970s traditionally conservative semi-professional Australian footballers started to agitate. On the one hand, a draconian cluster of zoning, recruiting, permit, registration and transfer rules tied players to specific clubs; on the other, the system of regulated payments barely compensated them for their training, travelling, or physical risk. In short, VFL rules effectively condemned players to master–servant relationships.[40] In 1970 two Collingwood stars, Des Tuddenham and Len Thompson, took a stand against 'the autocratic demands and paternalistic posturing of VFL delegates and club officials'. After demanding an increase in match payments from $25 to $300 per game, they went on strike for three weeks. Five senior Essendon players withdrew their services for one game. Their demands were more modest than the Collingwood pair: they wanted $40 per match and $3 for training. Although the League offered concessions, allowing long-serving players to negotiate higher pay and to sign contracts with the clubs, 'players were no longer prepared to accept the paternalistic pronouncements of a few crusty ex-players' and they formed their own association. Among the modest concerns of the VFL Players' Association were better ground facilities, injury compensation and insurance, legal advice on contracts and related matters and representation on the League's board.[41]

Athletes and players were not the only ones demanding change. Coaches, the engineers of the gold boom, also clashed with amateur officials over the administration of their sports.[42] Forbes Carlile condemned hypocritical amateurism and pointed to the vastly different 'interpretations' applied by the United States, Western Europe and the Soviet Union. He lambasted the ASU as 'an inflexible, iron-fisted oligarchy': 'it is common knowledge that a very thin line exists between the amateur and professional in sport. In swimming many officials patrol that line with zeal.' Amateur officials, for their part, likened the role of coaches to that of a 'classic French mistress': they tolerated their services but refused to legitimise them. As far as they were concerned, payment denigrated the noble structures of amateurism.

Spectators joined the chorus of dissent. Tens of thousands voted with their feet and walked away from traditional sports. Daily crowds at Sheffield Shield cricket matches dropped to under 3000 in 1967–68, compared with over 4300 in 1947–48; attendances at Melbourne Cups averaged less than 81 000 in the four years between 1965 and 1968, compared with just under 97 000 between 1945 and 1948; and aggregate attendances at VFL home-and-away matches fell from 2.7 million in 1963 to 2.4 million in 1969.[43] Spectators who stayed demanded better facilities. Australian football fans expressed ire at overcrowded grounds, primitive toilet facilities, congested and unhygienic drinking areas and poor seating.[44] Cricket crowds also became noticeably more unruly in the late 1970s. Match reports describe streakers disrupting play, fans throwing beer cans and fighting among themselves, and youths clashing with police. Police, historians and sociologists variously attribute the sudden change in behaviour to increased alcohol consumption, the rise of World Series Cricket which supposedly attracted a less knowledgeable and less informed type of spectator, and protests against the introduction of fixed seating in traditional working-class areas of grounds, notably Bay 13 at the MCG and the Hill at the SCG.[45] But cricket crowds were simply symptomatic of the broad changes taking place in Australian society and of youth, in particular, who were willing to express their discontent with traditional institutions. Relationships between surfers and surf lifesavers add further weight to this argument.

Craig McGregor compares the respective styles and attitudes of surfers and surf lifesavers in the mid-1960s:

> Board riding is an intensely individualistic sport, whereas club surfing is a team effort. The board rider is flexible, untrammelled, moving from beach to beach in search of waves; the surf lifesaver joins a single club, gives his allegiance to a single beach, stays there while on duty. The board cult has its large camp following of women ('fremlins'); the surf clubs are the last citadels of unrepentant Australian masculinity . . . (based on mateship, physical prowess, keg parties, grog-ups, uncertain relationships with women, a certain homespun philosophy of life) . . . The one is cool, modern, uncommitted; the other is traditional, hidebound, loyalist (OUR CHIEF PATRON: His Royal Highness The Prince Philip, Duke of Edinburgh). One is self-involved, even selfish, one is aimed at service; one is free wheeling, one is disciplined; one is with it, one is square . . . A whole strata of young Australians have chosen the first.[46]

*The malibu surfboard, introduced to Australia in the late
1950s, was mass-produced and light (about 10kg).
Riding waves became an accessible pastime for the
youth of the day. The malibu came to symbolise a
hedonism that directly challenged existing conformity.*
MARGAN & FINNEY

While McGregor largely ignores the tensions between 'alternative
lifestyle' and competitive surfing, and neglects the surf lifesaving movement's attempts to accommodate surfers,[47] his description of 'the beach
generation' supports the conclusions drawn from the experiences of
Dawn Fraser and Lorraine Crapp. First, traditional, pre-war, amateur-
style sports administrators demanded rather than earned respect, showed
minimal sympathy for alternative viewpoints, brooked no challenges to
their authority, were notoriously obdurate and mulish, and never shied
from exercising power. In its 'war' against surfers, the surf lifesaving
movement demarcated surfing zones, instructed inspectors to confiscate
boards, lobbied municipal councils for a surfboard registration scheme
whereby non-lifesavers paid five shillings for an annual licence, and in

some cases even advocated the prohibition of surfboards. The president of Sydney's Freshwater Life Saving Club advocated banning surfboards, which, he said, encouraged 'hoodlums' to the beach at the expense of families. Second, youth left the lifesaving movement *en masse*; active membership declined by over 7 per cent in the 1964–65 season and grew by less than 1 per cent between 1964–65 and 1969–70.

VIOLATING COMMUNITY TRADITIONS?[48]

In 1964 Carlton Football Club signed Ron Barassi, favourite son of the Melbourne Club, as its playing coach for three years. Barassi received a (then) staggering £20 000; his average weekly earnings from the deal were ten times that of the average VFL player. Outraged fans deemed the transfer an act of flagrant disloyalty, claiming the 'treacherous' Barassi had foresworn his home and violated community solidarity.

But material prosperity and demographic shifts in the 1960s and 1970s were already changing quite fundamentally the values and composition of traditional geographic communities. Financial demands by players and growing commercial opportunities merely compounded these changes. All the Melbourne-based clubs in the VFL had their home ground within a 10-kilometre radius of the central business district. By the mid-1960s, the geographic centre of population lay some 15 kilometres to the east of the city's centre. Not surprisingly, several clubs—including St Kilda, North Melbourne and Richmond—pursued spectators and moved to new grounds, even though this meant recruiting a different class of spectator who did not necessarily identify with the traditional community. Spectators alone would not provide the income necessary to pay demanding players, or to build more comfortable ground facilities for spectators. Clubs needed new sources of funding independent of gate receipts and club memberships. They turned to corporate sponsorship. In so doing, they further weakened community customs and tradition.

North Melbourne paved the way in Australian football. A former player, Allen Aylett, 'created a unique business structure' at the club. He employed a full-time fundraiser who 'expanded the social club, established a coterie of wealthy supporters, offered members and other supporters a range of travel and insurance services, and...delivered strong commercial support in the form of business sponsorship'. These revenues enabled recruitment of the best players and in 1975, within just three years of launching its new structure, the club won its first ever premiership. North Melbourne had produced a winning business formula which other clubs, and the VFL, quickly followed. The latter set up a properties division, based on a model developed by the American National Football League, to sell the League's logo and image to the highest bidder. Officially endorsed club scarves, beanies, jumpers, flags and emblems soon became an integral part of the match day spectacle and an important source of revenue. Sponsorships and television rights further boosted the revenue base. By the end of 1975, the VFL had entered a dramatic new phase in its development. Club traditions and local community connections were, in Bob Stewart's words, 'no longer the core values that guided the administration of the game'.

SPORTSWOMEN

Striking is the word for the prominent role played by women, especially in the olympic arena, in this golden era. At Melbourne in 1956, they won seven of Australia's thirteen gold medals. Between 1948 and 1960 women won seven of Australia's gold medals on the track, while men won one. What made these achievements even more remarkable was that women comprised only some 20 per cent of Australian teams, less than 25 per cent of olympic events were open to women, and nearly every social institution in Australia, from women's magazines to trade unions, agreed that their primary responsibility was motherhood. The 'laws' of motherhood, as we have seen, demanded that women marry, withdraw from the workforce and minister full-time to their children and husbands.[49]

Fundamental changes in the Australian economy in the 1950s recast the role of women and, in particular, their contribution to family life. New consumer durables—televisions, washing machines, refrigerators and motor cars—flooded the market after the war. These goods quickly became necessities rather than needs and, more importantly, wages were needed to buy them. Similarly, new technologies and economies of scale lowered the cost of food and clothing, which became increasingly uneconomical to make at home. In short, a second income contributed more to a family's standard of living, and, in a rapidly growing economy with an insatiable appetite for labour, women left the home in droves. Later, at the end of the 1960s, feminist critiques of the conventional family added further fuel to this social transformation of women's lives and family structures.

Marjorie Jackson and her mother are pals. Mum sees her off to work from their Lithgow home.

She rides her bike to the office each day, doesn't find that cycling affects sprinting.

At the office she is an expert typist. "Excellent and efficient," says manager Jack Crosby.

Home again after training. She helps Mum get the dinner while sister Beryl stands by.

A short game of cards is a relaxation in the evening. Mother is a keen spectator.

Then for a few quiet hours. Mother reads the paper while Marjorie does fancy work.

The 'ordinariness' of sprint gold medallist Marjorie Jackson. The media loved the plainness and homeliness of the working, dutiful daughter. They constantly attempted to restrict sportswomen to the image of the nice girl-next-door—someone who would avoid the 'excesses' of Annette Kellerman, Fanny Durack and, later, Dawn Fraser. SPORTING LIFE, DECEMBER 1949

Hardly masculine! Eighteen years old, slim, with a boyish haircut and a ready smile, this was Dawn Fraser as she began to break world records early in 1956. Rumours suggesting that she was masculine caused her 'irreparable damage'. During her career she was constantly subjected to rumour and innuendo about her sexuality. HARRY GORDON & DAWN FRASER, *GOLD MEDAL GIRL*

Sport reflected these changes. We have seen how the lure of gold initially enticed male sports officials to suppress their prejudices and select women to represent Australia. But even female gold-producing machines didn't stop commentators emphasising their domestic and family responsibilities. On her return from the 1954 Empire games in Vancouver, a reporter asked Marjorie Jackson's husband how she handled a broom; even as Shirley Strickland sprinted for gold in the 80m hurdles at Melbourne in 1956, with her three-year-old child Pip cheering from the stands, 'others in the crowd taunted her to retire and let someone younger have a go'.[50] Precisely as women gained greater economic and social freedom, critics turned their attention to female sexuality. Few sportswomen suffered in this area as did Dawn Fraser: the rumours suggesting that she was masculine hurt her deeply and caused her 'irreparable damage'. 'Trying to prove [my femininity] has

given me one of the greatest challenges I've had in my life.'[51] Despite
sweeping over the Australian social fabric, the tide of change clearly left
gender stereotypes and prejudice firmly in place, although happily Fraser
eventually triumphed to become a national icon.

SPORTING CITIZENS

The 1960s was perhaps the most important decade of this century for
Aborigines. Except for Queensland, all states and the Northern Territory
reconsidered and revised their Aboriginal statutes, either abolishing them
or ameliorating them. The 1967 referendum on Aborigines, misconstrued
and misrepresented as it was, nevertheless was *seen* as a new deal con-
ferring 'citizenship' or 'citizenship rights'.[52] In 1963 Charles Perkins led
a group of university (ABSCHOL) students on the famous 'freedom
rides' to break the rigid colour bar in social amenities—particularly
swimming pools and cinemas—in several towns in northern New South
Wales. Aboriginal pressure groups aired major grievances: the fate of
Aborigines at the Maralinga nuclear test site, drinking prohibition in the
Territory, forced removal of Aborigines from old Mapoon Mission in
Queensland, ongoing repression in Queensland, subsistence wages in the
cattle industry. They also helped stake the first of the major land rights
claims, at Yirrkala in Arnhem Land. The ABC played a part, with radio
and television reporters bringing light to much darkness in Aboriginal
affairs. A handful of academics, three of them immigrants (Diane
Barwick, Jeremy Beckett and Colin Tatz), began a systematic uncover-
ing and vivisection of some appalling policies and practices.

   Individual codes took the first tentative steps to recruit what they
would quickly realise was 'black gold'.[53] Long after the Nicholls era
ended at Fitzroy, VFL club Essendon grabbed the gifted runner, boxer
and footballer, Norm McDonald. He played in six grand finals, including two premiership sides. Geelong signed Graham 'Polly' Farmer, who
was removed as a child and who most consider the best ruckman of all
time. Barry Cable, multiple medal winner and brilliant rover, went to
North Melbourne, and David Kantilla journeyed from Bathurst Island
to play for South Adelaide and South Australia. A fellow Territorian,
Michael Ahmatt, also travelled south to Kantilla's new domain, and from
there to play basketball for Australia in Tokyo and Mexico, venues of
the 1964 and 1968 olympics. This was, indeed, emergence from the
incarceration on reserves. Rugby league also began to recruit a few

Aborigines. The first Aborigine to play for Australia was a Queenslander, Lionel Morgan—for two Tests in 1960; Arthur 'Artie' Beetson, who began life as a winger in Roma (Queensland), played fourteen Tests and as many World Cup matches for Australia.[54]

Wally McArthur's story probably epitomises the Aboriginal experience in sport after the war, as Aborigines began the excruciatingly difficult journey from their incarceration on reserves, missions and settlements. Born at Borroloola in the Northern Territory, and named after the local McArthur river, Wally was classified as a 'half-caste' and removed to the Bungalow mission school near Alice Springs. In 1942, the authorities sent him by train to Adelaide and then to the Aboriginal boys' home at Mulgoa, west of Sydney. He attended Penrith High and in 1948 won twelve of the thirteen events on the school's sports program. At the NSW High Schools' Championship, he was allowed to enter three events: the 100 yards, 440 and the long jump. He won all three—without shoes! Wally was again 'transferred', this time to St Francis's Anglican Boys Home in Adelaide. Thereafter he won the state 100 and 220 yards titles in the under-19 category. He was omitted from the state under-19 team to tour Tasmania in 1951, although others he had beaten soundly were selected. He complained—and was told that if he paid his own way he could go. A friend paid his fare. Wally duly won the national 100 yards title in the under-19 category. Second was Kevan Gosper, currently a member of the IOC in Australia, who ran for Australia at Helsinki the following year. Colour posed no problem for Gosper, but it was an endless obstacle for McArthur's amateur career. Charles Perkins insists that Wally was in line for olympic selection in Finland but 'was denied a place in the South Australian athletic squad because he was Aboriginal'. McArthur's solution was to turn professional, which he did in 1951. He won his first ten pro races. At Norwood Oval in Adelaide, he was matched against the NSW and Australian 130 yards champion, Frank Banner, whom he defeated. As the 'Black Flash', he went on to a sensational rugby league career in the United Kingdom in the 1950s.

Carlton football player Syd Jackson, yet another removed child,[55] and jockey Richard Lawrence 'Darby' McCarthy,[56] represented a fundamental and significant change in Aboriginal life in the 1960s: both were abrasive and aggressive about their Aboriginality. Darby recalls a 'bloke asking me about being coloured': 'No. I'm black, you're coloured. I was born black, stay black and die black. You're born pink, go white, get brown in the sun and finally end up grey.' Jackson and McCarthy offer a strong contrast to the men like Beetson, Cable and Farmer who lived in the shadows of assimilation. While the latter hesitated, or let their managers and administrators hesitate on their behalf, to proclaim their Aboriginality,[57] Jackson and McCarthy were up front and proud.

World bantamweight boxing champion Lionel Rose presents the best example of shifting white attitudes, perhaps even embryonic atonement, or even a sense of reconciliation, in the 1960s. Raised in a shack at Jackson's Track near Drouin in Victoria, Rose won his title against 'Fighting' Harada in Tokyo in 1968. Melbourne gave him an unprecedented homecoming—from the airport to Town Hall 250 000 tumultuous people massed, shouting 'Good on ya, Lionel! You beaut little Aussie!'. No boxer has ever had such a homecoming, said the press, 'not Joe Louis coming home champ to Detroit, not Sugar Ray Robinson returning to Harlem nor Marcel Cerdan to Paris'. The last quarter-mile of Swanston Street was jammed with 100 000 people, an attendance not even the Beatles could muster. Clearly, there was a strong sense of guilt about Aboriginal treatment that day. There was also a sense that Aborigines were now, somehow, part of the land.

Not unexpectedly, the boxing fraternity named Rose, Fighter of the Year. But it is his Australian of the Year[58] that raises bigger questions about Australian identity, race relations and sport, and indeed the inter-relationships between them. Rose's award came after that of the first recipient, Sir Macfarlane Burnet in 1960, followed, in order, by Dame Joan Sutherland, Jock Sturrock, Sir John Eccles, Dawn Fraser, Sir Robert Helpmann, Sir Jack Brabham and the Seekers: two biomedical research scientists, a soprano, a ballet dancer, a pop group and four sports stars! Other Aboriginal recipients have been Evonne Goolagong-Cawley (1971), Galarrwuy Yunupingu (1978), Lois O'Donoghue (1984), Mandawuy Yunupingu (1992), and Cathy Freeman (1998). Of the six Aboriginal recipients, three have been sports achievers. These awards raise two questions. What values underlie the fact that four out of the first eight winners were sportspeople? In light of this, what do white Australians perceive as 'serious' Aboriginal achievements—the intellectual, political, artistic, or the physical?

A NATIONAL IDENTITY?

Ethnic diversity, a major economic shift in trade and investment from Britain to the United States and Japan, and a reorientation of foreign policy away from Europe towards America and Asia, should have prompted Australians to raise crucial questions about their national identity in the postwar period. Surprisingly, they appeared remarkably indifferent to, and even complacent about, their status and place in the world. 'It seems', argues John Rickard, that 'the Australian temperament [is]...uneasy with nationalist gestures'. Rickard attributes this to the complexity of our historical relations with Britain and general feelings that any assertion of Australian identity runs the risk of being interpreted as a rejection of the British heritage. The result, he concludes, 'has often been not so much a cultural division within the community (though that does, in shadowy form, exist) as a deep seated scepticism about the values of exercises in the ritual and rhetoric of nationalism'.[59]

Robert Gordon Menzies, Prime Minister in 1939–41 and 1949–66, certainly shied away from asserting Australianness. He maintained an unwavering faith in British institutions and British civilisation, proudly declaring himself 'British to the boot-heels'. Nor was his position idiosyncratic: it was a platform upon which the Liberal–Country Party Coalition came to power in 1949 and retained government for the next 23 years. Unsettled by its language of political and economic independence and anti-colonialism, and apparent support for communist China, the electorate swept Labor from office. Labor's pronouncements and policy directions not only alarmed Protestants but also divided Catholics—to the extent that a group of young conservative intellectuals defected and formed the Democratic Labor Party (DLP). By the mid-1950s, postwar prosperity had significantly eroded the Catholic Church's historic attachment to the Labor Party and the DLP finally shattered the accord. By fragmenting the Catholic vote, the DLP also, paradoxically, helped break the 'pursed-lip silence' between Protestants and Catholics: its support for the Liberal–Country Party alerted Protestants to the fact that the Catholic Church was no longer a grand monolith.

Menzies and his followers couldn't escape the fact that relations with Britain had begun to crumble. Two events more than any other signalled the change.[60] First, in 1942 Labor Prime Minister John Curtin decided that Australia's defence would take priority and he refused Prime Minister Winston Churchill's request to station Australian troops in Burma. Second, in 1961 Britain began negotiations to enter the European Common Market, a move that ended any lingering notion of an eternal Australian dominion within the British Empire.

The Cold War divided the communist East from the capitalist West. In this hostile international environment, Australia turned to America for its security needs. Even as early as December 1941, John Curtin had said, 'I make it quite clear that Australia looks to America, free of any pangs as to our traditional links or kinship with the United Kingdom'.[61] Desperate to prove its credentials, Australia rushed to America's side in both the Korean and Vietnam wars. The best symbol of the growing relations between the two Pacific Rim nations was the production in Australia of the Holden car by the American giant, General Motors. The American influence was not confined to the military and manufacturing spheres; many young Australians adopted the culture of American protest—including its argot, music, clothes, drugs and mass politics.

GOVERNMENT POLICY AND INTERNATIONAL SPORT

Australians weren't aggressively nationalistic in sporting sentiments in this postwar period. Menzies believed that cricket affirmed Australia's commitment to the British way of life and to British cultural standards. In 1963 he described the game 'as part of Australia's rich British inheritance' in which the two countries are part of 'the same blood and allegiance and history and instinctive mental processes'.[62]

Consistent with this history, successive postwar governments left the control of sport in the hands of sports associations. According to this philosophy, 'sport was an area of free choice for the individual and beyond the realm of federal government responsibility'.[63] Thus not only did national sporting representatives have to raise their own money to compete abroad, but federal governments contributed nothing to the provision of sporting resources or facilities for the masses. Swimming pools, ovals, courts and tracks were a matter for negotiation between municipal councils and the states. In the inter-war years the federal government assisted national sporting associations with minor subsidies.[64] For example, Joseph Lyons' United Australia government granted the 1936 Australian olympic team £2000.

Exceptions were made where sports demonstrated a contribution to national defence and health. Colonial governments encouraged rifle clubs, and the Queensland and Victorian governments built rifle ranges at Victoria Park (1877) and Toowong (1887). Similarly, federal governments financially supported the Surf Life Saving Association and the Royal Life Saving Society. In 1941 the United Australia government passed the *National Fitness Act* which established the National Fitness Council and led to the expansion of physical education in the schools and universities.

Government involvement in sport escalated with the 1956 Melbourne olympics. The federal and Victorian governments and the Melbourne City Council provided £2.4 million for a capital works program, including the construction of swimming and diving pools at Olympic Park and the reconstruction of the arena at the MCG. The two governments also agreed to underwrite the £300000 deficit associated with the promotion and organisation of the games. In addition, the federal government gave the Victorian government a £2 million interest-free loan to build the olympic village.[65]

The Cold War had major ideological and structural ramifications on international sport, and especially the olympics. They became starkly ideological rather than nationalistic, tests of strength as the Russians and the Americans portrayed their victorious athletes as triumphs of Soviet-style social engineering and Western-style capitalism respectively. Traditional class-based amateur sport collapsed as the Soviet government gave state scholarships and American corporations awarded rich university scholarships to their nation's best athletic prospects. Australia still preferred to push the philosophy that 'sport and politics are separate': officials even boasted about saving the games from political disruption in the wake of the Suez crisis and the Soviet Union's invasion of Hungary.[66] 'An atmosphere of menace loomed in 1956', states the official report of the games, and 'clouds of international tension...burst into storm'. But,

> curiously, Australia's very remoteness...became...perhaps the saving grace of the Games. [The athletes] reached their destination to find world politics and massing war machines shrinking into mere paragraphs as Olympic weather forecasts, the prospects of athletics, the aspects of arenas, and problems of training, of teams and times, crowded them out of the headlines.[67]

The official report made no mention of the fact that Lebanon and Iraq boycotted Melbourne in solidarity with Egypt over the Suez crisis; nor did it describe the blood that stained the water during the infamous water polo final between Hungary and the Soviet Union. The report also offered no explanation for China's boycott: the Chinese refused to compete against the Taiwanese.[68]

In the international arena, European decolonisation of Africa had even greater implications than the Cold War for Australian sport. Resource-poor and lacking political influence, newly independent Africa seized sport as a policy weapon, especially against apartheid South Africa, a popular competitor with Australia in rugby and cricket.[69] There is much exaggeration, in sport and outside it, about this relationship. Hardly a brotherhood, it stems from positive images Australian Diggers had of South African hospitality, and hospitalisation, during war years. Apart from varying degrees of racial intolerance, there was and is absolutely nothing to connect Australians with 85 per cent of the population, which is African, Cape Coloured and Indian. All they share in common with two-thirds of the remaining 15 per cent of whites, the Afrikaners, is rugby. This leaves about 1.35 million English-speaking whites, some of whom happen to like cricket. Yet the myth of commonality and brotherly bonding between these nations persists.

In 1971, at the height of protests against the Vietnam war and con-scription, the South African Springboks toured Australia, shattering almost forever the shibboleth that sport and politics don't mix:

> Smoke bombs, flares, fire crackers and whistles were common; the chants of 'Sharpeville, Sharpeville' (where 69 black Africans died at the hands of the South African police) were countered with pamphlets handed out by the National Socialist [Nazi] Party of Australia which was pro-white South Africa. Rugby Union officials, players and supporters sided with the police in often brutal conflicts involving students, intellectuals, church groups and trade unionists. Barbed wire went up around playing areas in an attempt to prevent invasion by demonstrators.[70]

Joining the battle, Prime Minister Billy McMahon's Liberal–Country Party Coalition government transported the Springboks on RAAF air-craft and Joh Bjelke-Petersen's conservative Queensland government declared a state of emergency, the only example in Western history of the declaration of, in effect, martial law because of a two-week sporting tour. There is no better example in *our* history of sport dividing Australians, although the cataclysmic divide that the 1981 Springbok tour created in New Zealand is a worse example. At that moment, sport became a symbol of 'fiercely opposed ways of life, attitudes and beliefs'.

The postwar period also showed signs that Australian politicians recognised the political advantages of international sport. Menzies used cricket to 'advance his status within the Commonwealth'.[71] In 1954, at

The South African Springboks tours of Australia and New Zealand shattered the notion that sport and politics don't mix. They produced the worst violence ever seen in the sporting history of the two countries. In Queensland, Premier Joh Bjelke-Petersen introduced the equivalent of martial law in order to facilitate the presence of the Springboks for two weeks in the sunshine state. JOHN FAIRFAX GROUP

the behest of West Indian leader Eric Williams, Menzies urged the Australian Cricket Board to tour the West Indies on a mission of 'great diplomatic value' after an English tour the previous season which had been 'a social disaster at a delicate stage in the Caribbean's late-colonial political development'.[72]

Nonetheless, amateurism remained the preferred approach. Australians continued to believe that raw talent would secure gold. No one, according to the press of the day, better epitomised this approach to international sport than Marjorie Jackson, winner of two olympic gold medals at Helsinki in 1952:

> She wears simple clothing, bought at local shops and, like any Australian girl, she helps around the house, catches a bus to work and goes home for lunch...She is an altogether normal Australian youngster who just happens to spend her spare time showing the world that a genuine Australian amateur, without any of the advantages enjoyed by athletes of other countries, can take on the world's best and beat them almost effortlessly.[73]

A total of only six olympic gold medals at Tokyo in 1964, followed by five at Mexico City in 1968 debunked this myth. Australia's golden sporting era had passed and, notwithstanding the efforts of Shane Gould—who won three of Australia's eight olympic gold medals at Munich in 1972—natural ability alone would not produce a recovery.

8

A National Sports Policy

1973–1991

As regards the policy process for sport and recreation, there are few signs that an effective policy community exists and... policy development suffers from a similar degree of fragmentation to that found in other policy areas. For sport, the primary consequence of fragmentation is to enable the Commonwealth government to take a powerful policy lead on selected issues, but a secondary consequence is the absence of effective checks from among sports organisations on ministerial actions. For example, the resignation of Ros Kelly as Minister for Sport in 1994 was prompted by a critical report from the Auditor General alleging that the distribution of facility grants through the Community, Culture, Recreation and Sports Facilities Program was motivated less by identified need than by a desire to 'buy' votes in marginal constituencies.

—BARRIE HOULIHAN[1]

MYTHS AND NEW REALITIES

There are many myths in and about sport. Three interrelated myths are relevant here. First, sport is a social activity quite separate and remote from all of forms of human behaviour and endeavour. Second, therefore, it is divorced from politics, law, sociology and, until quite recently, from academia, literature and art. Third, therefore, sport is a purely private activity, a matter solely for the enjoyment and concerns of those who play, watch, broadcast and produce sport. The truth is that from the day colonial governors dipped into the government purse to buy sports land or to sponsor events there has been an interconnection between politics and sport. From the day teams went abroad or represented Australia here, under national colours, and often under direct patronage or imprimatur, such sports became arms of the nation–state, however innocuously. The real turning point came in the third quarter of the twentieth century, during which nearly every Western, Communist and Third World government developed a *national* sports policy. Successive Australian federal governments appropriated sport as an example of national virtue at the tail-end of this period. In the 1970s, in less than a decade, government involvement in sport transformed traditional notions of sport as 'a purely private affair'.

A 'mass movement of dissent' swept Labor to office in 1972,[2] after 23 years of conservative Coalition government rule. Gough Whitlam, the new leader, promised to replace the old Australian way of life with a 'new nationalism'. Although never explained precisely, the new nationalism 'related to a general pride in Australian achievement, and an increasing disquiet at the extent of foreign investment in Australia'.[3] But all this required a radical overhaul of both domestic and foreign policy.[4] Sport fitted Whitlam's domestic and foreign policy agendas. Labor initiated a sport-for-all policy, explicitly linked sport to foreign policy, and laid the foundations for an elite sports policy.

Three short years later, the conservatives returned to office: global economic turbulence, widespread unease at the pace and direction of Labor's change, and a major constitutional crisis ended Whitlam's visions.[5] 'Once again', wrote Manning Clark, 'the Australian electorate had demonstrated the truth that their history had fashioned them as sound conservatives: in a choice between the status quo and a mild change, they had opted very clearly for a conservative way of life'.[6] While Malcolm Fraser's Coalition government abandoned Whitlam's sport-for-all policy, as we will see, the effects of that policy on the structure of sport and the perceptions of its stakeholders were profound. On the other hand, Fraser enhanced and embellished the role of sport in foreign policy. Labor regained office in 1983. Unlike Whitlam, Prime Minister Bob Hawke focused on economic management rather than social reform. His Labor Party conceptualised sport primarily within a market-oriented, business framework.

Sport and Domestic Policy[7]

The Whitlam government developed the first coherent and comprehensive public policy on sport, and established the first Department of Sport, Recreation and Tourism. The new ministry provided capital assistance for sporting facilities and funding for travel, coaching and administration. This was a cosmic change. Whitlam linked sport and recreation specifically to urban social problems and, in particular, to health and fitness. A sporting culture, the government believed, would help improve the general quality of life, although it targeted low-income-earners living in the dormitory suburbs of major cities. These lacked essential quality of life resources, such as libraries, child-care centres, facilities for sport and recreation. Labor granted local authorities funds to provide floodlighting, resurface playing areas or replace obsolete mechanical plant. It also gave direct grants to national controlling associations to host, or travel to, world championships, or develop administration and coaching skills.

Labor mooted a national institute to train elite athletes. It presented a proposal in November 1975, the same month that the Governor-General, Sir John Kerr, dismissed the Whitlam government. Its philosophy emphasised mass participation and suburban facilities. According to the Minister for Sport, Frank Stewart, 'we have no intention of imitating some countries which regard success in sport as some sort of proof of the superiority of their way of life, ideology and race. Our task lies clearly elsewhere, in meeting more basic needs, in catering for masses, not just a small elite'. Tom Armstrong has high praise for Labor's sports policy:

The Whitlam government can reasonably claim to have seriously addressed the question of access to sport and recreation within Australia's urban environment. The period remains a mark against which policies of successive governments can be measured. The importance placed on the role of local government, the gradual progression through a series of initiatives, and the willingness to experiment and learn from mistakes, make it unique, not only in the history of Australian sport, but Australian politics in general.

Yearning to restore much of the Menzies era, Fraser dismantled many of Whitlam's reforms—including sport for all, and assistance to sports controlling bodies and local communities. Summing up the Coalition's philosophy, Barry Cohen, the shadow Minister for Sport, said that 'Mr Fraser gives the impression that all that is required to produce a fit and healthy nation is a pair of sandshoes and running shorts'.

Even in three years, Whitlam's policies produced positive effects. First, they alerted volunteer amateur sports officials to the importance of efficient and professional management. In the era of mass dissent, many traditional sports lost support and in the mid-1970s government funding offered welcome relief to struggling associations. For example, federal funds granted to Warringah Shire Council in 1974 enabled three life-saving clubs on Sydney's northern beaches to upgrade their clubhouses and facilities.[8] But eligibility required demonstrable management skills. There is a big difference between organising a chook raffle or a Saturday night dance and writing a thoroughly researched application or proposal for official financial assistance.

Second, the Whitlam policies encouraged local governments to invest directly in community sports facilities. Since the late nineteenth century municipal councils had provided their locals with public space and rudimentary facilities, notably grassed ovals for cricket, hockey and football, and the occasional swimming pool. Labor recommended that local governments take a more direct role by providing more, and a wider range of, facilities, especially for children, and by actively encouraging communities to make greater use of their resources. Local councils also agreed to consult more widely before constructing new facilities, and they employed recreation and sports officers. Many of the latter were trained in the universities, gaining qualifications in new specialist degree programs established in the 1960s and 1970s. Socially and environmentally sensitive and literate, they played a crucial role in fostering the social side of sport and leisure even when facilities and conditions were basic and less conducive to social intercourse than private facilities.

Third, the Coalition's withdrawal of Labor's financial lifelines to clubs and codes politicised previously apolitical sports officials. For example, 42 national governing associations formed the Confederation of Australian Sport in 1976 after the federal government announced it intended to slash funding for sport. The Confederation's 1980 'Master-plan for Sport' had all the hallmarks of Whitlam's sport-for-all policy. Under the plan, the Confederation launched specialist associations to promote sports administration and sports coaching, and initiatives to assist sport for children, women and veterans. Collectively, then, Whit-lam's policies, and Fraser's attempts to dismantle them, radically changed the traditional philosophy, structure and organisation of sport.

MULTICULTURALISM AND ITS MEANINGS

Despite his philosophical opposition to Labor's social reforms, Malcolm Fraser supported the Whitlam commitment to cultural diversity.[9] The Coalition considered immigrants 'vital for economic recovery and… broader national strategies'. In 1977 the Ethnic Affairs Council, created by the Coalition, published *Australia as a Multicultural Society* and Fraser commissioned a review, headed by lawyer Frank Galbally, to assess the government's provision of services to immigrants. Galbally argued that 'ethnic cultures must be preserved, not repressed'. Most commentators attribute the official policy of multiculturalism to the Galbally Report.[10] Certainly the Hawke government declared its support for 'the cultural, social and economic implications of a multicultural Australia'. Accord-ing to the new Labor Minister for Immigration, Stewart West, 'ethnic groups must be free to express their ethnic identity if they wish to do so, subject to Australian laws, without sacrificing their rights of equal access to the community's resources'.[11]

How exactly does one promote multiculturalism as a unifying social force? How does one reconcile the incompatible concepts of multicul-turalism and nationalism? Multiculturalism, for example, 'attempts to administer a consensus which, while propagating cultural diversity, glosses over the conflict promised by cultural difference'. A young Australian–Croatian soccer fan put it this way:

Multiculturalism is a big mumbo jumbo kind of thing...there is always
going to be trouble with it. How can it work? Take the Croatians and
Serbs as an example...you come here and are supposed to be Australian
now...but they still allow you to be Croatian and Serbian. The Croatians
come here and build their clubs and community, the Serbians come here
and build their clubs and community which support their Serbian philosophies and Croatians our philosophies. They expect there not to be some
anger between us...it's saying it's alright but they know the consequences
of it. Multiculturalism has just got too many consequences...it's a load
of shit I think...but it's good, like we can use it...take advantage of it,
if it's here...the Australian government wants it...we'll take advantage
of it.[12]

Most politicians, policy-makers and social analysts take care to avoid
these questions. In the end, they put 'Australianness' first, demanding
that immigrants relinquish their allegiance to former homelands. While
the Office of Multicultural Affairs recognises the cultural identity of all
Australians, its *National Agenda for a Multicultural Australia* sets 'carefully defined limits' on how immigrants express their identities.[13] At the
other end of the spectrum, soccer officials reject multiculturalism. They
say it contradicts notions of sport as the great social unifier and they
have made conscious efforts to Australianise and 'de-ethnicise' the game.

During the period of mass immigration, 'soccer clubs became a vehicle
and forum for the expression of nationalistic sentiment',[14] particularly
among Croatians and Macedonians concerned about the independence
of their former homelands. Sports violence associated with ethnic rivalry,
most of it grossly exaggerated by hysterical media, prompted officials to
consider banning ethnic club names in the 1960s.[15] In the 1970s a second
wave of proposals surfaced, culminating in the Australian Soccer Federation (ASF) banning ethnic club names in 1977. Rescinding the ban
in 1983, the Federation reapplied it at all levels of competition in 1992.[16]
Concerned about the game's image and eager to transform soccer into
a major football code, the ASF commissioned an investigation by James
Bradley, a University of New South Wales academic. The Bradley Report
blamed soccer's poor image on its close affiliation with ethnicity. He recommended breaking the ethnic backbones of clubs in the national soccer
league and emphasising geographic loyalties and identities. In essence,
this meant removing foreign and ethnic names, logos and emblems. In
the wake of the report, Sydney Croatia, for example, changed its name,
first to Sydney CSC (Croatia Soccer Club), and then to Sydney United.

Has the ban tempered ethnic rivalry? John Hughson says not.[17] Tensions 'simmer' between and within ethnic communities, and some continue to use forms of identification contrary to multiculturalism. He points to the Bad Blue Boys, a group of 'highly parochial supporters' who follow Sydney United and 'use soccer to parade a nationalistic allegiance to Croatia'. Why do these young Australian-born men 'choose to form their social identity in the image of their parents' culture'? Hughson blames 'exclusion from Australian sports such as rugby league and cricket'. The Bad Blue Boys feel 'ostracised from the dominant sporting culture' and thus 'band together with other Croatians and "wogs" to play soccer'. Ostracism also manifests in the Bad Blue Boys' indifference to Australia's national team, the Socceroos. By reserving their support for national players with Croatian backgrounds, the Boys express, at best, a secondary allegiance to the Socceroos.

Soccer nationalists chide those who don't give unqualified support to the Socceroos. In 1992 the *Australian*'s Ray Gatt accused Sydney CSC of failing to foster the game and using soccer to promote long-standing political issues. Similarly, Jeff Wells, then writing for the *Australian*, accused Sydney United of being 'brazenly Croatian': he named thirteen players who he said were Croatian. Sporting nationalists show very little, if any, comprehension of multiculturalism, something they equate with assimilation. According to the *Sydney Morning Herald*'s Mike Cockerill, for example, the 1992 Australian team was a 'microcosm of the multicultural society, proving how people can co-exist peacefully because they have left their traditional grievances behind'. A few months later Cockerill urged supporters of Sydney CSC to embrace 'assimilation' and throw away their 'national flags'.

Sporting nationalists refuse to concede the presence of 'cultural boundaries which might exclude some from membership of the Australian nation'. Nor do they understand the dynamic nature of communities—which always include subgroups living in relationships of a general communion.[18] Croatian–Australians embrace a host of political doctrines: from neo-Nazism on the far right to communism on the far left, with nationalists, democrats, trade unionists and different religious and peasant groups in between.[19] 'Being Croatian' or 'living out Croatianness' means different things to different subgroups. Thus, while the Bad Blue Boys consider the 1940s Croatian political leader and Nazi collaborator Ante Pavelic a 'freedom fighter', tertiary-educated and upwardly mobile Australian–Croatians of the same age bracket condemn

Club officials and supporters encourage ethnic loyalties, actively opposing attempts by the game's governing associations to nurture identities based on regional and national affiliations. Soccer counterpoints the belief that sport is a medium for cultural integration and multicultural tolerance. When Melbourne Croatia defeated Adelaide City 2–0 in the 1995 National Soccer League grand final at Hindmarsh Stadium (Adelaide), Melbourne supporters climbed the perimeter fence and waved Croatian flags, while fans of St George Budapest, Sydney, raised a banner reading 'Death to the NSL'. ROY HAY

the Bad Blue Boys' offensive behaviour. On the other hand, the Boys' parents take a less critical stance, attributing their behaviour to youthful 'exuberance'.

Just as different social classes, races and genders distinguish each other, so too do cultural groups. Neither assimilation nor multiculturalism, nor indeed sport, has altered this social reality. We do not condone the truculent nationalism shown by sections of some ethnic communities living in Australia; nor do we suffer illusions that Australia is ethnically neutral. As John Hughson reminds us, limits imposed on expressions of cultural identity mean privileging traditional Anglo-Australian culture, even if the content and values of the latter escape precise definition.

Multicultural soccer reinforces our principal theme of connection and disconnection. It highlights the fact that loyalty, devotion and 'fanhood' are based in the first instance on class, caste, religion, race, and colour and then on history and geography. In short, of all the criteria on which identity rests—including suburb, school, religion, family, nationality, ethnicity, culture and politics—sport is the *weakest*. Each person has his or her rank order of these criteria. Artie Beetson, the great rugby league forward, declared himself 'an Australian first, a Queenslander second and part-Aboriginal third' before he reversed the order.[20] Never did he define himself as a 'footballer'. Immigrants, their children, and even their children's children, and minority groups like Aborigines, have identification points that loom larger, consciously or subconsciously, in their beings than the externality and ephemeral nature of 'sporting identity'. They need two 'cultural' legs to stand on: when the going gets too tough in one, the mainstream, as it all too often does, there is always succour in the other, the society of home-ness and togetherness. Most Anglo-Australians simply do not comprehend these needs and these realities. This is especially true of sports entrepreneurs. Their artificial teams—what Stephen Alomes calls the 'non-existent teams'—of the Western Reds variety, do not inspire immediate adherence. As the short-lived Perth rugby league experience suggests, they are doomed unless they, like the Sydney Swans, can appropriate a pre-existing value system. Sydney's fan basis, for example, lies largely in the 'Sydney versus the rest' value system. Nonetheless, collective identities such as classes, ethnicities, races and genders are not permanently fixed; they must be continually reproduced. Of course, sport will reflect any changes.

Sport and Foreign Policy

Whitlam sought 'to convey both to Australians and the world a sense of…political independence',[21] and although Frank Stewart emphasised Labor's sport-for-all policy, Whitlam's government was the first to use sport as an overt tool of foreign policy. Subsequent Liberal and Labor governments developed and embellished this stratagem.

South Africa and Gleneagles

Six days after becoming Prime Minister, Whitlam declared that Australia would ostracise South Africa's minority, racist regime. Labor prohibited racially selected South African teams from playing in Australia; it also prevented them from landing in the country *en route* to New Zealand.[22] This was the first time an Australian government had used sport in such a manner in the international political arena.

A question of identity? Artie Beetson played fourteen Tests and as many World Cup matches for Australia, and he had a profound influence on Aboriginal youth. Beetson initially declared himself 'an Australian first, a Queenslander second, and part-Aboriginal third'. Later he reversed the order. Nowhere did he describe himself as a footballer. RUGBY LEAGUE WEEK

Contrary to his patrician image, society pedigree, and statements made when leader of the opposition, Fraser proved as uncompromising on South Africa as his Labor opponents. Twenty-two mostly African nations boycotted the Montreal olympics in 1976—in protest at New Zealand's close sporting relations with South Africa and the IOC's refusal to withdraw New Zealand's invitation to Montreal. Whereupon Commonwealth leaders discussed strategies to protect their respective national sporting interests from disruption caused by boycotts of, and protests against, South Africa. Led by Fraser, India's Indira Gandhi and Canada's Pierre Trudeau, they produced the Gleneagles Agreement the following year.

Gleneagles committed Commonwealth heads of government 'to combat the evil of apartheid by withholding any form of support for, and by taking every practical step to discourage contact or competition by their nationals with sporting organisations, teams or sportsmen from South Africa'.[23] Interpretation of the Agreement, and the machinery available to governments to control their sportspeople, varied between countries. Black states stuck rigorously to the spirit of the Agreement; Britain and New Zealand, as one would have expected, adopted 'looser' interpretations.[24] New Zealand posed especial problems for Malcolm Fraser. Keen to develop amicable relations with black Africa, he lobbied Prime Minister Robert Muldoon to cancel the 1981 South African Springbok rugby tour.[25] Gleneagles thus strained relations between Australia and New Zealand, already heightened by delicately poised negotiations on reform of the trans-Tasman free trade agreement, Muldoon's 'advice' to Fraser that he should look at 'racism in his own backyard' before condemning South Africa, and the 'underarm' bowling incident at the beginning of the year. With New Zealand requiring a six off the last ball to tie the third final of the 1981 World Series Cup, the Australian captain Greg Chappell instructed his brother Trevor to bowl a 'grubber' to New Zealand batsman Brian McKechnie, denying him any opportunity to score. Although technically legal, the incident sparked a furore between the two countries. That episode has lingered longer in the national sporting psyche than most other sporting events.

Despite Fraser's efforts in trying to win their support, black Africans mooted a boycott of the 1982 Commonwealth games in Brisbane.[26] This was not in solidarity with Queensland Aborigines: they opposed New Zealand's presence. While Queensland Premier Joh Bjelke-Petersen re-assured his supporters that the games would be a success irrespective of black Africa's attendance, Fraser appreciated the political symbolism of Africa's presence. He circumvented a potentially highly embarrassing African boycott by forcing the Commonwealth Games Federation to strengthen its constitution and adopt a 'code of conduct' (which pro-vided guidelines for national Commonwealth Games Associations to

'The underarm bowling incident': Australian cricket captain Greg Chappell ordered his brother Trevor to bowl the last ball of a match against New Zealand with an underarm action along the ground, so that there was no possibility of a six being scored to tie the match. One historian has called this incident 'an excess of caution'. It was hardly that. It will remain in the annals of twentieth-century sport as a black moment in Australian sportsmanship.
DREW FITZGIBBON/*HERALD & WEEKLY TIMES*

apply the Gleneagles Agreement), and by offering ten athletes from developing Commonwealth countries scholarships to the Australian Institute of Sport. It is worth noting that Aboriginal interests counted for nothing in either the African or Australian agendas for these games.

Africans were not the only ones to threaten the 1982 Commonwealth games. Despite lack of support, Aborigines used the games as an effective forum to protest and demand better conditions from the Queensland and federal governments, especially on land rights in the sunshine state. Queensland borrowed a leaf from Moscow in 1980, when the Soviet regime cleared that city of all Jews and possible 'dissidents' who might talk to foreign media. Queensland passed the *Commonwealth Games Act 1982* to keep Brisbane 'clean' of Aboriginal 'dissidents' during the games fortnight. The Act empowered police rather than government to declare a 'situation of emergency', to have police and people specially sworn in to seize persons and property, and to take finger-, palm-, toe-, foot- and voice-prints of suspected persons. It designated notified areas in which only accredited persons could assemble, and it imposed fines of $2000 or sentences of two years' gaol, or both, for 'offences' under the Act. It also indemnified from criminal or civil action those who were sworn in as deputies and who exceeded their authority. The purported objective of the Act was 'good conduct and order'. This draconian statute, which civil liberties bodies amazingly ignored, was not about law: it was about Bjelke-Petersen's extreme sense of political order. In the end, the Aborigines won several victories. They forced the Premier, against his will, to allow two lands rights marches through the city streets—activities hitherto banned vigorously. Of great significance, quality sports reporters—notably the Canadians and England's Ian Wooldridge—turned their attention from who would run in the women's 4 x 100m track relay to Aboriginal affairs and sports politics.[27] They filed land rights footage and interviews with Aboriginal leaders across the globe. The ABC's 'Four Corners' screened a land rights program on the first Saturday night of the games; it had a huge audience and it encouraged conservative white Australians to think about Aboriginal affairs. The games showed Aborigines, as other games have shown so many others, that sport is as good a venue to air grievances as any, and better than most. Hence our surprise that Aboriginal leaders failed to build on the Brisbane experience to wring concessions from governments before and during the 2000 olympics build-up.

Not surprisingly, Gleneagles produced many anomalies. The Fraser government allowed five South African cricketers playing county cricket in England to play World Series Cricket in Australia, but then banned two others still playing domestic cricket in South Africa.[28] Bob Hawke tried to smooth out anomalies and tighten Australia's position. He believed Australian sportsmen and women violated Gleneagles by competing against foreign sportspeople who had played with South Africa. In April 1985 Hawke threatened to cancel the passports of Australian rugby union players due to play against New Zealand in Auckland in June. At the time, New Zealand's All Blacks were preparing for an official tour of South Africa. Many commentators and analysts howled at this apparent gross violation of sportspeople's rights. But with sport now inextricably part of foreign policy, Labor's position was logical and right. After all, in the 1950s and 1960s government foreign policy prohibited Australian citizens from travelling anywhere in Eastern Europe or in any communist country. No one screamed 'violation'. Governments of the day also refused visas to sports teams from 'undesirable' countries—and no one yelled 'fault' or 'foul'.

The politicisation of sport made sportspeople much more aware of their rights and willing to assert them. Increasingly, they turned to the courts for clarification. World Series Cricket sponsor and promoter, Kerry Packer, persuaded several English cricketers to break their contracts with the Test and County Cricket Board and so force the court to judge the validity of the Board's contracts. The court subsequently found that clauses in the contracts constituted unreasonable restraint of trade.[29] Occasionally, such as when 'rebel' Australian cricketers played in South Africa in the mid-1980s,[30] sportspeople conveniently forgot about their obligations and responsibilities. Members of the 'rebel' cricket teams led by Kim Hughes erroneously believed that their rights to play under any conditions and circumstances justified defying Australian foreign policy. Hughes's 'rebels', many of whom confessed to being mercenaries,[31] posed a particular legal dilemma for the Australian Cricket Board. The Board initially turned to the courts for an injunction to stop the team from playing in South Africa, but it settled out of court, fearing ruinous litigation costs and knowing that its contracts imposed unreasonable restraints.[32] The rebel tours highlight important issues about what is representative and what is private sport. The rebels refused to tour as private individuals and teams; they insisted on representing Australia in full national colours and regalia. From its perspective, the South African government would not have accepted a private team with a fancy name like 'Azaleas' or 'Proteas': it needed to show its voters, and the world, that South Africa was still a valued member of the international cricket community.

THE AUSTRALIAN INSTITUTE OF SPORT

Elite sport is a system of international prestige. Not surprisingly, the Whitlam government proposed an increase in funding for elite athletes competing internationally. Professor John Bloomfield first proposed an institute of sport in a 1973 report commissioned by Labor. His report spawned a study group, chaired by Allan Coles, head of human movement studies at the University of Queensland, and which included former VFL player and coach Jack Clarke, olympic team physician Ken Fitch, and Socceroos coach Rale Rasic. In November 1975 the group strongly recommended 'the establishment of an Australian Sports Institute as a major step towards meeting the needs of sport in Australia, with respect both to mass participation and excellence'.[33] The group erroneously assumed that success in international sport would inspire greater participation among ordinary Australians. This assumption has grown into a fossilised axiom. Justifying increased expenditure for elite sport in 1989, Labor's Graham Richardson said 'these champions and potential champions provide an important inspiration for others to "have a go"'.[34] The history of Australian sport, however, suggests that gender, age, ethnicity, race, income and wealth are far more significant than elite role models.

The constitutional crisis and the sacking of Whitlam in 1975 prevented immediate progress. Fraser willingly seized sport as a political weapon against South Africa, but he was much slower to consider it as a means of winning international prestige. In this sense, he returned the Liberals to Menzies' 'minimalist' position, showing reluctance to assist the Australian team even financially at the 1976 olympic games. Outpourings of 'grief' and 'disbelief' over failure at Montreal prompted a reappraisal.

Australians came back from Canada with a miserly catch of one silver (men's hockey) and four bronze medals (equestrian three-day team event, men's 1500m freestyle, finn class yachting and 470 class yachting). Pundits had predicted a bounty of 30 golds. Not since Berlin, 40 years earlier, had Australians returned from an olympics minus gold. Several 'inquests' followed, with the foreign press gleefully reporting recriminations and painful exorcism. Britain's *Guardian* likened Australia to a 'middle-aged athlete gone flabby', reporting that the country had 'stumbled into a national identity crisis, stricken by self-doubt and torn by bitter recriminations over real and imagined failings'.[35] Ironically, the 'scientific' coaching methods that propelled Australia to glory in the 1950s and 1960s provided a model for other nations, particularly in Eastern Europe, to emulate. Whereas Australia continued to play down the contribution of its coaches, the Europeans recognised and duly rewarded their coaches as professionals.[36]

Failure in Montreal also exposed the dark side of a rapidly emerging Australian national sporting character: the poor loser. Symptoms of the poor winner—the arrogant, ungracious victor—first appeared in the bodyline era. Even the great Don appeared to fear failure. In a Sheffield Shield match in December 1931, Eddie Gilbert bowled Bradman for a duck. In a subsequent Shield game in January 1936, Ezra ('Boxer')

Wyeth, Gilbert's Queensland bowling colleague, recounted seeing an uninjured Bradman in the stand. Playing now for South Australia, he had dropped himself lower down the batting order, possibly, it is speculated, to avoid Gilbert's exceptional pace. Wyeth's personal letter to Ken Edwards states, in part:

> As I made my way into the building I saw Don sitting in an alcove with his pads on. His face was very white. For me it said he was in trouble and he fell down to size for me. He was concerned about Eddie. There had been some trouble for some time because of his criticism of Eddie and he expected Eddie to take care of it.[37]

Eddie did—he dismissed Bradman for 31, caught Wyeth.

By the 1960s the signs were more visible, even before the notion of new nationalism emerged. When place-judges ignored the timekeepers' watches and then overruled American protests to award John Devitt olympic gold in the 100m freestyle in Rome, Bill Berge Phillips, secretary of the ASU and swimming's representative on the Australian Olympic Federation (AOF), gloated: 'We rubbed your noses in it and we'll show you some more when we're through.'[38] No one felt the wrath of the ugly losing Australian at Montreal more than Steve Holland. Having broken twelve world records in distance swimming before the games, the media and public banked on the 'certainty' of Holland-gold in the 1500m freestyle. Despite swimming a tactically bad race, Holland nonetheless broke the world record again in the final. But his effort won only 'tainted' bronze. 'The transition from hero status to perceived failure was swift and unsympathetic'; Holland later described it as a 'terrible time, a time of agony. I felt alienated and ostracised, just because I came third. Australians don't like losers. I was made to feel guilty'.[39] Similarly, after his victory in the 1500m freestyle at Barcelona in 1992, Kieren Perkins described the psychological strain as 'unbelievable'. There were occasions, he said, when 'it got so bad I wanted to hide. If I didn't win gold, I didn't want to go home'.[40]

J. Neville Turner feels predisposed to exonerate Greg and Trevor Chappell for the 'underarm' ball against New Zealand in 1981, calling their action 'an excess of caution'.[41] It was hardly that. The incident confirms the desperation to win in the Australian psyche. An interesting comparison emerges in this context between the cricketing brothers' uncharitable and miserable action in 1981 and their predecessors' 'exaggerated' reaction to English bodyline bowling during the 1932–33 Test series. Neither new nor unanswerable (as Stan McCabe's 187 not out in 240 minutes in the first Test and Bradman's century in the second demonstrated), bodyline bowling only became an issue when the Australian team failed to match its own star billing given by the local press. The cricket community needed an excuse to explain unanticipated defeat: bodyline offered it.[42] Australia, it would seem, is 'robbed' more than any other nation!

Bob Ellicott, Minister for Home Affairs, nurtured sports policy in the Coalition government. In 1979 he asked his Sports Advisory Council to prepare a framework for a national sports policy. Cabinet eventually rejected the Council's recommendation, amended by various public service committees, for a coherent national policy, but Ellicott developed a strong vision for a national institute of sport after examining sports systems in China, England, Europe and North America.[43] The Australian Institute of Sport opened in 1981. Why did the Coalition establish a national institute for elite performers while refusing to commit itself to a national sports policy? The answer lies in the 1980 Moscow olympics.

When the Soviet Union invaded Afghanistan, President Jimmy Carter advocated an international boycott of the forthcoming Moscow olympic games. Twenty-five nations eventually joined the United States-led boycott. Interestingly, Britain's Margaret Thatcher and New Zealand's Robert Muldoon, who were only too happy to help their sports teams circumvent the boycott of racist South Africa, pledged wholehearted support for Carter's plan.

The boycott divided Australians as deeply as the Great War. A Gallup poll in June 1980 showed 52 per cent support for, and 41 per cent against, a boycott.[44] Pro-games people typically argued for the rights of sportspeople and appealed to the 'sanctity of sport'. Modern pentathlete Alex Watson complained that olympians were made to feel like 'traitors' betraying their nation when 'all we are doing is something towards which we have been motivated for the greater part of our young lives'; swimmer Michelle Ford pointed to the preciousness of the opportunity—'you can get a chance only once in four years, and it might be the only chance in your life'; an apparently nostalgic Dawn Fraser feared that a boycott would destroy the olympic movement. Far from painting the olympics as something extraordinarily special, Ford's description merely highlights the superficial and ephemeral nature of sport: her gold-medal-winning time of 8.28.90 in the 800m freestyle was but a fleeting moment in, rather than the essence of, her life and the lives of even the most ardent swimming fans. One also has to ponder the perennial argument of sportspeople that their years of preparation and hope are, somehow, greater and more precious than the preparations of others who meet disappointment in life and in careers.

Pro-boycotters looked beyond the desires of athletes and put sport into its proper social and historical context. As the *Australian* noted, a boycott 'is not about athletes winning medals. There are no medals for the dead in Kabul, only bullet holes in the chests of those who are fighting for their freedom…With hindsight, it is apparent that a boycott of the 1936 Berlin Olympics might have changed the course of world history'. Here, at last, was a semblance of maturity about priorities in the life of a nation.

Fraser put enormous pressure on a divided AOF. Even Australia's two members of the IOC disagreed: Kevan Gosper supported the government, while David McKenzie objected to the 'intrusion' of politics into sport, especially since the government maintained diplomatic and commercial relations with the Soviet Union. McKenzie's argument ignores the powerful, visible, symbolism attached to international sport and the succour that the olympics gave to an obnoxious regime and system on the verge of disintegration. There is little doubt the Federation would have submitted to a prime ministerial request as little as ten years earlier. But events during the previous decade had transformed Australia. Sports, in particular, had become more independent and assertive. The Moscow boycott issue reinforced these values. In the end, the Federation's eleven-member executive voted 6–5 to attend.

Attempting to draw attention away from his own defeat, and grossly overstating a situation that quickly receded into the footnotes of history, Fraser decried this 'sad day for Australia'. The issue produced no winners. A number of athletes, who had gathered outside the hotel to await the Federation's decision, celebrated. Their joy proved short-lived. The government offered financial compensation to national governing bodies to withdraw their teams; yachting, men's and women's hockey, equestrian, volleyball and shooting accepted.[45] (Shooters Yvonne Hill and David Hollister competed after the former successfully challenged the Australian Shooting Association in court—demonstrating once again sport's independence.) Moreover, the conflict cast long shadows: several individuals, including swimmer Tracy Wickham and sprinter Raelene Boyle, withdrew, citing stress; the basketball team 'sneaked out of the country' fearing that the government would confiscate their passports;

athletes left Russia wearing street clothes rather than the national uniform; and the team marched in the opening ceremony under the neutral olympic rather than the Australian national flag. If ever there was an event of shame, guilt, ignominy, despair and anguish, this was it. And if Australian sport was ever 'a ceremony of innocence', it was certainly drowned there and then.

Shortly after Moscow, the Fraser government rushed through plans to establish the Institute. It opened its doors in January 1981 to Australia's best athletes to train, full-time, at public expense. Its objectives were clear: to appease the domestic sports lobby smarting from the Moscow affair and to restore Australia's international sports profile.

Successive governments in the 1970s transformed the role of sport from an essentially independent social activity to a political object of government policy. By the early 1980s, the Coalition government and the Labor opposition viewed sport as a tool for national development and unity. Fraser spelled this out in a speech made at the 1982 Commonwealth Games. Australia's elite athletes, he said, represented 'the true co-operative spirit of the Australian Commonwealth', a 'truly multicultural society', and 'intense national pride'.[46] Officials and athletes didn't necessarily welcome government intervention: while some enjoyed greater financial assistance, they feared loss of independence. To this end, they increasingly turned to the courts. But there was no question of governments retreating. On the contrary, they became more involved, sinking larger amounts of money into elite sport, and especially the Institute, to satisfy the lust for olympic gold and as an economic investment.

SPORT: RUNNING WITH THE MARKET

Despite promises and reassurances, economic conditions continued deteriorating in the Fraser years. The Coalition couldn't stem inflation or unemployment. An estimated two million lived in poverty in 1982—in a population of 15.28 million.[47] To deal with worsening economic conditions, the Coalition fell in behind Britain and other Western governments in discarding Keynesian economic principles[48] in favour of *laissez-faire* theories. According to the latter, governments shouldn't interfere with the 'free working' of the economy but should allow individuals to pursue self-interest, with full confidence that the 'invisible hand' of the market would, somehow, preserve the 'common good' and the social fabric. Thus the Coalition and Labor governments in the 1980s committed themselves to financial, industrial and trade deregulation, smaller government, and to transferring responsibility for social policies to the private sector.

Concomitant with this economic shift, the administration and structure of Australia's main professional sports codes underwent trans-formation. The VFL offers a good example.[49]

The Victorian Football League[50]

After his election as president in 1976, Allen Aylett, the man who saved North Melbourne club, set about reforming the VFL. His vision included a smaller number of modern, first-class grounds, a national competition with teams based in other capital cities, fewer Melbourne-based clubs, and a smaller, 'independent' management structure overseeing the administration of the League. The latter, known as the VFL Commission, came to fruition in 1984, Aylett's final year as president. The Commission produced numerous reports, including one presented to the clubs in 1985, entitled *Football: Establishing the Basis for Future Success.* Prepared with assistance from consultants and market researchers, the report acknowledged that a viable competition required strong member-based clubs. But it also noted the emergence of a new type of spectator: the 'theatre-goer'—the patron 'who attended a few matches a year as part of leisure activity that may also include a movie, children's activities or a barbeque in the hills'. In other words, the report identified whole-sale changes in leisure and entertainment patterns as weakening the traditional local community structure of football. This was a perfectly correct assessment. Once football dominated Melbourne's barren cultural landscape. In the 1970s Melbourne grew into a rich, dynamic cosmo-politan city. By the 1980s football competed with a host of diverse recreational and leisure activities. For those interested in sport the choices numbered in the hundreds; the majority avoided sport altogether, choosing instead to work in the garden, visit an art gallery, listen to a concert, wander around a museum, read a book, relax in a coffee bar or contemplate by the water's edge. Gloomy James Hogan needn't have feared: the Melbourne Public Library was assuredly not an endangered or useless institution.

Even with support from the entire population, Melbourne couldn't sustain an elite competition that adequately compensated professional athletes playing a high-risk body-contact sport. Declining support put Australian football's premier competition in a precarious situation. In 1983 the League's operating expenses exceeded the operating revenue by nearly $2 million, six clubs were on the verge of bankruptcy, and the Corporate Affairs Commission had asked several clubs to explain why they continued to trade. In 1982 the League relocated the South Melbourne club to Sydney. The club had less than 1500 paid-up members and its finances were in disarray. Interestingly, most senior players supported the move: when the 'Keep South at South' group, which opposed the Swans' pending relocation, gained control of the club at a special general meeting, the players threatened to walk out.

To the consternation of traditional fans who despaired at the loss of their suburban-based competition, the VFL had, by the early 1990s, implemented Aylett's vision of a national competition. (In 1989 the VFL changed its name to the Australian Football League for the 1990 season.) Disgruntled fans lashed at the League, accusing commissioners of not understanding football, inappropriate use of corporate language and principles, and allowing entrepreneurs to destroy community sport. Yet, of all the changes, only the turn to entrepreneurs failed. In 1985 the VFL sold the Sydney Swans to Geoffrey Edelsten, a (some time) Sydney medical entrepreneur, for $6.5 million; financial troubles associated with the 1987 stock market crash forced the League to buy back the Swans— for $10! Eventually, in 1993, the club returned to public ownership. In 1986 the League also sold the licence for a Brisbane club to a private consortium headed by actor Paul Cronin. Continuing financial problems and a succession of owners, including the (now exiled) entrepreneur Christopher Skase, saw Brisbane also restructured as a membership organisation by 1992.

Australian entrepreneurs turned to sport in the mid-1980s on a scale previously seen only in the late nineteenth and early twentieth centuries. Whereas amateur officials once thumbed their noses at entrepreneurs, in the 1980s governments encouraged entrepreneurial involvement: *laissez-faire* economic theory regards entrepreneurial activity as essential to a healthy economy. The archetypal sporting entrepreneur in the 1980s was Alan Bond. A British-born immigrant turned big businessman, Bond headed a Western Australian business syndicate whose yacht, *Australia II*, won the America's Cup in 1983. The 'auld mug' had resided with the New York Yacht Club since the first race in 1851.[51]

The America's Cup[52]

Very few Australians showed interest in the early stages of the 1983 America's Cup challenge: fewer than 1 per cent of the population participate in sailing, and the 12-metre yacht racing variety is one of the most expensive sports in the world, inevitably the toy of millionaires. An advertisement for Tag Heuer watches captures well the abundance of 'offshore racing', comparing it to 'standing in a cold shower tearing up twenty dollar bills'. Few gave Bond's syndicate a realistic chance of beating the Americans on their home turf after 132 years. Interest grew when *Australia II* reached the final round, then receded after the Americans established a 3–1 series lead. But in the early hours of 27 September 1983, *Australia II* started the seventh, and final, race of the series and 'millions of Australians, few of whom had ever seen a 12-metre yacht, sat bleary-eyed in front of their television sets'. When the boat won, many Australians engaged in patriotic displays not seen since the end of the Second World War. The media saturated the country with 'stories extolling the heroic virtues of the yacht's owner, designer, skipper and crew'.

Bob Hawke, a populist Prime Minister and the first to effectively use sport to connect with the general population,[53] seized the opportunity to congratulate 'Bondy', and 'that marvellous Australian Ben Lexcen' (*Australia II*'s designer), on behalf of 'every Australian': he called it 'one of the great moments in Australian history'.[54] Amid the euphoria of that fleeting moment, Hawke probably did speak for, if not every single Australian, at least the overwhelming majority. The real importance of the victory was the credibility it lent to the entrepreneur—the cornerstone of *laissez-faire* economics. The usually sober broadsheet dailies gushed. The *Age* asked: 'is this [victory] not a demonstration of the important truth that in a dynamic society talent will prevail over privilege?'; the *Australian* suggested that 'dedication and sacrifice paves the way for a fulfilment, not only of personal dreams, but of our concept of nationhood'; the *Australian Financial Review* called it 'a celebration of individual achievement and excellence' necessary 'if we are not to decline into a lazy, isolated, self-indulgent society of parasites. *Australia II*'s victory should remind us what a bit of guts and effort can do'. The Melbourne *Herald* had the final word: 'Patriotism was on the line today', and then added what sums up the essence of modern sport, and 'so was Newport's tourist economy'.[55]

Market-driven televised sport, like the Hollywood tradition, needs 'stars'. If the talent isn't there, it must be manufactured. In 1968 the late Ian Turner, historian and writer on Australian football, wrote that 'the Australian people made heroes of none, and raised no idols, except perhaps an outlaw, Ned Kelly, and Carbine, a horse'.[56] He was right. Thirty years earlier that great novelist and short-story writer, Paul Gallico, gave up sports writing. In farewell, he said that the sports writer has few, if any, heroes: 'We create many because it is our business to do so, but we do not believe in them. We know them too well.'[57] More so than the print industry, television insists on idols and icons as a stratagem to keep viewers glued. Sport offered a plethora: Bond became a super-hero overnight. Dawn Fraser and Lionel Rose found themselves described as 'national treasures', a Bradman cult grew to bizarre pro-portions and, symptomatic of the whole trend, Australians hailed boxer Jeff Fenech, a man of few charms, as a messianic hero figure of what was, by then, a generally despised and unpopular sport. In the 1990s the Shane Warne artifice became the ultimate in fictional heroism, sur-passing, at times, that astonishing Greg Norman industry known as the Great White Shark Enterprises.

Like all sporting moments, the yacht euphoria faded, quickly: it couldn't, for example, sustain the nearly four million struggling on ben-efits. More dramatic was Bond's, and the entire 1980s generation of entrepreneurs', fall from grace. The eighties 'dynamic' entrepreneurs who won praise on talkback radio, in pubs, boardrooms and cabinet meet-ings, were predominantly paper millionaires who simply bought assets with borrowed money, revalued them, and borrowed against the higher value to buy more assets. When the stock market crashed in 1987, the hitherto profligate banks became more cautious. They refused to lend and they called in debt. Bond's net worth plummeted from $400 mil-lion to around $50 million and Bond Corporation Holdings owed the banks more than $6 billion. By 1994 Bond languished in gaol, convicted on charges stemming from his various dealings. Christopher Skase was to 'exile' himself to Majorca, the subject of unending, often comic, efforts by government to extradite him.[58]

Subscribers to *laissez-faire* economics initially explained the stock market crash as evidence of the free market at work. They welcomed the market's 'self-correcting mechanisms' for ridding the economy of less fit entrepreneurs. They were less sanguine when Australia lumbered into recession in 1990, and then vented their spleen when Labor's treasurer, Paul Keating, flippantly dismissed the economic downturn 'as a recession that Australia had to have'. Elected in 1996, John Howard's Coalition would continue to stoke the flames of *laissez-faire* economics. Elsewhere, Western governments, troubled by the consequences of high unemployment and social crises far greater than anything seen in the 1970s, have begun dusting off Keynes's 'discredited' theories. But sport will not return to the past. In the last quarter of the twentieth century, sport has acquired more of the characteristics of entertainment, and grown as a prop for economic development and an art-form of political distraction.

POLITICAL CIRCUITS

The cliché about keeping politics out of sport took a long time to die. Paradoxically, in the process, sport began to infuse politics.[59] No matter the party, said George Orwell in 1946, their political language 'is designed to make lies sound truthful and murder respectable'. But in the 1980s, the sports metaphor increasingly sanitised and depoliticised politics. No longer the art of governance, decision-making and the adjudication of conflicting interests, politics emerged as a television script, with the voters cast as spectators and politicians as gladiators.

The phenomenon derived from overseas politics, particularly from Richard Nixon's predilection to talk about his 'team', with himself as quarterback, working out 'game plans' to reach the 'goal line' and so win 'the ballgame'. In the Watergate scandal, he was merely 'a team player'. The British followed, wallowing in sports imagery as the British 'came from behind' to take out 750 Argentines as against 226 down in the Falklands war.

Australians followed, assigning excesses in the same mould: giving to immoral decisions and bad politics meanings normally applied to quality sport, and asserting that only pros have the skill to plan victories, 'to manage the economy', 'to control the unions'. Endless cartoons showed the key contenders in and out of the ring, on and off the pitch, in and out of the scrums. Headlines read: 'Fraser v Hawke', 'Hayden relegated to Second XI', 'Keating bowls Howard'. Even worse was the typical Alan Jones commercial: 'I wouldn't trust my country to an inexperienced driver, stick with the experienced driver who's got a proven record.' To these ends, the Liberal Party, in particular, began a (mercifully short-lived) program of assembling sports stars in their advertisements. When the Nationals in Queensland unilaterally included rugby league star Wally Lewis in one of their campaign ads, he threatened legal action, as a member of the opposition party. That, at least, seemed to put an end to these particular sanitation exercises. But milking the sports metaphor remains—whether it be the popular Bob Hawke attending all and every sports occasion to the point where the crowds booed his appearances, or John Howard doing guest commentaries on cricket and proclaiming that the most prestigious achievement possible in the nation is to be made captain of the Australian cricket team!

Sport is not only the sanitising of politics but the distraction of, and from, politics. In the 1980s Premier John Bannon of South Australia discovered a sure-fire way of winning elections: stage a Formula One grand prix in Adelaide and an election around the same time. He staged both, successfully, in 1985 and again in 1989. The issues—schools, hospitals, unemployment and poverty—paled in the face of the grandiose events, which Bannon, and other premiers, avow as the perfect vehicle for putting their cities 'on the map'.[60] Jeff Kennett of Victoria 'stole' the grand prix from Adelaide and then wrested the motorcycle grand prix from New South Wales (on the technicality that the latter state wouldn't allow tobacco advertising). Premier Ray Groom even drove in his state's newly acquired Targa race in Tasmania. Since 1991 Queensland has had an IndyCar grand prix. Even the Northern Territory ran a (disastrous) Cannonball Run in May 1994, a month before their election. In what Gabrielle Harrison, until 1999 the Labor Sports Minister, described as 'the most scandalous waste of taxpayers' money in the state's history', the Liberals in New South Wales spent $140 million on the Eastern Creek raceway. The 1995 Eastern Creek race returned a mere $4 million into the economy!

What all this signifies is that 'big events are really often not that big' and that 'the numbers and the dollars are often rubbery'. Petrophiles are not as thick on the ground as the public relations people would have us believe. Queensland put $86 million into the IndyCar race between 1991 and 1994: these events *cost* money rather than produced wealth. Nor do they produce the magic formula for 'jobs, jobs and more jobs'. The circus and circuits philosophy may well be reconsidered when the Sydney olympic hangover sets in.

9

'Market Stakes'

1977–2000

Sport, as it has for a century, will continue to grow in popularity. It will also continue to submerge racial or cultural barriers, not strengthen them. One reason for this optimistic view is simple economics: the world is getting both richer and, in terms of telecommunications, smaller. As a country develops, so its people acquire both leisure-time and the means to enjoy it. East Asians now play and watch sport in numbers that were inconceivable even one generation ago. Where Asia leads, Africa and the rest of the developing world will follow. A second reason for optimism is technological. As digital TV becomes common, it will need programs to fill its plethora of channels—and sport is the obvious filler. Moreover, digital TV will enable sport to sell itself and its sponsors to viewers in new ways. In tennis, a viewer will be able to choose from which end of the court to watch. The accessibility and dazzling tricks offered by new technologies will make sport more alluring than ever, lessening the latent prejudices of race and culture. But the greatest justification for believing in sport's rosy future is that gender gaps will certainly narrow. For sponsors and sports promoters alike, women are the next market, one which is huge, barely exploited and—if properly developed—is as likely as the men's to be both loyal and profitable.

—ECONOMIST [1]

At the beginning of the twenty-first century market forces guide the world economy—at least in theory, if not always in practice. Today nation-states and regional trading blocs are committed to trade liberalisation and the removal of restrictions on the free movement of goods, services and capital. This global trend affects every aspect of life— including sport—as entrepreneurs, sports administrators and federal and state governments seek greater shares of the market. The best local examples of market-driven sport are the new national competitions in Australian football and rugby league, and rugby's southern hemisphere-based Super 12 tournament. The National Rugby League (NRL)— formerly the Sydney-based NSWRL—currently includes teams from east-coast Australia and one from Auckland. Many commentators predict the inclusion of New Zealand-based teams in the National Basketball League and the AFL in the not too distant future.

In the previous chapter we briefly noted the socio-economic conditions which compelled the AFL to adopt a market model, and the macro-economic climate under which the Hawke Labor government encouraged sport to look more closely at market approaches—in the national interest. In this chapter we examine in more detail the politics of the market, beginning with World Series Cricket (WSC) and the Los Angeles olympics. Unlike the *Economist*, we do not view sports markets as apolitical and culturally neutral operations. As our examples show, politics and culture saturate sporting markets.

WORLD SERIES CRICKET

Before the 1970s sport derived most of its revenue from gate receipts and memberships. In the 1970s major sports supplemented these traditional sources with television broadcast fees. By the 1980s television had become the major source of revenue. In 1976 television paid the NSWRL $15000 to telecast the grand final; in 1990 Channel Ten paid $45 million to televise rugby over three seasons. Television also attracted greater corporate sponsorship. In the 1980s corporate assistance to the

Queensland Rugby Union never exceeded $20 000; by the mid-1990s it had grown to $2.1 million.[2]

The small-screen industry played a particularly important role in reviving cricket in the 1970s. When the ABC provided national coverage of the entire Test series in 1970–71, an estimated one million people watched play each day. With these numbers, cricket immediately appealed to the commercial network: it offered a perfect vehicle to attract more advertising and to meet the 'legislatively required Australian content levels at an economically viable level'.[3] Kerry Packer's Nine Network made the first move. However, the ACB ignored Channel Nine's overtures and refused the network exclusive rights. Packer responded swiftly and decisively. He signed most of the world's leading players and launched the WSC to rival the International Cricket Conference (ICC) and the ACB's Test match series. At first the ICC ignored WSC. It then banned players who joined WSC, before finally challenging the new competition in England's High Court. Defeated at every turn, the ICC and the ACB capitulated within two years and 'Packer got everything he wanted', including exclusive broadcasting rights to domestic cricket for ten years and a say in which teams toured Australia.[4]

Packer's WSC turned sport into a new site of corporate politics as big companies fought each other for exclusive control of competitions. A good example is the (ongoing) corporate 'cereal war' between Kellogg and Uncle Tobys. Both use lifesaving's Ironman event to increase their market share of breakfast cereals.[5] In the summer of 1986–87, the Surf Life Saving Association of Australia (SLSAA) and its principal sponsor, Kellogg, launched a circuit of six endurance events for its top 'ironmen'.[6] While welcoming the circuit, many of the ironmen expressed dissatisfaction at the low prize money and the failure of the SLSAA to promote the events adequately. They formed a rebel event, the Ironman Super Series, and designed new courses specifically for television and spectator entertainment. Led by Michael Porra, a former lifesaver, the rebels sold their concept to Channel Ten, which wanted a summer sport to compete against Channel Nine (which has exclusive rights to Australian cricket) and Channel Seven (tennis), and to Uncle Tobys, which wanted a high-profile vehicle to compete with Kellogg.

Corporate rivalry reached its apogee in 1995 with the introduction of pay television. It magnified the value of sport as a corporate commodity because it introduced a new form of communication technology that has the potential to fundamentally alter the way Australians conduct their lives. In the mid-1990s, rugby league became the site of a struggle between two pay television networks, Foxtel and Optus Vision, and two communication giants, Telstra and Optus. Just as the former conceived sport 'as a battering ram' and 'a lead-offering' in the pay television stakes,[7] the latter viewed pay television as an ingredient in the highly lucrative communications industry that includes the Internet, on-line banking, home-shopping, home-based entertainment and telecommuting. Thus sport, and movies, are important vehicles to secure pay television subscribers and to introduce them to technology that will, in the not too distant future, organise and define the lives of significant numbers.

In the first instance, Rupert Murdoch's Foxtel, a joint venture between News Corporation and Telstra, needed a 'product' to lure subscribers. Given his association with the game in Britain, Murdoch chose rugby league. He was unsuccessful in his approach to the Australian Rugby League (ARL), which at the time had a contract with Kerry Packer's Channel Nine. Packer owned the free-to-air and pay television rights to rugby league and he warned the ARL that he would not hesitate to defend his contract through the courts. Packer also held a small interest in Optus Vision, with an option to significantly increase his holding. Optus would later replace Winfield cigarettes as the ARL's principal sponsor when the federal government banned tobacco companies from sport. Rebuffed, Murdoch launched a corporate raid, which the (then) president of the ARL, Ken Arthurson, likened to the Japanese attack on Pearl Harbor in the Second World War. He signed up some of the strongest clubs and the best coaches, players and referees to his rival Super League.[8] True to his word, Packer turned to the courts and embroiled Murdoch's Super League in two years of court action. Thus the Super League did not begin until 1997.[9] Packer, a popular villain twenty years earlier during his WSC foray, suddenly became the people's hero in the war against Murdoch—who was no longer a dinky-di Aussie but a dirty corporate American raider.

Super League survived but one season; in 1998 the two competitions merged into the NRL.[10] Australia simply doesn't have the population to support two elite rugby league competitions. The feuding and politics associated with Super League decimated the game at all levels as disillusioned fans and estranged sponsors fled, and a resentful print media reduced its coverage. 'We've tested public enthusiasm for rugby league', wrote *Inside Sport* at the start of the 1997 season, 'and the result is just in: the winner is apathy'.[11] In Sydney and Brisbane many former fans turned to Australian football; in Canberra they switched to rugby. Such was the plight of the game that the two corporate rivals, Optus–Optus Vision and Telstra–Foxtel, feared losing a valuable commodity and elected to negotiate. Under the existing agreement, Channel Nine holds free-to-air rights for three years and Foxtel and Optus Vision share pay television rights. But the majority of Murdoch clubs survived the merger, thus giving him a direct say in the organisation and administration of the NRL. Perhaps the most remarkable feature of this corporate war was Packer's opportunism: after the courts sanctioned Super League, Packer abandoned the ARL and televised both the Optus Cup and the Super League on free-to-air television! Without Packer's financial support, the ARL had no option but to deal with Murdoch.[12]

Corporations with monopolistic ambitions were not the only entities to intervene in sport. Other economic units, associated with nation-states, also intruded. In 1978, the year after Packer launched the WSC, Los Angeles secured the 1984 olympics. But unlike Packer, who applied a 'stick' to the ACB, Los Angeles' games organisers offered sports administrators irresistible 'carrots'.

THE 'PRIVATE' OLYMPICS

In the late 1970s the future of the world's biggest sporting pageant looked uncertain. A succession of threatened and actual boycotts, beginning with Mexico City in 1968, political violence in 1972, and burdensome debts, had scared most potential host cities away from the games.[13]

In 1978 Los Angeles lodged the sole bid for the 1984 olympic games after the only other competitor, Teheran, withdrew. Denied state funding, the Los Angeles organising committee privatised the games; it sold television rights to American, European and Japanese networks, demanded that sponsors make a minimum pledge of US$9 million each, and licensed companies to sell 'official' olympic products—everything from hamburgers to camera film.[14] The result was a US$220 million profit, an immediate revival of interest in hosting the games—six cities entered the 1985 race to host the 1992 summer olympics[15]—and, most importantly, a total re-evaluation of the economic value of international sport. Los Angeles offered coalitions of governments, entrepreneurs and sports administrators a perfect model to turn major sporting competitions into 'hallmark' events.[16]

In the late 1970s Sydney and Melbourne launched short-lived bids for the 1988 olympic games. In 1979 the New South Wales government withdrew its support for Sydney, citing concerns about costs; similarly, two years later the federal and Victorian state governments withdrew backing for Melbourne.[17] But interest quickly revived after Los Angeles, and Brisbane—led by Mayor Sallyanne Atkinson—plunged head first into the race for the 1992 games. Brisbane never stood a real chance against Barcelona and Paris,[18] but after the vote Atkinson explained her real objectives: 'we put our city and our country on the map. It was a small investment.'[19] Similarly, the Department of Sport, Recreation and Tourism's annual report for 1986/87 noted that Brisbane's bid 'focus[ed] world-wide attention on Australia, its tourism potential, its excellent sporting facilities and its professional sports administration'.[20] Notwithstanding third place, Brisbane collected more votes than Belgrade, Birmingham and Amsterdam, inspiring senior officials of the Australian Olympic Federation and federal and state politicians and bureaucrats to encourage further bids. Melbourne submitted an unsuccessful bid for the 1996 games,[21] before Sydney won the 2000 games in 1993.

Just as Packer's WSC turned sport into a site of corporate rivalry, as big companies fought each other for exclusive control of competitions and sports, so Los Angeles' financial success launched bidding frenzies among cities bursting to capitalise on the apparent economic potential of the olympics. Sporting gold assumed new meaning after Los Angeles. Federal and provincial governments around the world reappraised the employment and tourist prospects of nearly every sporting event; governments, sports officials and their commercial backers formed alliances to compete for the right to host the events that international sporting federations now regularly offered for sale. But as the Sydney olympic bid reveals, the competition unleashed a new, aggressive and unscrupulous politics, hitherto unknown in sport.[22]

In its quest for the 2000 games, China presented the IOC with a priceless terracotta soldier.[23] Explaining the invaluable donation, Chen Xitong, chairman of the Beijing bid committee, said 'we look upon the IOC as God—their wish is our command'. In their desire to satisfy the 'Gods', bid committees lauded, indulged, coddled, duchessed and pampered—in short, bribed—IOC members. Dossiers identifying IOC members' personal wants and tastes are mandatory bid committee tools. Bob Scott, chief executive of Manchester's bid committees for the 1996 and 2000 games, once boasted: 'I even know the shoe size of the second daughter of one particular IOC member'! Early in its campaign for the 2000 games, Berlin's committee apologised for investigating IOC members' sexual preferences. Members of Sydney's bid committee willingly partook in this deceitful, corrupt and shameful game.

While the style and intensity of lobbying is antithetical to the noble sporting ideal of fair play, some IOC members happily exploit this deferential treatment. They fashion opulent lifestyles from all-expenses-paid 'investigations' of cities bidding for (summer and winter) games, and from the pilgrimages of gift- and favour-bearing delegations who arrive at IOC meetings and even members' homes. An official of the Barcelona organising committee summed up the behaviour of IOC members: 'they're used to getting what they want, to having their demands met— their motto is "we all want more".'

At century's end, the IOC and the whole olympic movement is in crisis, its credibility in tatters. Olympism has nothing left but greed and a win-at-any-cost mentality by those who seek only power or financial benefit. The 'educational value of good example' and 'respect for universal fundamental ethical issues'—ideals in the olympic charter—are bereft of credibility. Olympic officials have responded with promises to redress and reform themselves. But their obvious lack of resolve leaves many sceptical about any serious change in olympic culture. Scepticism and cynicism arise from the obvious unwillingness of IOC officials to allow anyone other than themselves to oversee reform. Damian Grace says it well: 'The IOC does not see itself as accountable to anyone but itself. It is ethically narcissistic: the IOC holds a mirror to itself and makes its own adjustments.'[24]

MARKET SPORT AND THE POLITICS OF RESTRUCTURING

Traditionally, sport connected and distinguished social groups—such as classes, communities and genders—and deferred to 'barrackers' who intimately identified with 'their team'. Market-oriented sport, by contrast, puts barrackers and old-fashioned club supporters behind corporate sponsors, merchandisers, media barons and 'consumers'. Whereas traditional sport offered 'barrackers' a means to affirm and reaffirm their identities, sports consumers merely seek quality entertainment.[25] To attract the largest number of 'consumers', market-driven sport produces entertainment packages that attempt to dilute, and even transcend, existing group affiliations and identities.

The ARL employed African–American performer Tina Turner 'to promote the game to a wider audience in campaigns that integrated Anglo-Saxon heritage with multiculturalism and a repackaged masculinity portraying footballers as dedicated professional gladiators'. According to the NSWRL's marketing manager, Graeme Foster, 'the Tina Turner campaign was the culmination of a three year marketing plan to give rugby league a more contemporary image. It was a ballsy [sic] campaign that appealed to women and young men, and reached in to the white collar audience without alienating league's traditional blue collar supporter base'.[26] Nearly all Australia's major sporting competitions now use 'show-business' formats for games which include 'complementary' entertainment like fireworks, music, team mascots and dancing girls. In some cases entertainment appears to have supplanted the actual game, as this description of a Sydney Kings basketball match suggests:

> There were dancing girls and a court jester mascot, before he was dumped for a lion. The kitsch meter peaked with a man in an electric-light cowboy suit riding a horse around the court with socks over hooves. He sang 'Rhinestone Cowboy' and shot a couple of baskets. Everywhere you looked...it was logo a-go-go. The players' shirts became a patch-work of corporate symbols...Sponsors' banners hung high and shoulder-to-shoulder above the stands. And at half time, a Mitsubishi car would descend from the ceiling to just sit there...Basketball was almost a sidearm of Kings Inc.[27]

Television offers further evidence of the remodelling of sport as entertainment. In the 1960s and 1970s, Australian football replays, match previews and post-mortems—notably 'League Teams' and 'World of Sport'—were institutions in Melbourne. Today they have been replaced by entertainment programs like 'The Footy Show' and 'Live and Kicking'. The two genres are worlds apart. As the *Sunday Age* notes, 'the commentators and experts have become entertainers and vaudevillians. What once passed for gravitas has long since given way to the pursuit of the sharp one-liner and, of course, ratings points'.[28] Not infrequently, sports entertainment degenerates into boorish puerility, such as when Sam Newman blackened his face in an attempt to parody Aboriginal player Nicky Winmar for his non-appearance on 'The Footy Show'. Enormous public and media pressure led to a reluctant acceptance that this wasn't just 'fun' and to a somewhat unconvincing apology. Clearly, sports 'entertainers' have yet to learn that racial vilification is as unacceptable on the screen as it is on the field.

Throughout this book we have shown that philosophical differences over the meaning of sport have historically divided administrators and served as a source of tension, even conflict, between players and administrators, and entrepreneurs and volunteer administrators. Not surprisingly, the introduction of market approaches exacerbated many of these political tensions.

While some administrators—notably Allen Aylett (VFL), Phil Coles and John Coates (AOC) and Michael Porra (Ironman Super Series)—actively encouraged and willingly embraced the market model, others—like members of the ACB and SLSAA—clung desperately to the past, fearing the breakdown of traditional authority structures and loss of power. Divisions between Sydney officials and those from Queensland and provincial New South Wales helped fuel the ARL–Super League battle, with the former mostly supporting the ARL and most of the latter siding with Murdoch. Similarly, olympic officials John Coates and Kevan Gosper clashed over the introduction of a market-based system of financial rewards for Australian athletes. According to Coates, the athletes 'generate the television and sponsorship revenues' and 'it is only fair' that they receive compensation for lost study and career opportunities. Gosper disagreed. Financial compensation, he said, 'devalues the medal' and cheapens the 'honour and glory'.[29] Early in 1991 Coates replaced Gosper as president of the AOC and Australian medallists at Barcelona received $31 250 for gold, $12 500 for silver and $6250 for bronze.

The WSC, Ironman Super Series, and Super League all capitalised on players' grievances, which included low financial rewards for demanding, sometimes crippling, training regimes, exclusion from management structures, and inadequate benefits like superannuation and retirement opportunities. Indeed, the lack of attention paid by traditional sports administrators made players perfect recruits for entrepreneurs and corporations who promised to develop and market events, build media profiles and public awareness, attract sponsorships, and increase prize money.

The market model offended many traditionalists. The WSC outraged cricket officials, former players, journalists and academics. Most portrayed the event as a media mogul hijacking Australia's national game. Keith Windschuttle's polemic was typical:

Limited over cricket resembles an inferior quality generic brand of a supermarket product; it may be a big seller now, but it exists courtesy of the demand created by the original product or the real thing. Packer's product is inferior because it has broken the conventions of the game, turning the ritual and drama of traditional cricket into a mere spectacle. The taste for spectacle, however, is always short-lived because it is inherently unsatisfying. Test cricket, on the other hand, has endured for more than a hundred years because it grew from and expressed national and community needs, particularly those related to our dependent colonial status. Test cricket is about life; Packer cricket has been aptly dubbed a 'circus'... Though it may take a few more seasons, Packer cricket must eventually end up the same as television wrestling, a derided display shown on Saturday mornings only because no cheaper programs are available.[30]

But dismay at 'Packer's product' remained relatively confined, and the game not only survived but thrived. A recent survey of Year 11 students from a range of socio-economic backgrounds in Victoria and New South Wales reported a definite preference for one-day cricket and a request for more of this variant—and less Test cricket.[31] Far from denigrating cricket, the limited-overs game injected a new lease of life by breaking outmoded conventions. Consistent with the prevailing seventies-style nationalism, players and fans wanted change: players demanded rewards commensurate with their efforts and skills, and fans welcomed attractive, vital, fast-paced, exciting sport. Contrary to Windschuttle's claims, Test cricket was the product of a staid, pre-war, white middle-class Anglo-Australian culture. As we have seen, multiculturalism and affluent baby-boomers progressively undermined and transformed this culture.

Like the opponents of the WSC, critics howled at the VFL's market-driven initiatives. Football attendances, as a percentage of Melbourne's population, continued to fall in the early 1980s. In 1983 the VFL's operating expenses exceeded the operating revenue by nearly $2 million, six clubs were on the verge of bankruptcy, and the Corporate Affairs Commission had asked several clubs to explain why they continued to trade. Determined to reverse the decline, the VFL's commissioners launched a campaign to encourage 'theatre-goers'.[32] The strategy involved new marketing and licensing initiatives, merging clubs, relocating clubs to bigger population centres, and improving grounds. Barrackers especially opposed the relocation of South Melbourne to Sydney; they accused rapacious administrators, sponsors and media barons of browbeating them—the 'rightful owners' of football. Bogged in nostalgia, barrackers completely ignored the football, demographic, economic and social realities of inner Melbourne, south of the Yarra. At the time of relocation, the South Melbourne club had not won a premiership for some 50 years, it had not appeared in a grand final for nearly 40 years, its membership stood at only 1500, and it lacked a solid financial foundation. Barrackers also glossed over the facts that South Melbourne club officials applied to play home games in Sydney, and that most players supported relocation.

In the end, opposition came to nought. The VFL–AFL's market approach proved, like the WSC and limited-overs cricket, a popular and financial success. In 1997 the AFL earned $83 million in revenue, and attendances in 1998 for all official matches topped the seven million mark. Crowds in Sydney averaged 35 810 compared with the AFL's average of 34 767.[33] As former Swans' Brownlow medallist and fierce opponent of relocation, Fred Goldsmith, recently conceded, 'it's better' that the club now plays in Sydney to full houses every week.[34] Players are also better rewarded. In 1997 player payments totalled $55.6 million, with 31 per cent earning more than $100 000. In late 1988 the VFL employed one marketing manager and a secretary, and retail sales for licensing activities amounted to $13 million. A decade later the latter amounted to $91 million, with the principal sponsor, Coca-Cola, paying the AFL in excess of $5 million per annum.[35]

Responding to his critics, Mike Wrublewski, owner of the Sydney Kings basketball team, notes that in the early 1980s 'nobody was interested in the game. By providing a package, which entertains as well as presents the sport in its most competitive light, we've introduced basketball to so many people. I think we should be proud that a night out at the basketball is an entertaining night out'.[36] Wrublewski can indeed boast: his club has '130 sponsors' and 'there's a waiting list for people to buy sponsors' boxes'.[37] Barrackers who malign corporate sponsors will, of course, scoff at these facts. But as the AFL's chief executive Wayne Jackson reminds us, 'their dollars' are effectively a subsidy: we charge spectators 'less than the cost of putting on the actual show'.[38] Similarly, a month's subscription to pay television is often cheaper, and more convenient, than attending a live event.

On the other hand, smaller crowds at NRL matches and successful opposition by Australian football barrackers to the proposed mergers of the Footscray and Fitzroy clubs,[39] and the Melbourne and Hawthorn clubs, should alert sports administrators, sponsors and media barons that there are limits to restructuring. Barrackers clearly overstate their case, as when Dave Nadel calls the survival of the Footscray Football Club (now the Western Bulldogs) 'a victory for old style tribal, suburban football over corporate football, national football and "theatre-goers"'.[40] But there is no doubt that under some circumstances the release of pent-up community frustration can, if not reverse significant socio-economic trends, at least prompt modifications. By painting a glowing picture of fabulous benefits, the disciples of market sport have cleverly countered many of the concerns and hence much potential opposition.

The Sydney, Brisbane and Melbourne bid committees painted the olympics as an economic panacea.[41] Touting calculations made by KPMG Peat Marwick, the Sydney bid committee, for example, claimed that the 2000 olympics would inject $7.3 billion into the Australian economy over fourteen years from 1991, with the tourism, hospitality and construction industries reaping windfalls. Not surprisingly, the vanguard of Sydney's bid committee comprised leaders of the transport, construction, hotel and tourism industries, the financial sector and the commercial media. Among the members were Peter Abeles (TNT), Kevan Gosper (Shell), John Ward (Qantas), Eric Neal (Westpac), Kerry Packer (Consolidated Press), John Alexander (Fairfax) and Kenneth Crowley (News Limited).

Any notion of sport as an economic cure-all requires careful evaluation. As impressive as KPMG Peat Marwick's 'most likely' economic scenario looks at first glance, it represents a minuscule average annual increase in national output of $500 million, or *one-eighth of 1 per cent* of an Australian economy worth $400 billion per annum. Max Walsh, the respected economics commentator, gave the figure further context when he observed that the fall in the value of the Australian dollar in the second and third quarters of 1993 and the consequent rise in foreign debt wiped out the projected benefits of the games. Most of the 156 000 jobs predicted by KPMG Peat Marwick for the 2000 olympics are temporary, low-paid and unskilled jobs in construction and hospitality. In short, no modern games have had anything other than a minimal effect on national or regional economies.

Moreover, the true costs of staging the games are unclear. The NSW Auditor-General has criticised the organising committee for shrouding costings in 'unnecessary secrecy' and accused it of violating freedom of information laws and guidelines on public disclosure set down by the Independent Commission Against Corruption.[42] According to his calculations published in early 1999, the games will cost the government \$2.3 billion, \$700 million more than official estimates.[43] Much of the debate over costing concerns disagreements over what should be included and excluded. For example, during the bid, the government maintained that the cost of staging the games was \$1.697 billion. Yet when Sydney won it admitted that the total cost, including essential infrastructure (principally at the main site of Homebush Bay), was \$3.232 billion. Then Premier John Fahey initially said that redevelopment of Homebush Bay was part of a capital works program 'independent' of the 2000 games decision. But this argument misled taxpayers because Sydney's victory condensed and converted a twenty-year discretionary project into a seven-year essential project. Redevelopment of Homebush Bay will not produce an economic return and it will compete with other capital works programs associated with health, education, housing, transport and policing. Coincidentally, the same day that Sydney won the hosting rights to the games, the New South Wales government announced closures at the Prince Henry, Royal South Sydney and Royal Women's hospitals, at a cost of 225 beds and 800 jobs.

The economic myths of sport don't survive in a vacuum: they are carefully propagated, nurtured and defended. For example, an aggressive pro-games lobby effectively silenced those who asked searching questions about the economic, social, political and environmental costs of the 2000 olympics. In July 1993, just before the ABC's 'Four Corners' program went to air with its investigation into the bidding process, Bruce Baird, the NSW Minister for Transport and the Olympic Bid, bellowed a warning: 'if anybody gets in the way of the bid, then all I can say is watch out.' The bid committee angrily denounced Max Walsh for challenging its revenue estimates and expenditure on infrastructure, and Premier Fahey called treasury officials 'bean counters' and the NSW Labor Party 'anti-games' after they challenged financial costings. The admonishing tones insinuated that critical analysis of the Sydney games is un-Australian and that those who don't want to be 'on the team' must be anti-Australian.

Even the benefits bestowed on sport by the olympics need careful scrutiny. In 1987–88, on the eve of the Barcelona olympics, the Hawke Labor government significantly increased the size of its grants to individual codes. Olympic sports such as swimming (\$183 000), athletics

($174 000) and basketball ($157 000) received the highest amounts.[44] In mid-1994 the Keating Labor government began a $135 million, six-year program to improve the performances of olympic athletes. The long-term objective of the program is to win 60 medals, including 20 gold, in Sydney. Funds are distributed on the basis of past success and future prospects. Thus, after winning a bronze medal at the Atlanta olympics in 1996, softball earned a 'category one' classification, guaranteeing it $1.4 million (for management, coaching, international competition and direct athlete support) in 1997/98. Other category one sports in 1997/98 included rowing ($3.4 million) and swimming ($3.1 million).[45]

Somewhat surprisingly, given its fervent commitment to *laissez-faire* economics, John Howard's Coalition government, coming to office in 1996, retained Labor's olympic program: even Howard could not resist the allure of olympic gold. But sport should not expect the party to continue after 2000. The Coalition has already savaged the budgets of non-olympic sports and umbrella administrative associations. The Australian Schools Sport Council, the Confederation of Australian Sport, and the Australian Universities Sports Federation are three notable losers with their 1996/97 budgets slashed by between 50 and nearly 80 per cent.[46] Even during the Hawke and Keating Labor governments—when total funding for sport rose from $41.2 million in 1984/85 to $86 million in 1992/93—grassroots sport made few gains. In 1995/96, for example, the Australian Sports Commission allocated only 11.3 per cent of its budget to this end.[47] Even more surprising, and worrying, is the air of naive complacency and 'unreality' observed among local sports organisations. According to Barrie Houlihan, they seem oblivious to 'the consequences of even a modest withdrawal of public funding, let alone the scale of reductions that are likely after 2000'.[48]

ACCESSING THE 'MARKET STAKES'

Notwithstanding the *Economist*'s rosy picture of racial and cultural barriers in sport weakening under the impetus of market forces, serious questions remain. How, precisely, will the market increase access for groups traditionally discriminated against like working-class children, women, particularly those from non-English-speaking backgrounds, Aborigines, gays and lesbians? Will the market really connect these groups with the dominant white Anglo-Australian male sporting culture?

Will market-driven sport transcend the major differences in caste, class, colour and ethnicity and become the great unifier of the nation?

Children

Policy-makers, politicians, educationists and the medical lobby claim that children's sport is a national priority. Children's sport, they say, is an insurance policy for the physical and mental health of the future nation, a solution for delinquency problems, and the richest source of olympic gold. Yet they show little understanding of the mechanisms by which children gain access to sport, or, indeed, what attracts them in the first place.[49]

Parents are the key to children's sport in Australia. The whole structure depends on their time, money and emotion. And these are, in the first instance, functions of economic class and social status. Among the lower-income classes, money is a scarce resource and children's sport is often unaffordable. Children's sport is expensive: money is essential for equipment, uniforms, travelling, medical care, competition fees, club memberships and coaching. Most parents spend over $1000 per sport per year; many spend between $2000 and $3000. And the expenses rise dramatically if the child represents the region or the state.

While good incomes obviously make it easier for parents to absorb the economic shock of children's sport, time is equally important. Taxiing children to sport is a full-time occupation. As one netball parent explains, 'there is no way we could manage with one car...especially with Bob working afternoon shifts. If he's not home there is no way I could get the kids to training. It would be impossible'. As well as taxiing there is spectating, waiting, officiating, fundraising, general duties and coaching. Time forces many parents to pull their children out of sport. One parent stopped her three children playing hockey: they trained for swimming two nights a week and hockey two nights and played hockey on Friday nights. It was simply 'too much. I was sometimes falling asleep at the wheel of the car', she said. Not surprisingly then, as a group, children of single parents enjoy the least access to junior sport. Single parents who want their children to play need high incomes and access to a support network—friends, family—to cope with time and transport arrangements.

Parents' cultural beliefs can also exacerbate the economic problems associated with children's sport. For example, many Vietnamese-born Australians consider sport, at best, peripheral.[50] 'Economically marginalised and of low social status', their first priority is to improve their children's standard of living. This means work and study. Cultural values, such as pride in the extended family and a Confucian respect for authority, not only reinforce the strong work and study ethic, they also weaken the desire and passion for sport. According to teachers, winning the support and interest of Vietnamese parents is a 'difficult obstacle': 'we can get the Vietnamese kids to play [at] school...but [not] to represent the school. The kids say "Mum and Dad don't want us to go—we'll miss out on school".' And many Vietnamese parents are simply unwilling, or unable, to transport their children.

Clearly, market approaches, which tend to emphasise self-help, will not rectify the problems associated with children's access. Even easy access does not explain participation, which for many children is a function of personal choice dictated by the very nature of sport.[51] The reality is that most Australian children avoid voluntary sport because they dislike the win-at-all-costs philosophy, the unbearable pressures, boredom, lack of fun, long hours, and overbearing, masochistic coaches. Teenagers, in particular, talk of conflicts of interests with work, study and non-sporting interests, the high cost of equipment and travel, and declining parental interest.

The non-English-speaking

Although studies suggest that a significant percentage of young adults voluntarily return to sport, existing sporting structures still preclude some groups. The most notable exclusions are women from non-English-speaking backgrounds.[52] While they make up nearly 15 per cent of the population, they are grossly underrepresented in sport. In 1993 an Australian Bureau of Statistics survey reported that only 8.4 per cent of females from non-English-speaking countries had played some form of sport during the previous year. This compared with 26.7 per cent of Australian-born women. Language difficulties and religious and cultural hurdles confront many. Women without English skills may not know about sporting programs, may not be able to follow coaches' or instructors' commands, and may feel uncomfortable about expressing their feelings and ideas. Many Muslim women will not engage in physical exercise or sport in the presence of men; they require female-only facilities. Lastly, a Greek woman explains how cultural expectations excluded her from sport: 'There's double standards, girls have to stay home and

learn to cook and all that stuff and the brothers go out and do all the
boy things—girls aren't encouraged to have that get up and go.'

The absence of immigrants, and in particular immigrant women,
from Anglo-Australian sport highlights the principal theme of this book,
namely that sport primarily connects pre-existing social groups and
communities. This fact helps explain the prevalence of immigrant- or
ethnic-based sporting federations in Australia: the long list includes the
Croatian Soccer Association of Australia, the Pan-Hellenic Athletic
Association of Australia, the Council of Polish Sports Clubs in Australia,
the Maccabi Movement, the Scottish Caledonian Games Association,
and the Gaelic Athletic Association. All host their own sporting events
and carnivals.[53]

The ambitions and experiences of second- and third-generation
immigrants informs us that material success, social mobility and elevation to middle-class status is a prerequisite for the adoption of traditional
Anglo-Australian sports. Nicholas Doumanis refers to second- and third-
generation Greeks who, as members of the Perth-based Macedonian
Greek Brotherhood, Megas Alexandros, formed cricket and netball teams
out of a conscious 'desire to participate in mainstream Australian sports
at the community level'.[54] Similarly, an Italian immigrant describes one
of her cousins, an 18-year-old second-generation Australian female, playing soccer: 'the oldies don't see it as something appropriate for young
ladies', she says, but 'it is changing'.[55]

Aborigines

Cultural decisions about whether to connect or disconnect with disparate
groups are one thing, government neglect and racial discrimination are
another. In *Obstacle Race*, Colin Tatz describes at length the sporting
facilities and opportunities available for Aborigines in 90 towns or communities across Australia. The well off are few and far between.
Australian football thrives in the Tiwi communities at Nguiu and
Milikiparti (on the islands north of Darwin); in Port Lincoln (South
Australia), Aborigines own Mallee Park Football Club and 19 acres in
town, complete with oval and licensed restaurant-clubhouse; Cherbourg,
some 280 kilometres north of Brisbane, is a celebrated centre of Aboriginal sports culture, producing not only Eddie Gilbert and Frankie
Fisher, but no less than three boxers at the 1962 Commonwealth
games—Jeff Dynevor (who won the gold), Adrian Blair and Eddie
Barney (Gilbert's son)—and later, rugby league star Steve Renouf. By

contrast, 32 towns or communities have absolutely nothing in the way of grounds, facilities, equipment, coaches, transport, money and, above all, opportunities to compete.

In most Aboriginal communities it is impossible to distinguish anything that can be called a 'sportsground'. Lombadina and Djarindjin, in north-western Western Australia, play Australian football on a saltpan marked only by goalposts made from twisted saplings. Kalumburu has a paddock that, literally, lies under water for more than half the year. Gingie Reserve, in New South Wales, has an 'oval' covered in wild bushes. What passes for 'ovals' at Kintore and Mt Liebig in Central Australia are cleared patches of dusty red earth, with no markings, locker rooms, showers, stands or scoreboards. These conditions do not reflect rational choices made in a free market: they are symptoms of the despair and hopelessness faced by Aboriginal communities torn asunder by unemployment, alcoholism, domestic violence and outrageously high levels of youth suicide. They are also symptomatic of an attitude in ATSIC in its early years and the Australian Sports Commission (at present), that elite sport is all that matters.

While facilities in major towns and in the small and large cities vary, Aborigines constantly confront white authorities and officials who deny them access to public parks and playing fields, even in the suburbs of Perth. Equally racist are the white youths who flock to other sports rather than compete against Aborigines who predominate or shine. Bourke is an example: white youths recently switched to rugby union, although a number of Aborigines have followed. In 1998 Aborigines ceased playing football in Bourke: league and Australian football clubs refused to play against local Aboriginal sides, despite the local police commander offering to pay team expenses and to patrol matches.

Aborigines in remote communities pay more per capita for their sport than any other Australians. In 1982 the Townsville Rugby League admitted the Aboriginal community of Palm Island, with a population of just under 3000, to its competitions, subject to the Palm Islanders paying the cost of the visiting teams—$3000 for a plane, $2000 for a sea launch. Over seven years, Palm Islanders spent nearly $400 000 on their players' away game expenses and on visiting team fares. They spent a further $25 000 on jerseys, ground equipment, shoulder pads and the like. It was an unsustainable expense for a community struggling on subsistence incomes, deriving almost exclusively from social service benefits. Since 1988 the Island's four clubs have had no option but to play each other.

On the eve of the olympics, and with olympism's leaders promising redefinition and invigoration, it will be interesting to see whether the
Australian Olympic Committee, with its guaranteed $100 million fund-
ing bonanza from olympic revenues, will spend a single cent on
improving Aboriginal facilities and access to mainstream sport.

Women

For most of the twentieth century Australian women have had to mediate
two contradictory messages. The first informs them that sport is unfeminine and not conducive to beauty; the second tells them that exercise
is a prerequisite for an attractive figure. The *Australian Women's Mirror*
explained this contradiction as early as 1924:

> the woman who goes in for sport generally does it so strenuously or it
> might be more correct to say stridently, that she becomes too muscular
> and ungainly to ever attain the grace, ease and smoothness requisite for
> the ideal of feminine loveliness. Yet moderate sports are the ideal mode
> for keeping fit and young, provided one eats judiciously and cares for the
> skin and hair at the same time.[56]

Feminists and the medical profession mounted the first serious and
sustained challenge of the 'moderate sports' dictum in the 1970s.
Feminists urged women to understand, celebrate and take responsibility
for their bodies, while medical practitioners, concerned about rising cir-
culatory and coronary diseases, advised women to take exercise with
vigour. A new generation of women's magazines responded with regular articles on jogging, cycling, rowing and aerobics: fat was out, thin
was in and, for the first time in history, women were no longer intruders
in what had been a virtually exclusive male domain. By the mid-1980s,
women could compete, risk their bodies, and sweat in public. Even the
notoriously chauvinistic SLSAA, under pressure to increase its declining
ranks, opened the clubhouse doors to women lifesavers.[57]

Women made further gains in the early 1990s when the medical profession recommended strength and weight training as prerequisites for
good health. Again the media intervened, with advertisers increasingly
showing images of active women with well-toned and sculpted bodies:
muscles became functional and fashionable. The strong sportswoman
became more visible and more self-assured and proud. Former Commonwealth gold medallist Lisa Curry-Kenny, a trend-setter in the muscle
stakes, reports getting 'lots of letters from women who have watched

For most of the twentieth century, Australian women have had to
steer through contradictory messages about the 'unfeminine' nature
of sport and the benefits of exercise. In the 1970s, feminists urged
women to understand, celebrate and take responsibility for their
bodies. By the 1990s, women's bodies had become well-toned and
sculpted; muscles became functional and fashionable. Here Carol
Grahame shows her form in 1987. PAUL TATZ

what I have done, read my books and done my videos and now feel
good about themselves'.[58] In the late 1990s, muscular strength is a
symbol of female power.

But power is rarely absolute. Sexist men and conservative women still
intimidate and stigmatise sportswomen. Muscular women still walk a fine
line between what the guardians of sexuality—men and women who

claim that they are protecting women to ensure they fulfil their destinies as wives and mothers—consider aesthetically pleasing and excessive muscular development. Some female athletes are still reluctant to 'bulk up'. Sprinter Melinda Gainsford doesn't want muscles although she concedes that 'I have a job to do and I have to make sacrifices. That sacrifice could mean muscles'.[59] The guardians of sexuality still demand that sportswomen prove their femininity. And feminine remains code for heterosexual. Sexist men and women use homophobia—disgust and hatred of lesbians—and the 'butch' label to effectively police women's behaviour. Unfortunately, too many sportswomen respond with silence, denial, apology and overt heterosexual behaviour; they denounce lesbians and hire male coaches. In their desperation to avoid the taint of lesbianism, officials instruct girls to keep their hair long, shave their legs and to wear makeup, nail polish, perfume, jewellery and skirts. The Australian Women's Cricket Council, for example, opted for culottes rather than trousers to counter 'dyke' stereotypes and to present a more acceptable feminine image. In other sports, officials ban 'severe' haircuts, discourage public drinking and smoking, scrutinise social engagements and living arrangements, impose evening curfews, and hire chaperones and 'experts' who teach players how to look like the girl next door.

Lastly, eroticism continues to undermine muscular feminism. Some media portray muscly women as erotic, while old-fashioned sexist sponsors and advertisers still prefer their women to adopt submissive poses in scanty swimsuits.

Paradoxically, the liberation of the muscular sportswomen has also introduced new social pressures. Popular notions that bodies are machines capable of fine tuning, or that bodies are infinitely malleable and can be resculptured at will, place intense pressure on women. Bodies are not pistons, hinges and levers; bodies have genetic limits. Muscular bodies, like wafer-thin fashion bodies, lie well beyond the grasp of most, but this doesn't stop women from trying. Unfortunately, for many women trying to achieve the impossible means lives of hard labour under punishing and excessive exercise regimes.

Homosexuals

Homosexual and bisexual men and women have, of course, always played sport and participated in physical activities. But the prevailing sports culture ensured that they hid their sexuality.[60] Sport made young men fit to reproduce the white race and to serve the nation—whether it be on the battlefield or the sportsfield; sport made young women fit for marriage and motherhood. In this inhibited environment alternative sexualities had no place.

The sexual revolution, which began in Australia in the 1960s, gave gays and lesbians new space. They began to step out of the closet and invest their time, emotion and money in their own sports activities and associations. But it was the AIDS crisis which provided the catalyst for gay and lesbian sport. In several key sports, AIDS created an immediate protest about playing against homosexual players, for fear of contamination or infection. That began to wane, with better health information. AIDS also created a greater awareness of the health benefits of exercise and fitness among homosexuals. In the last decade they have departed drab, smoke-filled bars and dingy nightclubs *en masse* for clean, freshly aired gyms and health studios. One survey claims that gays, lesbians and bisexuals spend 250 per cent more on health and fitness than heterosexuals. Homosexual gay and lesbian sporting associations now host gay games and 'world cups' in ice hockey, soccer, tennis, ten pin bowling and volleyball. Sydney attracted 1059 competitors to the eighth Australian Gaymes in 1997 and will host the international gay games in 2002. Organisers expect more competitors at this event than the 2000 olympics.

While public acceptance of gay and lesbian sport owes much to a handful of high-profile stars such as Greg Louganis, Martina Navratilova, and Billie Jean King, the market has played a crucial role. In Australia, Ian Roberts came out much later in his rugby league career. Big corporations—such as Philips, US West and Veronica (a Dutch cable TV channel) which sponsored the 1998 gay games in Amsterdam—recognise their sheer spending power. Roger Le Blanc calculates that gays and lesbians contribute $1.1 billion to Australia's leisure and recreation industry, which is worth $12 billion, per annum. Given their financial clout, it is hardly surprising that even conservative administrators now welcome gays. As one rugby league club manager puts it, gay fans 'represent good value for money': they consume copious alcohol, they're loyal and, unlike many young straights, they're non-violent.

Throughout this book we have shown how, at different historical junctures, different groups—colonial governors, publicans and entrepreneurs, and middle-class amateurs—have had profound effects on the meaning and structure of sport. Few will disagree that at the beginning of the twenty-first century the market is the dominant force. While we believe that the market has had, and will continue to have, many positive benefits for sport, we nonetheless warn against embracing the *Economist*'s optimistic picture of the future. In one field alone, there is simply no 'lessening the latent prejudices of race'. Markets are not the politically neutral forces that their disciples claim. On the contrary, they are intensely political. Clearly, there will be many losers in the 'market stakes'; in some cases, hopefuls won't even make it to the starting line.

10

The Australian Way of Sport

Australia does have this aggressive desire to succeed, to beat other nations, to exert its national ego, and this has been channelled tremendously through sport. The public has this desire for success and the champions are lionised to such a degree that there are few dividends for failure. Australian sportsmen have a fanatical desire to win with a killer instinct not often equalled by other nations.

—KEITH DUNSTAN[1]

If we could just get rid of the Aborigines, we wouldn't have any drama. We wouldn't have no problem then, would we?

—ROBERT HESSION, the manager of St Kilda's Peter Everitt,
who was suspended for four matches for racial vilification
(*Inside Sport*, no. 90, June 1999)

Is there an Australian sporting identity, a distinctive Australian way of sport? We have given examples of sport reinforcing boundaries between cities and states, and of sport both highlighting and accentuating ethnic, religious, sexual, political, racial, class and local cleavages. We have shown how very different groups—women, immigrants, Aborigines, workers, militant Protestants, Catholics, and all manner of progressives and conservatives—have constructed and reconstructed sport as a way of asserting their identity and affirming their social status. But we have also cited several instances where sport has furthered the common interest and national identity. Millions cast aside all differences to celebrate the *Australia II* victory. In that moment in 1983, Australians affirmed themselves as one: the race evoked, synthesised and embellished national stereotypes. In that moment Aussie mates sank the insufferably rich and arrogant Yanks.

Defining the Australian national identity is beyond our scope here. But in broad terms, at least, we can talk about a national quality in sport. Regrettably—and this is not for want of trying—we find little to celebrate in the Australian sporting character, propped up as it is by pampered and temperamental 'stars', uncharitable and biased journalists, unprincipled, unscrupulous and over-indulged officials, and increasingly obnoxious crowds.

HARD 'HEROES'

Australia has produced scores of sporting champions, men and women who have held world records or titles.[2] Yet few meet the criteria for real hero status—as opposed to what the perceptive Paul Gallico called manufactured hero status. Journalist Richard Hinds says there are so many more heroes today 'because we expect so damn little of them'. For Hinds, a contemporary hero is anyone merely good at something, who drives a sports car, wears Gucci clothing, is 'champagne-swillingly rich', 'chicked up to the hilt', and 'just intelligent enough not to embarrass themselves on celebrity *Sale of the Century*'.[3] His list could also have included anyone photographed by the press or who appears on television.

Our standards are considerably higher. For us, heroes distinguish themselves, display courage, or perform outstandingly in adversity. They are magnanimous; they ennoble and enhance humankind by what they do; and most importantly, they inspire and motivate, and often change people's lives for the better. They have visions of the way life ought to be lived, and often show greater concern for humanity than about competing in their chosen arenas. They certainly don't take bribes from anonymous bookmakers, appear regularly before disciplinary tribunals, sledge and vilify their opponents, bend or break the rules, smash motel rooms, conceal their eyes behind mirror sunglasses, spray champagne, or swagger with all manner of 'support staff'. Not surprisingly then, only a few qualify in our sense. They include the boxer Dave Sands, cricketers Bill O'Reilly and Keith Miller, tennis player Evonne Goolagong-Cawley, athlete Cathy Freeman, Australian footballers Jack Clarke and Michael Long, rugby Wallabies Mark Ella and Nick Farr-Jones, and swimmer Shane Gould.

After swimming to immortality with amazing grace at the 1972 olympics, Shane Gould retired and began a new life, one admirable for its Christian values. Widely regarded as one of the world's best bowlers in the inter-war years, Bill O'Reilly was forthright, erudite, gregarious and perceptive, skills he also applied as a journalist at the end of his cricket career. Although he clashed with cricket authorities, Keith Miller's gentlemanly disposition and broad range of interests made him one of the most popular players of the postwar period. After playing 263 games for Essendon in the 1950s and 1960s, Jack Clarke coached the club for three seasons. He not only played with skill and grace, but as a coach taught the importance of integrity and loyalty. Clarke also involved himself in youth affairs. Nick Farr-Jones captained the Australian Wallabies with distinction in the 1980s and early 1990s. He led by example and refused to compromise on questions of leadership.

It is not altogether surprising that half our candidates are Aborigines. When Sands was killed, at 26, boxing writer Ray Mitchell's funeral tribute captured qualities few can match:

> Dave was loved by all ... [He] was a shy, quiet, modest fellow; he had no vices; he never spoke disparagingly of anyone; he always gave credit where it was due; he was a great sportsman, who never took an unfair advantage, in the ring or out.[4]

Virginia Wade, the very tough British Wimbledon champion, summed up Evonne Goolagong: she 'played with a kind of giddy pleasure ... she

Shane Gould has an astonishing olympic record: she won gold in three individual races in world-record times. At one point she held every swimming record from 100m to 1500m and she either broke or equalled eleven world records. After swimming to immortality at the 1972 olympics, she retired (at 16!) and began a new life. She is one of the handful of genuine heroes in Australian sport. TONY DUFFY/AUSPORT

had no drive for money or power or stardom. She played because she loved it...She's still in people's minds...memorable...someone you always wanted to win...there was not a single false thing about her... people just loved her'.[5] Cathy Freeman is not only an inspirational talent:

she is generous, gracious, handles defeat easily, cares about her fellow human beings and actively promotes Aboriginality. Her approach to sport and to people is one of joy, not ruthless ambition. Mark Ella played 26 rugby Tests and captained Australia in nine of them. He did what few sportsmen do: he retired at the top of his powers. He remains in the memory while passing into history. He was Young Australian of the Year in 1982 and remains Australia's only representative in the International Rugby Hall of Fame. With no enemies, apart possibly from Alan Jones who deposed him as captain, his claims to hero are many. Perhaps it is his attitude to the game that stands out: why play, he asked, unless one is doing so for fun and enjoyment? Michael Long has done what few Aborigines before him have done: outshone and outplayed the opposition, won medals and premierships without boast, and successfully fought the fight against racism in sport without rancour.

In the present era of sport as entertainment, an appearance on television confirms one's 'star' billing. Paradoxically, television tends to destroy the properties, traits, characteristics and messages that first bring individuals to its attention. A classic example of this phenomenon is Roy Slavin and H. G. Nelson. On ABC radio they used parody and humour with brilliant and devastating effect to dissect sport. On television they achieved less success because they, rather than their subject matter, became cult figures; the vibrant and captivating personalities, the merry demeanours of 'Roy & H. G.', became the show. Their messages—aimed at deflating egos, and removing the pomp and pretentiousness from sport—were lost in the hype and schlock of television. In a similar vein, the player or the athlete who wins the game, the race or the championship, suddenly appears very ordinary and mortal when unprepared for the penetrating glare of television lights. Unfortunately, instead of leaving their performance on the field, court or track, and to the memory, our best sports men and women expect, even demand, public approbation and adoration. But their insatiable lust for unconditional praise and glory lures them to the very medium that exposes their mediocrity. Some of our sports stars do have more to offer than an athletic performance. Some are 'devoted to family' and do visit the sick, aged, lonely and dying; some do inspire others. But very few have visions. In Australia the lives of sports stars too often begin, and end, with 'playing hard'.

Playing hard is a conspicuous Australian trait. It is far more than good-natured pluck and determination, or selfless pride in, or honest commitment to, a representative team. It has become a euphemism for a win-at-all-costs mania that despises defeat and lacks any, often all, sense of perspective. At the 1992 Barcelona olympics, Clint Robinson defeated Norway's twice world champion Knut Holmann, for the 1000m kayak gold. Four years later in Atlanta, in less favourable circumstances, his fanaticism collapsed into petulance: 'People just don't realise my disappointment', a teary-eyed and inconsolable Robinson blurted after being beaten into third place. 'I've always been a believer that while second and third is fantastic, it's the start of the losers. A lot of people have said, "hey, you've won a bronze medal"...but when you have won gold and a world championship, it's hard to cop.'[6] Here is but one of many examples of Australian stars who believe they have an inalienable right to gold because they try, because they train and sacrifice, and because they're Australian. Sports psychologists, managers and agents could well moderate these values and, ultimately, help produce a more mature nation. They could inculcate a sense of perspective and proportion into the lives of our sports representatives. But this, of course, would require them first to admit that they, and their clients, have social responsibilities to the society of which they are members.

Playing hard also involves spite and malice. The current national cricket team has few peers in this game. Paul Sheehan calls it 'one of the worst sledging combinations in history'.[7] Australian cricketers 'can come out with some pretty disgusting things', says South African cricketer Jonty Rhodes.[8] New Zealand Test cricketer Chris Cairns was the target of one particularly sickening bout during a batting spell in a 1994 Test. At the crease after the recent death of his sister in a train accident, a devastated Cairns listened to members of the Australian team chant 'choo-choo-choo-choo-choo-choo'.[9] The contrast with a different age and place is stark. In 1953 New Zealand fast bowler Bob Blair lost his fiancée in a horrific Christmas eve train smash at home while he was on tour in South Africa. Two days later, in the second Test between New Zealand and South Africa in Johannesburg, the players and 'the 25 000 at Ellis Park silently stood to him'.[10] How sharp, too, is the contrast with Don Bradman's 'Invincibles': in 1948 they played 34 matches, were never beaten, winning by skill alone. Bradman, as hard as they come in sport, had no need to resort to a single word of sledging throughout the tour, and neither did his opponents.

Australians have always played hard. In 1930 the *Manchester Guardian*'s cricket writer, Neville Cardus, opined that

There has never been a comic character among Australian players... They are men of war most times. Even when the Australian batsman is brilliant to watch, he is at the same time a dour fellow. The Australians have shown us many handsome batsmen, but one and all they have worn their plumes with a difference. They have hit the ball hard and beautifully—but they have also hit the ball vindictively. Lust for spoils, not some power above mortal combat, has been the motive force. Even Victor Trumper was a conquistador, and there was little humour or graciousness about the incomparable Macartney.[11]

Playing hard assumed a distinctly odious aggressiveness in the 1960s with the rise of what Bill Mandle calls 'the ugly Australian hero', the one who 'ignores the spirit behind the [rules]'. Mandle's chief culprits were swimmers Dawn Fraser and Linda McGill, and tennis player Bob Hewitt. But they were pale imitations of Australian cricketers in the 1970s, in particular Ian Chappell, Denis Lillee and Rodney Marsh.[12] Former West Indies captain Viv Richards retains vivid memories of Australian cricketers during the 1975–76 Test series and their 'extreme savagery' and 'extreme racism'.[13]

Australia's 'hard' sportsmen and women consider 'sledging' a form of 'gamesmanship'. They justify it as a legitimate part of the game. Former Collingwood footballer Tony Shaw once described racial abuse as just another tactic: 'It's business out there... I'd make a racist comment every week if I thought it would help win the game.'[14] Indeed, the traditional ethos of sport, with its code of stoic honour, even convinced victims of abuse that sledging was a legitimate tactic and that the only response was to turn the other cheek. 'If you got into a fight about every stupid comment that was made', argued football legend Graham 'Polly' Farmer, 'you would have four or five fights a day'.[15] A new generation of Aboriginal footballers would prove Farmer wrong: just one well-fought campaign would radically transform the culture of racial sledging in the AFL.

Social changes in the 1950s and 1960s all but destroyed sport's traditional code of inured silence. In the early 1970s even Ted Dexter, captain of the England XI, complained about the Australian 'style': they 'throw off all their 180 years of civilised nationhood; they gaily revive every prejudice they ever knew, whether to do with accent, class consciousness or even the original convict complex, and sally forth into battle with a dedication which would not disgrace the most committed of the world's political agitators'.[16] Others were more blunt. West Indian cricketers took to calling Australians 'fucking white coward[s]'.[17] In a totally different milieu, Hawaiians laid siege to Australian surfers in the northern winter of 1976–77, refusing to supply boards, physically assaulting them, and threatening to burn down their accommodation. Two champion Australian surfers, Ian Cairns and Wayne Bartholomew, felt sufficiently intimidated to barricade themselves in a hotel. Tensions eased only after intervention by Eddie Aikau, the respected Hawaiian elder surfer. He effectively spoke for the entire international sporting community when he advised 'you Aussies' to 'learn to be humble'.[18]

Racial sledging increasingly drew the ire of the ever-growing number of Aboriginal footballers.[19] In 1995 Essendon's Michael Long insisted that Collingwood's Damien Monkhorst had called him a 'black cunt'. 'Why do we have to put up with it?' asked a furious Long, adding:

> That's not part of the game; it's not why I play. It's not what we should have to put up with. I think any racial or verbal abuse concerning colour or about your parents directed at you is wrong...Aboriginal people have been copping it for too long and I wanted to make a stand—not just in relation to what happens on the football field but off the field in day to day life.[20]

Ross Oakley, then the AFL's chief executive, believed that subsequent mediation 'presented a perfect resolution' to the racial abuse. Long thought otherwise. He seized the occasion at Oakley's media conference to tell Australians that, far from apologising, Monkhorst had simply said, 'you took it the wrong way, mate'. Public outrage extracted an apology from Monkhorst, while strong criticism from the federal Minister for Immigration and Ethnic Affairs, Nick Bolkus, forced the AFL to put more teeth and determination into the racial vilification code.[21]

The AFL's hesitancy in acting is just one of many examples of officials, media, agents, sponsors and clubs conniving in the protection and immunisation of stars from due legal process. (The relative immunity of football stars from police prosecution is both legion and legendary.) Another recent example was the ACB's belated appointment of Rob O'Regan QC, former chairman of the Queensland Criminal Justice Commission, to inquire into its handling, nearly four years earlier, of bribery allegations against Shane Warne and Mark Waugh.[22] While O'Regan castigated the ACB, and in particular its failure to suspend Warne and Waugh for what he correctly called serious offences,[23] he didn't address more fundamental questions about the elevation of sportspeople to demi-gods and the long established tradition of shrouding singularly unattractive 'stars' in cloaks of respectability. The Victorian government immortalised larrikin footballer Ted Whitten with a state funeral; another Australian footballer, Gary Ablett, employed the mantle of Christianity to conceal court appearances, drinking bouts and gambling binges. As long as they confuse sporting skills with heroism and conflate sporting success with social worthiness, Australians will retain a distorted sense of themselves and their place in the world.

Professionalism is the catchcry of the modern sports man and woman. As such, they insist there should be no limitation on their right to play who and where and how they want. Greg Chappell defended the underarm ball on several grounds, including the point that 'there was a lot of money at stake'. Players push the line that they have an unchallengeable right to earn their living, a right beyond question and criticism, a right even beyond suspensions imposed by sports judiciaries. There is, of course, another dimension to professionalism—unprofessional behaviour. Our players have yet to learn that there are no absolute rights in these matters, hence the ignorant squawks when footballers are fined for racism or for fouls that blatantly transgress the rules of their game, or any game. The laws of sedition, national security, libel, blasphemy, equity and a sense of decency impose limits on what we write, teach and broadcast; those limits apply equally to sportspeople, something they may well have to learn as the law and legal processes rightly intrude more and more into what was once considered the untouchable, sacralised domain of sport.

THE DRUG ISSUE

Senior Australian sports officials present themselves as being in the forefront of the war against drugs in sport. They boast that we do not have state-sponsored drug programs such as in the former East Germany, or the unpoliced use of drugs as in China. But the Australian record is less than clean. There are frequent revelations about drug use by athletes, footballers, cyclists and weightlifters. While these incidents are a constant embarrassment, officials maintain that they are merely aberrations. By insisting on Australian virtue, they fail to address the essence of the issue, and they refuse to consider alternative approaches.

Australia is hypocritical in its drugs and cheating argument. We do not ban 'drugs' which stop or delay the onset of menstruation, or interfere with diets which deliberately keep the bone density of young gymnasts low. At present we accept the increasing number of triathletes who arrive at meetings with inhalers, accompanied by medical certificates confirming sudden-onset asthma. We do not concern ourselves with substances which increase strength, improve stamina, boost speed, steady nerves, instil confidence, assist recuperation, celebrate victory, or mask defeat—substances which do not happen to find their way onto the banned list.

Officials ban performance-enhancing drugs for two reasons: they allegedly damage athletes' health, and they constitute cheating. We ask why sports officials, coaches and fans are so concerned about the health of athletes and players who take drugs, yet ignore other pressing health issues. Who protests when football coaches send concussed players back onto the field? Who really cares when parents surrender their children's childhoods to the sweat factories that are called 'sports institutes'? Why do sports bodies define carbohydrate loading as a 'natural training method' when it has such obvious health implications, including symptoms such as poor muscle coordination, listlessness, irritability, mood swings and hyper-activity? Why do sports bodies seek sponsorship from Coca-Cola, a soft drink containing caffeine which is a highly-addictive stimulant? Clearly there is a 'one-eyedness' about what constitutes 'good health'.

Sports officials could inject some realism into the drug issue and distinguish between use and abuse. After all, society approves the use of alcohol and rightly polices its abuses. Why not apply the same model to performance-enhancing drugs in sport, and tackle head on the illicit trade, black marketeering, and above all, chronic misuse which can lead to serious disease and even death?

Official Indulgence

Recently, the Australian Sports Commission inadvertently appointed Alan Jones, former Wallabies coach and talkback radio host, as its new deputy chair, which means he will automatically sit at the helm in two years. Approved initially as a general member of the Commission's board, a clerical error resulted in Jones's name being transcribed on the letter inviting the head of the ACB to fill the position. It was an appalling mistake. Bullying is a Jones trademark, whether it be on air or on the rugby league or union fields.[24] Among those seeking to transform sport's *ancien régime* of crude authoritarianism, uncomplicated choices and un-divided loyalties, Jones's elevation as one of Australia's most senior sporting officials is both bizarre and regressive, clerical errors notwith-standing. Yet, as the Sydney olympic bid, and its aftermath, confirm, there seems little realistic prospect of reforming this blinkered world of elitist pomp and over-indulgence.

Sydney's Olympic Bid Committee fawned on IOC members for their votes.[25] Its lobbying program, modelled on the successful Atlanta 1996 bid and euphemistically referred to as the 'let's-be-friends' campaign, consisted of bestowing royal treatment on visiting IOC members and, particularly in the case of Third World members, building profile and status in their countries. Visitors flew first class to Australia, were cleared through customs before the plane 'docked', and driven in limousines to five-star hotels. According to Perry Crosswhite, executive director of the AOC, they were free to structure their itinerary and 'nominate anything special that they, or their wives, wanted to see or do. We encouraged them to do what they were interested in; some were interested in art, some were interested in jewellery, particularly opals'. They dined at the best restaurants and were entertained at the Opera House; at least seven members spent time at luxurious resorts, including the Sheraton Mirage in Port Douglas and Lizard Island on the Great Barrier Reef. However, 'the full extent of spending on IOC members will never be known': some expenses 'never [went] through the bid's accounts', some 'were paid directly by sponsors or private individuals', and some 'were made on private credit cards and claimed back from the bid office under the broad definition of "hospitality"'.[26] Even access to these papers through freedom of information laws has been closed—on the dubious ground that the paperwork is the property of private accounting and consulting firms to which New South Wales' information laws do not (yet) apply.

The Bid Committee lobbied IOC members round the globe. It assigned senior officials to different regions. Phil Coles, a member of the committee, secretary-general of the AOC and an IOC member, lived in Paris for several months in 1993. Members of the Bid Committee actively bought votes. John Coates, a vice-president of the Bid Com-mittee and president of the AOC, offered three months' training at the Australian Institute of Sport to two athletes from eleven different African countries. He also arranged a place at the International Catering Insti-tute (Sydney) for Nomsa Sibandze, daughter of the IOC member for Swaziland, David Sibandze, and offered to accommodate Kenya's

Charles Mukora at the luxury Dorchester Hotel in London on his way to Monaco for the vote. Bruce Baird, the NSW Minister for the Olympic Bid, persuaded the State Rail Authority to employ Nick Voinov, son-in-law of the IOC member in Romania, Alexandru Siperco; at the time the Rail Authority had no vacancies for a person with Voinov's engineering qualifications. Frank Sartor, the committee's vice-president and Lord Mayor of Sydney, likened the lobbying process, particularly in the final week before the vote, to prostitution. We 'prostituted ourselves to try to get one more vote for Sydney', he said. He described the Hotel de Paris in Monaco, where IOC members stayed, as the 'Brothel de Paris'. But even those who expressed revulsion embraced the lobbying game. As one official put it, 'you shut your eyes and think of Sydney in 2000. We decided that as we had to do it, we would be the best whores you could find between Rome and Marseilles'.

Few officials felt or saw shame or any sense of the unethical. Baird insisted that bid members provided social assistance rather than opportunities for personal gain and enrichment: 'we recognised that African athletes did not have advantages of athletes from Western countries. It's an entirely different scene and one I don't have a problem with.'[27] The notion that helping African countries to field teams at olympic games constitutes development aid trivialises, even mocks, the socio-economic plight of hundreds of millions of people. It also misconstrues what really amounts to a preferential exchange between social elites, a point Coates conceded when he tried to justify the favoured treatment given Sibandze:

> I have known her father for 10 years. He is president of Swaziland's National Olympic Committee as well as being the country's IOC member. I am the father of six children and I hope that one day my contribution to the Olympic movement can be acknowledged by one of my kids studying overseas. Isn't this what the Olympic family is all about?

Coates sought refuge in semantics to cover his actions in offering Kenya's Charles Mukora accommodation: that didn't constitute corruption, he said, because Mukora never accepted the offer![28] Interestingly, signatories to the OECD's convention combating bribery in international business transactions think otherwise. The convention makes it a 'criminal offence for any person to offer an undue advantage to a foreign public official in order to win an improper advantage in the conduct of international business'. Offers, promises and gifts, irrespective of their acceptance, constitute an unfair advantage.[29]

The Salt Lake City bribery scandal exerted fresh pressure on Australian olympic officials to explain how, precisely, the Sydney Bid Committee won the hosting rights for the 2000 games. As the bribery scandal began to unfold, Salt Lake City media alleged that the daughter of a recently deceased member of the IOC, Rene Essomba (Cameroon), had received educational assistance from the Salt Lake City committee that successfully bid for the 2002 winter olympics. The allegations prompted the Salt Lake City Organising Committee (SLCOC) and the IOC Juridical Commission to conduct separate investigations into the allegations. The SLCOC reported its findings to the IOC executive on 10 December 1998. Among its findings was evidence of a systematic 'support program' organised by the Salt Lake City Bid Committee (SLCBC) aimed at 'helping' olympic officials from developing countries. The IOC immediately expanded its investigation and established an *Ad Hoc* Commission. Adding further urgency to the IOC's response were allegations by Marc Hodler, the IOC's member in Switzerland. He claimed that bribery had been a part of every olympic bid in the last decade.

The *Ad Hoc* Commission found that the SLCBC gave 'gifts' worth US$600 000 to IOC delegates. As well as tuition fees and university scholarships, the 'gifts' included cosmetic surgery, investment real estate in Utah, sexual favours and travel. Further allegations following the release of the *Ad Hoc* Commission's first report in late January 1999 led to a second report in mid-March 1999. A day after the release of the second report, the IOC held a special meeting to consider recommendations made by the *Ad Hoc* Commission. Members subsequently voted to expel six members. It also endorsed the Commission's recommendations that warnings, of varying degrees of severity, be issued to nine members, including Australia's Phil Coles.[30]

As more olympic bribery details became known, Jacques Rogge, the IOC official responsible for overseeing the 2000 games, suggested that Sydney's financial support to African athletes had breached the spirit of IOC rules.[31] Australian officials and former olympic athletes loudly proclaimed their innocence and dismissed all accusations and insinuations. Former olympic marathon runner Robert de Castella thought that the African deal was 'a way of raising the status of Australian sport in the eyes of other countries', while former olympic swimmer John Konrads described the Sydney bid as 'perfectly run': 'if we are privileged and we have the resources to help under-privileged athletes as part of the bid,

I think it's a brilliant way of doing business.'[32] Coates maintained that he only did what he had to do to win the games for Australia:

> We didn't win [the bid] on the beauty of the city and the sporting facilities we had to offer and we were never going to because, while that is important to the developed national Olympic committees, while that is important to the 40 national Olympic committees who will win medals at the games, it isn't important to those who will have a couple of representatives in a couple of sports.[33]

Clearly Coates shows no sense of proportion: winning is the only thing.[34] Like many other officials, he displayed deficiency of judgement and flagrant disregard for the spirit of the olympic ideal.

But it is the case of Phil Coles, one of the IOC's two members in Australia, that presents the best example of official indulgence.[35] In its report into the bribery scandal, the Board of Ethics of the Salt Lake City committee responsible for organising the 2002 winter olympics accused Coles of treating his visits to Salt Lake City 'like vacations'. The second IOC *Ad Hoc* Commission subsequently reported that Coles made five visits to Salt Lake City between 1990 and 1997 and accepted hospitality worth more than $60 000. On two occasions he took his partner and her two children. They stayed at expensive hotels and enjoyed a recreational program that included a visit to a Super Bowl game in Miami, an NBA All-Star basketball game, and a skiing trip to an exclusive Utah resort. The SLCBC paid for everything from ski pants and jeans to luxury accommodation, even tips to the housekeeper.[36] Coles's own hand confirmed his greed: 'We had an absolutely fabulous time and loved every minute of it', he wrote in a thank you letter to one of his Salt Lake City hosts. 'Who could ask for more—warm and friendly people, wonderful hospitality, basketball, skiing, snowmobiling! It was just the greatest fun. One complaint, however, your food is too good and we ate too much.'[37]

Despite all the evidence against him, Coles refused to concede impropriety. Far from showing repentance, remorse or shame, he said, simply, that he had been 'careless'.[38] And in the time-honoured tradition of sporting mateship, Coles's olympic colleagues and associates rushed to his defence. SOCOG's chief executive Sandy Hollway insisted that he is 'a good bloke...basically a very honest bloke', while John Coates called him the eternal 'battler from Bondi'.[39]

Politicians were a little more wary of defending Coles's free-loading.

Responding to the public outcry, the NSW Minister for the Olympics, Michael Knight, appointed Tom Sheridan, a retired auditor-general from South Australia, to inquire into the Sydney bid and how the committee spent $25 million wooing the votes of IOC members. Dressed up in excessive legal argument and pontification, Sheridan's report was a charade and quickly confined to the footnotes of the bid and the organisation of the games. After reading the report, a more relaxed Michael Knight happily admitted that 'Sydney's bid was not perfect'. But 'all in all', he insisted, 'it was pretty clean'. Former NSW Premier Nick Greiner agreed: Sheridan's report was 'of marginal consequence, not of great seriousness', while the bid was 'within the spirit of the rules'.

Sheridan's findings did not relieve the pressure on Coles, who remained an embarrassment and a political liability to SOCOG. Calls for him to resign from SOCOG intensified. He steadfastly refused, even in the face of new allegations that he accepted gold and diamond jewellery valued at nearly $10 000 from a Greek businessman associated with the 1996 Athens bid and, more damning, evidence that he gave confidential information about individual IOC members to Salt Late City officials in return for lavish hospitality. Under the terms of its initial warning, the IOC should have acted immediately on the new evidence and expelled Coles. High-ranking members of the IOC, however, refused to consider his expulsion. Finally, after months of delays, senior members of the IOC brokered a 'compromise': Coles would remain on the IOC on condition that he resigned from SOCOG. According to the official IOC press release, disclosure of the dossier (as distinct from its compilation) amounted to 'serious negligence' but that the 'facts at issue' dated from events 'from which [Coles] has already been sanctioned'! It was, in the words of the *Sydney Morning Herald*, a 'grubby compromise'.[40]

The actions of Phil Coles and his indulgence by colleagues support our argument that there is no philosophical or ethical substance in olympism. Whatever the historical essence of olympism, today it is little more than a biblical injunction to win whatever is available, and to acquire and retain non-accountable power, prestige and privilege—all, of course, for the sake of sport and the 'legacy of the athletes'. Nor, as the Sheridan and O'Regan reports testify, is there the slightest desire to analyse the culture of sport that nurtures excessive behaviour at every level. At its special meeting in March 1999, the IOC announced a number of reforms including a new method of choosing host cities, and

the appointment of a 24-person commission of eminent people to consider structural reforms to the IOC. 'We promised to clean house', the IOC president said, and 'we did it. We promised an Olympics united. It's done'.[41] We do not anticipate any significant changes. Among the 'global personalities of unquestioned fame' mentioned by Juan Antonio Samaranch to help refurbish his tarnished IOC was none other than President Richard Nixon's esteemed 'team-mate' and adviser—the architect of the secret bombing of Cambodia and the destabiliser of the democratically elected Allende government of Chile—Dr Henry Kissinger![42]

'ASHAMED TO BE AN AUSTRALIAN'

Australian sporting crowds have reputations for obnoxious, often appalling behaviour. It is a recent reputation, dating only from the 1970s. While Australian cricket crowds had always been 'fairly noisy', they generally remained 'good humoured' and were 'not exceptionally partisan'. In the early 1970s they became noticeably irascible. At the SCG during the seventh Test of the 1970–71 tour, England paceman John Snow felled Terry Jenner with a bouncer. A heated exchange then developed between Snow, his captain Ray Illingworth and the umpire, who warned the bowler for intimidation. The Hill crowd entered the fray, hooting, jeering, and heaving bottles and cans. Illingworth instructed his team to sit down until the noise subsided. When play resumed, Snow fielded on the boundary. An intoxicated spectator grabbed his shirt and attempted to drag him over the fence. England players ran to Snow's defence and the crowd pelted them with cans and bottles. The *Age*'s Peter McFarline, who saw the events at close quarters, summed up the sentiments of many when he wrote that the incident made him feel 'ashamed to be an Australian'. Illingworth, too, considered the crowd's behaviour unacceptable and led his team off the field.[43]

Derogatory comments on players' sexuality also emerged in the 1970s. Victorian state player Trevor Laughlin remembers the comments made by a Western Australian spectator after he used a protector-box when fielding close up. Walking to the boundary at the end of the over, he put the box in his back pocket and heard the spectator call out, 'always knew you were a poofter, Laughlin, with your balls in your back pocket'. Such comments represented 'a vulgarised and conservative response to the gay rights movement'.[44]

Crowd behaviour hasn't improved since the 1970s. John Woodcock, editor of *Wisden*, soundly admonished a 'discordant and unattractive' SCG crowd at the conclusion of a day-night limited-overs match in 1982, which he said had 'drowned' England in a 'sea of jingoism': 'By 8.30 any resemblance between what was happening and any normal game of cricket was coincidental... The sounds of fury, the beating of boards, and the booing of Englishmen was orgiastic. This was not so much sport as jingoism.'[45] South African cricket reporter Neil Manthrop recently referred to 'nauseatingly jingoistic' Australians, while the *Australian*'s Mike Coward nominates our one-day crowds as 'the worst behaved in the world'.[46] Certainly racial vilification of foreigners has worsened. Despite the International Cricket Council clearing Sri Lankan spinner Muttiah Muralitharan's unorthodox bowling action, Australian cricket crowds continue to jeer him. 'The crowds have been really bad', commented Sri Lankan captain Arjuna Ranatunga, adding that 'this problem only seems to happen in Australia'.[47]

Glenn James, a Vietnam war veteran, became the first black 'Man in White', refereeing two Australian football grand finals in the early 1980s. He was subjected to gross racial vilification from fans and players, so much so that lawyer Greg Lyons posed the serious question of whether the abuse of James—specifically, spectator screams that he was 'a use-less fucking boong'—amounted to a criminal offence.[48] In 1982 Michael Gawenda, now editor of the *Age*, reported that every time North Melbourne's Jim Krakouer went near the boundary line he could hear the chorus of 'you black bastard'. Martin Flanagan tells of how 'nice young men in the Members' Stand went pink from the exertion of yelling "hit him" every time a black player came near the ball'. 'Go sniff your petrol' was a commonplace, as was 'you black fucking cunts'—not from the outer, but from middle-aged ladies in the main stands.[49] Seventy-four-year-old Mary Millard was one who called Krakouer a 'black bastard'. While she played down the significance of her words—'it's all part of being at the footy on a Saturday arvo. It's just a way of letting out your feelings'[50]—they reveal her complete insensitivity to the feelings of others and, in a collective sense, confirm what social critic Humphrey McQueen labels the jingoistic and viciously racist Australian character.[51]

Despite efforts to broaden and homogenise the spectator base of sport, it is highly unlikely that market approaches will ever ameliorate those who are generally considered the worst behaved group of spectators: young 19–25-year-old, men mostly from low socio-economic backgrounds. Of the 1500 people arrested between 1960 and 1985 on charges relating to crowd disorder at the motorcycle championships at Bathurst, the overwhelming majority were young males either in manual occupations or unemployed.[52] This same cohort comprises most of the drunk, jeering, taunting and bottle, can, fruit and ice-throwing spectators at one-day cricket.

Why does this group behave so? It is hardly or simply 'the beer talking', as former national cricket captain Greg Chappell once opined. Aggressive forms of masculinity are the principal means by which young lower-class youths and men bond and interrelate with each other. Aggressive masculinity stresses courage, strength, dodges, trickery, invective, the ability to bear pain, and the consumption of vast quantities of alcohol. These norms and behaviour patterns are the basic ingredients of much (but not all) crowd disorder. On the other hand, it is no coincidence that the definitions of 'disorderly conduct' come from the middle classes who control the institutions of law (courts), order (police) and virtue (church and media). They subscribe to different social values, engaging in less collective bonding, less personal and more functional inter-relationships, and they know that strict self-control and self-discipline are essential preconditions for success: convictions for disorderly conduct have destroyed the employment prospects of many middle-class boys.[53] While there is nothing romantic about young lower-class men 'letting themselves go'—by any standards their conduct can be sickening —much of the behaviour which the media labels 'threatening' or 'moronic' is in fact purposeful and ritualised. Peculiar unspoken 'rules' typically govern what at first glance seems impulsive anarchy. Individuals perform specific roles: novice, rowdy, chant leader, tough guy, organiser, clown, nutter, scapegoat. Similarly, most of the aggression is verbal and ritual: rules allow groups to express belligerence and hostility in play forms, while friends restrain potential combatants.

Paradoxically, market approaches to sport contribute further to disorderly behaviour. Sponsors, advertisers, sports officials and governments market big sporting events as popular carnivals. The louts, to use a pejorative shorthand term, view carnivals as places to escape the normal social order, to let themselves go, to turn the world upside down, and to mock and taunt their social superiors. They attend sport, irrespective of the code, to represent themselves against the outside world. They mark the 'cheap seats' as their territory—a site from which they taunt opposing fans and teams, and middle-class toffs. An irony is that crowd control measures (fences, tickets, turnstiles, segregated seating, attack dogs, police) merely highlight lower-class 'territory' and the 'disorder'. Attempts by authorities to reclaim this territory, such as Bay 13 at the MCG and 'The Hill' at the SCG, simply aggravate the situation. The same thing happened at Bathurst in 1979 when the authorities built a police compound on an area previously used for camping and informal games. Administrators and marketeers have yet to learn that 'carnivalism' provokes, rather than soothes, emotions and that disorderly behaviour flourishes amid cacophonies of circus and sound—the products of incessant public address babble, blasting music, pre-match and half-time sideshows, avalanches of advertisements, and manufactured artificial tension induced by constant replays on giant screens.

ONE-EYED KINGS

For 150 years sport has been the principal means by which Australians have portrayed their way of life and beliefs and attitudes to the international community. Some commentators despair at the prominence of sport in this role. They consider it a manifestation of national immaturity. Keith Dunstan hopes that

> as the nation becomes older and more sophisticated, the desire to express its ego on the sporting fields should become less desperate; the need to show our physical greatness should be less anxious. Prime ministers also should be able to gain public approval without having to pull on football sweaters. The nation will discover that publicity by other means can be equally rewarding—touring orchestras, touring ballet groups, perhaps even roving scientists, writers and poets.[54]

In part, Dunstan overstates his lament. Sport does have the potential to convey a range of positive national attributes. Sport is not just what happens on the field. As hosts of the 2000 olympic games, Australians have the chance to display their national wealth of ideas and culture, technical expertise and organisational competence. Swarms of foreign journalists, international tourists, dignitaries and athletes will visit and, consciously and unconsciously, cast critical eyes over every aspect of our natural and built environment, our regional and national politics, our culture and social life, our very civility. They will judge us by our politeness and willingness to help strangers, our ability to make guests feel comfortable, and how we organise and handle mundane matters like mass transport and crowd control; they will study our culture for signs of superciliousness and cockiness; they will look at how we intermingle and treat each other; and some will seek signs of social inequality, tension and division.

We do, however, share much of Dunstan's lament. Some visitors will find Australia and Australians wanting. In many domains—Aboriginal land rights, general illness and mortality, Aboriginal living conditions, urban sprawl, water and air pollution, forest clearance, overgrazing— there is strong justification for criticism. Dunstan is right when he implies that too often Australians use, and rely on, sport to hide these realities. Certainly the respective views of Prime Minister Howard and five-time olympian Dennis Green that the captain of the national cricket team represents 'almost' the 'pinnacle of human achievement' in Australia, and that Phil Coles is a man of 'character and determination' because he was an olympic athlete, are arrant nonsense.[55]

Novelist Patrick White once observed that 'it seems as though life itself now depends on sport'. He asked whether 'this passion for perpetual motion' was 'perhaps for fear that we may have to sit down and face reality if we don't keep going'?[56] White may be correct. But we prefer another interpretation drawn from a considerable history that is less than flattering to the Australian way of sport: in the land of the blind, the one-eyed are kings.

Notes

All citations and references have been abbreviated, listing only author(s), dates (where they are needed to distinguish multiple titles) and page numbers. See the Bibliography for the full citation.

Prologue

1 Dening, 75.
2 Gallico, 9–10. Gallico was an outstanding sportswriter. In 1938 he published *Farewell to Sport*, after which he had a most successful career as a fiction and film scriptwriter. His noted short story is 'The Snow Goose'.
3 Matthews, 3.
4 Nadel 1998a; 1998b; Harms 1999, 11.
5 *SMH*, 20 March 1999.
6 Harms 1999, 10–11.
7 Cashman 1995.
8 Matthews, 4.
9 Grossberg, 7–8.
10 Marcus, 18.
11 Geertz, 27.
12 Harvey, 240.
13 Fischer, 4.
14 Carr, 11.
15 Gordon 1988.

Chapter 1—Sporting Connections

1 K. Inglis 1993, 148.
2 Herbert, 65, 68.
3 Trollope, 286.
4 *SMH*, 6 January 1999.
5 Balibar, 96.
6 Jarvie, 74.

7 Ford, 8.
8 Horne, 11.
9 In imperial money, before the dollar was introduced in 1966, the pound (£) was the main unit of currency. Four crowns made twenty shillings, or a pound (£1). A half-crown was 2.5 shillings. A guinea was always a fancy price used in horse-racing and in the sale of art works: it was 21 shillings. A dollar was, in theory, ten shillings, or half a pound.
10 K. Inglis 1993, 153–60; O'Hara, *OCAS*, 284–5.
11 Jarvie, 76.
12 Mandle 1973b, 236–7.
13 Gordon 1994, 429.
14 White, 115–19.
15 McGeogh, 131–2, 216–37.
16 The burial place of Shih Huang-ti, China's first sovereign emperor.
17 *Sun-Herald*, 14 March 1993.
18 *SMH*, 6 March 1999.
19 See, in particular, the ABC's 'Four Corners' program, 'Blood Sport', February 1999.
20 According to Simmel, relationships between organically connected people are based on 'the similarity of just those specific traits which differentiate them from the merely universal'. Later he

asserts that to 'the extent to which [social] similarities assume a universal nature, the warmth of the connection based on them will acquire an element of coolness, a sense of the contingent nature of precisely this relation—the connecting forces have lost their specific, centripetal character'. See his essay 'The Stranger'.

21 Jutel, 75–6.

22 Ken Burns produced the definitive television series on the history of baseball.

23 Kaplan, 177–8.

24 Lamont, 35–6.

25 Gordon 1988, 466.

26 Lipset, 38.

27 Stoddart 1986, 38–9.

28 Barnes, 140.

29 Stoddart 1986, 34.

30 Ibid., 44–5.

31 Holt, 93; John Hargreaves, 67.

32 Cashman 1984, 30–2, 135–42; Harms 1998, 42–9.

33 Veblen, xvi–xvii.

34 O'Hara 1988, 7–8.

35 Alomes & Jones, 21.

36 Ibid., 69–70.

37 Ibid., 48–9.

38 White, 83.

39 Traikovski, 1–6.

40 Fraser, 117.

41 McKay 1997, 91.

42 Fraser, 117.

43 Burroughs et al.

44 Dow, 134–42.

45 White, 15.

46 Booth & Tatz, 7.

47 Stokes, 159.

48 Tatz 1995, 154.

49 See A. McGregor for a full discussion of this event.

50 In 1992 the High Court ruled in the *Mabo* case that native title did exist at the time of the British invasion and that it had continued to exist in the Torres Strait. The federal Labor government responded by passing the *Native Title Act 1994*, which acknowledged that native title existed on all land and that it would continue to exist where the Crown had not acted inconsistently by alienating such land. It also created an Indigenous Land Corporation to purchase land in areas unavailable for claim.

51 Booth & Tatz, 7.

52 In December 1996, the High Court declared in the *Wik* case that Aborigines had conjoint rights with pastoral lease-holders, but that in the event of conflict between such rights, those of the lease-holders would prevail. Newly elected Prime Minister Howard immediately implemented a legislative response to effectively extinguish any native title rights on pastoral leases. The 'Ten-Point' Wik legislation was passed in 1998, after bitter debate, particularly over the federal Coalition's false claims about the vulnerability of white property rights.

53 The word 'barrack' is originally a negative term. Everywhere else, one barracks against, meaning to poke fun at, hence to shout derisively at and so disconcert players and spectators. Only in Australia does it mean to root and cheer for a player or team. A barracker is also a died-in-the-wool fan.

54 Adam MacDougall, Wayne Richards, Robbie O'Davis.

55 *Australian*, 8 July 1998.

56 Stoddart 1986, 49–50. He identifies another paradox here. While 'communities are dynamic...under the pressure of social and economic trends', clubs tend to remain static, 'maintaining ideas and practices in a social setting where they may have become inappropriate'.

57 M. Phillips 1998b, 43–4.

58 Marshall, 258. Marshall distinguishes between legal citizenship (equal treatment before the law), political citizenship (the right to vote and stand for office) and social citizenship. The German sociologist Jürgen Habermas argues that a strong, well-defined system of law is a foundation for forging consensus among ethnic and racial groups about the language, procedures and conventions for the legitimate exercise of power in a shared political arena, where there is competition for resources. He calls this consensus constitutional patriotism. According to Habermas, constitutional patriotism is a prerequisite for a nation of citizens, which he argues is a real nation as distinct from an artificial ethnic-cultural nation. Harbermas, 118, 146, 225. Habermas's notion of constitutional patriotism has particular relevance in explaining many of the recent political advances made by Aborigines, as discussed above.

59 McKay 1997, 105.

60 Epstein, 28.

61 K. Inglis 1993, 171.
62 M. Phillips 1998b, 46.
63 Cashman 1995, 197–9, 168.
64 *SMH*, 10 April 1999.
65 In 1998 it emerged that in the tour of Pakistan in 1994, both Warne and Mark Waugh had accepted sums of US$5000 and $6000 from an illegal Indian book-maker named 'John'—allegedly in exchange for weather and pitch infor-mation. The ACB fined both players, in private. Both players told a press con-ference that they were 'naive and stupid'. The press took a much harsher view: for example, the *SMH* published several articles under the heading 'Betting Scan-dal', and Patrick Smith's piece was headed 'Greedy pair have made Australia a laughing stock' (10 December 1998). A subsequent inquiry by Rob O'Regan QC castigated the Board for not sus-pending them. In the final Test against the West Indies in April 1999, McGrath was fined $2500 for spitting at, or near, an opposition batsman. See also note 22 in Chapter 10.
66 Ford, 226.
67 *SMH*, 14 January 1999.

Chapter 2—Currency and Sterling

1 Cumes, 9–10.
2 K. Inglis 1993, 47. White refers to the Presbyterian minister as an 'ardent proto-nationalist with the attachment of a proselyte to his adopted country' (26).
3 Alomes & Jones, 50.
4 Ibid., 53–4.
5 Cumes, 49.
6 Clark, 77.
7 G. Inglis, 73, 74.
8 Mosely 1997a, 26.
9 Serle 1970, 265–72.
10 Gordon 1988, 53.
11 K. Inglis 1993, 16, 32, 85.
12 Rickard, 103.
13 Ibid., 103, 104.
14 Atkinson & Aveling, 271.
15 Cumes, 40.
16 Cashman 1995, 114.
17 Rickard, 28–9.
18 Cumes, 40, 81.
19 O'Hara 1988, 13.
20 Alomes & Jones, 11.
21 Bakhtin, 10–11.
22 O'Hara 1988, 15.
23 Cumes, 51–7.

24 Daly, *OCAS*, 220.
25 Cumes, 146.
26 Ibid., 40.
27 Rickard, 78.
28 Ibid., 29.
29 Ibid., 26–7.
30 Clark, 24.
31 Dunning, 3–8.
32 O'Hara 1988, 10.
33 Cumes, 16–17.
34 O'Hara 1988, 18.
35 Gordon 1988, 62.
36 Clark, 56.
37 Atkinson & Aveling, 236–7; K. Inglis 1993, 84.
38 Rickard, 78–9; Clark, 77; White, 29–30, 34.
39 K. Inglis 1993, 18.
40 Daly, 36.
41 Cashman 1995, 25.
42 Atkinson & Aveling, 236.
43 Cashman 1995, 25–6.
44 Cumes, 18, 38.
45 Cashman 1995, 24. It is not clear how Cashman might reconcile this statement with a later warning against 'exaggerat-[ing] the degree of commercialisation in sport before the 1880s' (189).
46 K. Inglis 1993, 148–51.
47 Ibid., 148.
48 Atkinson & Aveling, 269.
49 Ibid., 270.
50 K. Inglis 1993, 44. Currency denoted inferiority to 'sterling': when local traders issued paper money to eke out the ster-ling coinage, it was worth less than its face value.
51 Clark, 55.
52 K. Inglis 1993, 25.
53 Ibid., 20.
54 Clark, 46.
55 K. Inglis 1993, 47.
56 Cashman 1995, 26–8.
57 Clark, 56.
58 K. Inglis 1993, 51.
59 O'Hara 1988, 33–5; Cumes, 126–31; K. Inglis 1993, 153.
60 Gordon 1988, 33.
61 K. Inglis 1993, 10; Rickard, 27.
62 Rickard, 27.
63 K. Inglis 1993, 106.
64 Clark, 48.
65 K. Inglis 1993, 104.
66 Stell, 1.
67 The sources are Cumes, 95–6, 206, 212. Other historians also question the accu-racy of Stell's work on related grounds (Adair & Vamplew, 49).

68 Rickard, 27–8.
69 Alford, 440.
70 K. Inglis 1993, 243, 245.
71 Ibid., 246–9.
72 O'Hara 1988, 68.
73 Ibid., 76–7, 114–15, 141.
74 Main & Holmesby, 239.
75 *Age*, 8 June 1993.
76 Blainey, 95–6.
77 This doctrine was finally put to rest in 1992 in the monumental decision of the High Court in *Mabo v The State of Queensland (Number 2)*.
78 Rowley, 19.
79 For a full discussion of early white–Aboriginal relations and the genocidal phase of Australian history, see Tatz 1999.
80 For a full discussion of Aborigines and cricket, see Tatz 1995, 45–86.
81 Mulvaney & Harcourt 1988.

Chapter 3—Morality and Muscularity

1 Mangan 1981, 9.
2 Atkinson & Aveling, 271.
3 Trollope, 499–500, 430–1.
4 K. Inglis 1993, 137.
5 White, 45.
6 Daly, 120.
7 R. & M. Howell 1992, 266; see also 192–5.
8 Daly, *OCAS*, 221.
9 Stoddart 1994, 79–80.
10 Harker, 80.
11 G. Inglis, 123; Brown 1987, 173.
12 Jenkins, 211–12.
13 Brown 1987, 173; Brown 1986, 21.
14 Holt, 93.
15 Mangan 1981, 7.
16 Daly, *OCAS*, 23.
17 Moore & Phillips, 62.
18 Daly, 86.
19 Mandle 1973a, 533.
20 Grow 1998a, 39.
21 Cashman 1995, 59; Adair, 177–80.
22 John Hargreaves 1996, 67.
23 Clark, 162.
24 Blainey, 29.
25 Stremski, *OCAS*, 37–8.
26 Grow 1998b, 48.
27 Ibid., 53–4.
28 Ibid., 54–5.
29 Ibid., 71–3.
30 Hess, 111–12.
31 Hickie, 22; de Serville, 58.

32 The material following comes from Hickie, 118, 126–9, 139, 179–81.
33 The SRFU was the second rugby association established outside England, with the first created in Scotland.
34 Cunneen, 295; M. Phillips 1994, 197.
35 Cunneen, 304.
36 M. Phillips 1996, 161–2.
37 Cunneen, 297–300.
38 The League boasted that it paid injured first-, second- and third-grade players £2 per week. M. Phillips 1998b, 30.
39 Cunneen, 302.
40 G. Inglis, 196.
41 M. Phillips 1994, 203.
42 Cunneen, 301–2, 304.
43 Sandercock & Turner, 13.
44 Mangan 1986, 18; Mangan 1981, 135–6.
45 McAleer, 44.
46 Hickie, 147.
47 Grow 1998a, 25.
48 M. Phillips 1996, 160.
49 Atkinson, also Jennifer Hargreaves.
50 The following material comes from Stell, 3, 6–7, 12, 16.
51 K. Dunstan, 209–10.
52 Tatz & Stoddart, chapter 4.
53 Stell, 52.
54 Vamplew 1994, 15.
55 Crawford, 188–9.
56 Ibid., 185–6.
57 Traikovski, 1–6; Crawford, 185–9, 191, 195–6.
58 The following material comes from Tatz 1995, chapter 6.
59 These views were not unanimous: the secretary of the Australian Amateur Athletics Union, for example, felt it was contrary to the ideals of amateur athletics to disbar a man 'merely because he was an aboriginal'.
60 Cunneen, 295.
61 Grow 1998a, 17.
62 Cashman 1995, 24.
63 K. Dunstan, 70–3.
64 Ibid., 228.
65 Ibid., 230.
66 Gordon 1998, 182.
67 Broome.
68 Broome & Jackomos.
69 Stell, 16–17.
70 Hess, 89–90.
71 Bradley, 42.
72 White, 43.
73 Stell, 29. See also Grow 1998b, 80.

Chapter 4—Community and Nation

1 Mandle 1973a, 525–6.
2 Grow 1998a, 33.
3 Grow 1998b, 69.
4 Hickie, 7.
5 Hickie, 19–20; Cashman & Hickie.
6 Cashman & Hickie, 40–1.
7 Ibid., 38.
8 Dow, 169.
9 Cunneen, 293.
10 White, 55, 63.
11 Cashman 1995, 106.
12 K. Dunstan, 51.
13 Grow 1998b, 67.
14 Ibid., 66.
15 Hess, 96.
16 Hickie, 9. Wills made his suggestion in 1858 in a letter to *Bell's Life in Victoria*.
17 White, 47.
18 Ibid., 38.
19 Ibid., 108.
20 K. Inglis 1993, 7.
21 White, 37, 38, 40, 56.
22 K. Inglis 1993, 9.
23 K. Dunstan, 9.
24 M. Phillips 1996, 161. For a discussion about the effects of the environment and climate on the Australian character see Brown 1988, 151–3, and White, 70–3, 75–6.
25 Headon, *OCAS*, 260–1.
26 Alomes & Jones, 9.
27 Ibid., 53.
28 K. Dunstan, 15.
29 Brown 1988, 154.
30 Ibid., 157.
31 Roderick, 20–21.
32 Clark, 174–5, 180.
33 Adair & Vamplew, 43.
34 Lawrence & Rowe, *OCAS*, 300.
35 White, 73.
36 Hickie, 15.
37 White, 111; see also Gordon 1994, 2.
38 Gordon 1994, 2–13, 30, 35.
39 For the full story of Mackintosh see R. & M. Howell 1988, 22–3 and Gordon 1994, 37–9. The term 'sports patriot' comes from Max Howell 1994, 35, where he criticises our analysis of the successful Sydney olympic bid.
40 Guttmann, 22.
41 Gordon 1994, xxiii–xxvi.
42 Crawford, 203.
43 Women gained the vote in South Australia in 1894, Western Australia 1899, New South Wales 1902, Tasmania 1903, Queensland 1905 and Victoria 1909. The Constitution conferred the Commonwealth franchise on all those entitled to vote in their state elections.
44 Stell, 38, 44–5.
45 The following material comes from D. Phillips, 10–21.
46 The following material comes from Raszeja, 41–4, 54–60, 65–9, 72.
47 Gordon 1994, 80.
48 Raszeja, 72, 81.
49 The following material comes from D. Phillips, 25, 29.

Chapter 5—The Great War Game

1 Blair 1998, 114.
2 Bean, 607.
3 Serle 1982, 44–5.
4 Alomes & Jones, 163–81.
5 *SMH*, 20 February 1999.
6 Although it had a mutual defence treaty with Belgium, Britain was the real villain according to Niall Ferguson. Britain, not Germany, was responsible for the greatest error of modern times (Ferguson).
7 Clark, 225.
8 Rickard, 118.
9 White, 125; Rickard, 118–19.
10 White, 112.
11 The 'Little Digger' sobriquet reflected Hughes's small stature and a visit to the Western Front in 1916. Clark describes Hughes as a person without 'affections for his fellow-man'. 'The pitilessness... experienced in his own struggle for survival', Clark argues, 'deadened' his human and social attachments (226).
12 Ibid., 232.
13 White, 130; Phillips & Moore, 106–7; Alomes & Jones, 176.
14 In the 1916 referendum the 'no' vote totalled 1 160 037 and the 'yes' vote 1 087 557. The next year the 'no' vote was 1 181 747 and the 'yes' vote 1 015 159. Clark, 232, 234.
15 Phillips & Moore, 108–9.
16 McKernan, 1, 3.
17 Blair 1998, 116.
18 McKernan, 3.
19 Mangan 1996a; Mangan 1996b.
20 M. Phillips 1997, 86–9.
21 Grow 1998a, 27.
22 M. Phillips 1997, 88.
23 McKernan, 1.
24 Ibid., 17.
25 M. Phillips 1996, 158, 170.

26 McKernan, 4, 14.
27 Blair 1998, 114; Blair 1995, 93–4; McKernan, 5.
28 McKernan, 5.
29 McKernan, 12–13; Phillips & Moore, 104.
30 McKernan, 7.
31 Phillips & Moore, 102; K. Dunstan, 167–8.
32 Phillips & Moore, 109.
33 Corris, 72.
34 Darcy was as much a victim of a personal vendetta by the sports entrepreneur and publisher Hugh McIntosh, as Protestant hostility. McIntosh offered to organise a tour to America for Darcy but the boxer declined. According to Darcy's trainer, Mick Hawkins, McIntosh became 'as mad as a hornet. Very few people bucked H. D. in those days, and he was sore. He threatened us there and then. Said he'd move heaven and earth to stop Les getting fights if he went to America under his own steam'. McIntosh's two newspapers, the *Sunday Times* and the *Referee*, both published vitriolic attacks of Darcy including one under the title 'Cold footed Les Darcy bolts from Australia to escape home defence' (Phillips & Moore, 105–6; K. Dunstan, 168).
35 Darcy's last letter to a friend, 21 April 1917 (Gordon 1988, 212).
36 Gordon 1988, 212.
37 K. Dunstan, 170.
38 McKernan, 14–15.
39 Phillips & Moore, 107.
40 Blair 1995, 100.
41 M. Phillips 1996, 172.
42 McKernan, 2.
43 M. Phillips 1996, 166–7, 170; McKernan, 7.
44 McKernan, 7; Stremski, 64.
45 McKernan, 16.
46 Ibid., 3.
47 M. Phillips 1997, 78.
48 Ibid., 79.
49 Ibid., 81. Of the 416 809 Australians who enlisted, 331 781 went to the front, 59 342 died, and 152 171 suffered wounds (Clark, 235).
50 M. Phillips 1996, 166–71.
51 Stremski, 58, 62, 64.
52 Ibid., 61, 63.
53 McKernan, 9.
54 Ibid., 10, 12.
55 Blair 1995, 96–7.

56 McKernan, 12.
57 Blair 1998, 133.
58 Blair 1995, 97; Stremski, 65.
59 M. Phillips 1996, 170.
60 M. Phillips 1997, 89–90.
61 Ibid., 90.
62 D. Phillips, 33.
63 Stell, 49–50.
64 Ibid., 72.
65 Ibid., 73.
66 Travelling exhibition, entitled 'Too Dark for the Light Horse'.
67 For an account of Aborigines in the armed services, see R. Hall. The travelling exhibition, in the footnote above, is most informative.
68 For a full account of Aborigines in boxing, including more detail on Jerome, see Tatz 1995, chapter 7.

Chapter 6—Empire First, Australia Second, Aborigines . . . Last

1 Rickard, 192.
2 White, 47.
3 D. Dunstan, 12.
4 Nauright, 122, 129; K. Inglis 1979, 150, 155 and 162. In the nineteenth century English cricketers toured Australia in 1861–62, 1863–64, 1873–74, 1876–77, 1878–79, 1881–82, 1882–83, 1884–85, 1886–87, 1887–88, 1891–92, 1894–95, 1897–98. Tommy Wills coached the Aboriginal cricketers before they went to England in 1868 and colonial Australian cricketers toured England in 1878, 1880, 1882, 1884, 1886, 1888, 1890, 1893, 1896 and 1899.
5 K. Inglis 1979, 149, 151–2, 155, 165–6, 169.
6 Ibid., 171; see also Mandle 1973a, 525–6.
7 K. Inglis 1979, 170.
8 Rickard, 120.
9 The inaugural Australasian championships was a triangular event between New South Wales, Victoria and New Zealand. The Victorian connection was Basil Parkinson. After arriving in Melbourne from England in the mid-1880s, he established the Melbourne Harriers and was a founding member of the Victorian Amateur Athletics Association. Parkinson also encouraged Edwin Flack to compete in the first modern

olympic games in Athens in 1896 (Gordon 1994, 3, 25–6).

10 Gordon 1994, 16.

11 Guttmann, 7–14.

12 By settling in Launceston in 1899, Cuff effectively removed himself from national and international sports administration.

13 Despite New Zealand's push for independence, Gordon notes that in 1913 the chairman of the New Zealand Olympic Council, Arthur Marryatt, cast a deciding vote against his organisation breaking away from the Australasian yoke (Gordon 1994, 51). The following material comes from Gordon 1994, 48–9, 51, 52, 57.

14 Henniker, 3; Moore 1989b, 189; Gordon 1994, 47.

15 Henniker, 5–6.

16 Nauright.

17 Moore 1989b, 188, 189–90.

18 The following material comes from Gordon 1994, 23–7.

19 Paul Hoch, *Rip Off the Big Game: The Exploitation of Sports by the Power Elite*, 1972; Jean-Marie Brohm, *Sport—A Prison of Measured Time*, 1975; Alan Tomlinson & Gary Whannel, *Five-ring Circus: Money, Power and Politics at the Olympic Games*, 1984; Vyv Simpson & Andrew Jennings, *Lords of the Rings: Power, Money and Drugs in the Modern Olympics*, 1992.

20 Gerard Henderson, *SMH*, 12 January 1999.

21 Moore 1989b, 196.

22 Guttmann, 21–9.

23 This quote and the ones below come from Gordon 1994, 49–51.

24 Henniker, 10, 11.

25 Alomes & Jones, 182.

26 Clark, 247.

27 Ibid., 249.

28 Now the Commonwealth games, the former Empire games have undergone several name changes which reflect the growing disparity of members: British Empire games (1930–54), British Empire and Commonwealth games (1954–70), British Commonwealth games (1970–78), and now Commonwealth games.

29 Gordon 1988, 269–71.

30 Dheensaw, 8–9; Moore 1989a.

31 Gordon 1994, 161.

32 Sandercock, 379.

33 D. Phillips, 40.

34 Stoddart 1987, 386.

35 Guttmann, 53–66.

36 Gordon 1994, 148–50; D. Phillips, 49.

37 Gordon 1994, 150.

38 Stoddart 1979, 126.

39 Cashman 1984, 30–1.

40 Ibid.

41 K. Inglis 1979, 153–4.

42 Cashman 1984, 97.

43 Stoddart 1979, 124.

44 Stoddart also refers to the 'common social bonds' among the thirteen-member Board, at least half of whom had attended prestigious private schools and then proceeded to university. The Board comprised four lawyers, two medical practitioners, two stockbrokers, a pastoral agent, the managing director of a timber company, and the director of a bread company (Stoddart 1979, 126, 137–9). The following quotes also come from Stoddart 1979, 139–40.

45 Letter on show in an historical cricket exhibition at the Mitchell Library, Sydney, December 1998.

46 Ryan, 52–6.

47 Gordon 1998, 277.

48 Stoddart 1979, 140–1.

49 Grow 1998b, 51–2.

50 Ibid., 80.

51 Rickard, 183.

52 Holmesby, 147.

53 D. Phillips, 39.

54 Flemming, *OCAS*, 324; Holmesby, 150.

55 Harriss, *OCAS*, 76–7.

56 *SMH*, 7 January 1999.

57 Gordon 1988, 372–3.

58 Stoddart 1979, 131.

59 Stell, 104–11.

60 D. Phillips, 40; Stell, 47.

61 Stell, 60.

62 D. Phillips, 41.

63 Stell, 109–11.

64 D. Phillips, 46.

65 Sandercock, 379.

66 Most of the following material comes from Tatz 1995.

67 Alomes & Jones, 242–4.

68 Here we identify Jimmy Callaghan (roughriding and equestrianism), Alby Roberts and Rollo Hinton (national professional boxing champions), George Green, Dick and Lin Johnson (all rugby league players), Leo Appo (woodchopping), Eric, Bill, and Maley Hayward (all Australian footballers and professional

runners), Doug Nicholls (Australian football), Lynch Cooper (professional athletics), Eddie Gilbert (Shield cricket), Ron Richards (professional boxing), Edna Crouch and Mabel Campbell (women's cricket), Glen Crouch (rugby league), Alec Hayden and Jimmy Williams (roughriding), and Cec Ramali (rugby union). For more details see Tatz 1995.

69 Bradman, 48, 288.

70 A. McGregor.

Chapter 7—Prosperity and Turbulence

1 C. McGregor, 24–6.

2 Clark, 295.

3 Frank Sedgman, 22 grand slam titles in singles, doubles, mixed doubles; Lew Hoad, Wimbledon singles title 1956, 1957; Ken Rosewall, four Australian, two French, two US opens; Rod Laver, first Australian to win grand slam of tennis, 1962; Dawn Fraser, four olympic gold; Lorraine Crapp, two olympic gold; John Devitt, two olympic gold; Murray Rose, four olympic gold; Jon Hendricks, two olympic gold; John Konrads, one olympic gold; Marjorie Jackson, two olympic gold; Shirley Strickland, three olympic gold; Betty Cuthbert, four olympic gold; Herb Elliot, one olympic gold, never beaten over the mile or 1500 metres; John Landy, one olympic bronze, central figure in race to break 4-minute mile; Ron Clarke, one olympic bronze, seventeen world records, carried torch and lit olympic flame in Melbourne; Richie Benaud, Test captain, first player to make 2000 runs and take 200 wickets in Tests; Alan Davidson, all-rounder, 44 Tests, batting average 24.59, bowling average 20.53; Neil Harvey, 79 Tests, batting average 48.42; Wally Grout, 51 Tests, 187 dismissals; Norman O'Neill, 42 Tests, batting average 45.56; Jack Brabham, Formula One world champion 1959, 1960, 1966; Peter Thomson, five British Opens, 1954–56, 1958, 1965; Russell Mockridge, two olympic gold, Paris Six Day event 1955; 'Midget' Farrelly, official world surfing champion 1964; Bill Roycroft, one olympic gold. For details see name entries in *OCAS*.

4 Wind 1960a, 84.

5 The material following comes from Gordon 1994, 195–9.

6 D. Phillips, 76; Wind 1960b, 80–1; Houlihan, 26–7.

7 D. Phillips, 76.

8 Woodman, *OCAS*, 103.

9 D. Phillips, 38.

10 Gordon 1994, 156; see also D. Phillips, 37–8.

11 Horton, *OCAS*, 89. Carlile also represented Australia in the modern pentathlon at the 1952 olympic games in Helsinki.

12 Gordon 1994, 175.

13 K. Dunstan, 13; H. Phillips, *OCAS*, 212–13.

14 K. Dunstan, 14; R. Stewart, *OCAS*, 94.

15 Stewart, 177, 182.

16 Clark, 292, 296.

17 Australia's population stood at 12.75 million in 1971 (Price, 9).

18 Martin, 61–7.

19 Rutland, 225–43.

20 Rickard, 225, 227.

21 Decision taken by Commonwealth and state ministers at the Native Welfare Conference, Canberra, 26–27 January 1961. See Tatz 1964, 11–28.

22 Price, 9.

23 Rickard, 235; Mosely 1994, 34; Jones & Moore, 24, 32.

24 Mosely 1997c, 159–62; Hay 1994, 70.

25 The material here comes from Mosely 1997c, 155, 162–3.

26 Stewart et al., 191.

27 Mosely 1997c, 167.

28 Mosely 1997b, 204–5.

29 Stewart et al., 192.

30 Caldwell, 37–8.

31 Lawton, 220.

32 The number of children attending school aged 14 years and over more than doubled between 1959 and 1969 from just under 300 000 to more than 650 000. Bachelor degree enrolments nearly quadrupled between 1955 and 1968 from over 21 000 to around 84 000 and then increased by another 50 per cent in the following decade to nearly 129 000 (Grundy & Yuan, 342, 344).

33 Booth 1994, 264.

34 Clarke et al., 67.

35 On the eve of her departure for Rome, Crapp married in a small, private ceremony. When news of her marriage became public, after the games began, swimming officials expressed their dis-

approval, subjecting her to constant surveillance and imposing strict curfews. The material in this section comes from D. Phillips, 78–81.

36 Fraser, 178–9.

37 Gordon 1988, 406.

38 Fraser, 198–9.

39 Gordon 1994, 262–3; D. Phillips, 84.

40 Stewart, 169, 179.

41 Stewart, 195–6; Stremski, 220–3; Dabscheck, *OCAS*, 438–40.

42 The material in this paragraph comes from Gordon 1994, 248–9.

43 Vamplew 1987, 383–6. These declines are even more dramatic when considered as a percentage of a growing population enjoying rising wages and increased leisure time. For an illustration see Nadel 1998a, 222.

44 Stewart, 178–9.

45 Adair & Vamplew, 130.

46 C. McGregor, 285–6.

47 The material here and following comes from Booth 1994, 265–70.

48 The material following comes from Stewart, 185–98.

49 The material here and following comes from Curthoys, 309, 316.

50 Stell, 180, 185.

51 Fraser, 117–18.

52 The 1967 referendum was promoted as, but was not in fact, a 'new deal' for Aborigines. It resulted in an overwhelming 'yes' vote to two questions: whether the federal government should have power to make laws for Aborigines in the states (concurrently with such states), and whether Aborigines should be counted in the national census, from which they were excluded in 1901. It is quite wrong to refer to this referendum as giving Aborigines 'citizenship rights', including the vote. Voting rights were available in all states by 1965 and the federal vote was granted in 1962.

53 Most of the material following comes from Tatz 1995.

54 Several critics rate him as the best forward in the history of the game. Later he became a national selector and a popular broadcaster.

55 Jackson played in three grand finals: 1969, 1970 and 1972.

56 McCarthy won three Stradbroke Handicaps, a Doomben One Hundred Thousand and in 1969 achieved the remarkable double of the AJC Derby and the AJC Epsom in successive races at Randwick.

57 Percy Hobson, who won the high jump for Australia at the 1962 Commonwealth games in Perth, was told to hide his dark, Bourke origins.

58 This is the National Australia Day Award, not to be confused with the *Australian* newspaper's Australian of the Year Award, which began in 1971.

59 The material here and following comes from Rickard, 203, 208, 220, 232, 234.

60 This material following comes from Rickard, 203–9 and Clark 268–9, 291.

61 Alomes & Jones, 264.

62 Cashman 1995, 120–1.

63 Armstrong, *OCAS*, 188.

64 The material here and following comes from Cashman 1995, 117–21. The University of Melbourne established Australia's first course in physical education in 1937 under the directorship of Fritz Duras, a former director of the Institute for Sports Medicine at Freiberg University. After the Nazis removed Duras from this post because of his Jewish ancestry, he emigrated to Australia (Gordon 1994, 265).

65 Organising Committee, 35, 39. At the conclusion of the games, the Victorian Housing Commission variously sold or rented the 365 houses and 841 units: see 121–2.

66 After Egypt seized the Suez canal from British and French interests the latter two governments convinced Israel to attack Egypt, thus giving Britain and France a pretext to invade Egypt to 'protect' the canal. When Prime Minister Imre Nagy proclaimed Hungary's intention of renouncing its alliance with the Soviet Union, the latter sent tanks and troops to Budapest.

67 Organising Committee, 23.

68 Ibid., 37. Interestingly, Egypt withdrew from the games for financial reasons prior to the Suez crisis. For details of the 'two Chinas' saga see Hill, 44–6.

69 Espy, 94–106.

70 The quotation and the paragraph following come from Stoddart 1986, 74.

71 Cashman 1995, 121.

72 Stoddart 1986, 66.

73 D. Phillips, 62.

Chapter 8—A National Sports Policy

1 Houlihan, 31.

2 Clark, 307.

3 Richard White argues that the Second World War discredited earlier ideas about a national type, given their close association with Nazi ideology. The heterogeneity of the American population, with which Australians came into closer contact during and after the War, also made it hard to reconcile a national type. Thus in the 1950s and 1960s Australians began to talk more about 'the Australian way of life'. This shift also corresponded with Western thought at the onset of the Cold War, which further encouraged ideological debates about identity (White, 157, 169).

4 Within its first month in office, Labor recognised the government of the People's Republic of China, ended Australia's military involvement in Vietnam, and announced an independent stance in foreign affairs. It also said it intended to make pre-school education available to every child, increase spending on teacher training, abolish university fees, introduce a universal health insurance system, establish a prices justification tribunal, and grant Aborigines land rights. See Rickard, 216; Clark, 310.

5 Inflation and unemployment both rose in Australia: between 1972 and 1975, inflation rose from 4.5 per cent to 16.9 per cent, and unemployment from 2.5 per cent to 4.5 per cent (Clark, 318; Withers et al., 150). After the opposition blocked supply in the Senate and Whitlam refused to test his party's support at the polls, the Governor-General, John Kerr, dismissed the Labor government.

6 Clark, 320.

7 Most of the material following comes from Armstrong, *OCAS*, 188–9; Semotiuk, 154–6, 189; Houlihan, 68–77.

8 Brawley, 178.

9 Rickard, 246. Ironically, while Al Grassby, Whitlam's Minister for Immigration, challenged what he called the 'mindless process of assimilation' and advocated greater 'respect' and even 'preservation' of migrant cultures and customs, Labor terminated Australia's mass migration programs. Under increasing attack for a policy which critics said contributed to inflation, Labor cut the immigration target from 140 000 in 1972 to 50 000 in 1975 (Martin, 71–2).

10 Martin, 72. Galbally's arguments repeated those made by Grassby.

11 Ibid., 74.

12 Hughson 1997a, 181–2.

13 Ibid., 169.

14 Hughson 1997b, 54–5.

15 Hay 1994, 70–1; Mosely 1994.

16 Mosely 1997c, 169–70.

17 Most of the material following comes from Hughson 1997a, 169–2; Hughson 1997b, 58–60. See also Brabazon, and Hage.

18 For a state of the art discussion of the concept of community and its application in an Australian sporting context, see Andrews 1998 and 1999.

19 Hay 1998, 59.

20 Tatz 1995, 26.

21 Rickard, 216.

22 Australian Society for Sports History, *Bulletin*, 19, 1993, 21.

23 The Gleneagles Agreement on Sporting Contacts with South Africa, London, 1981. Heads of government made the agreement during their biennial meeting at Gleneagles, Scotland.

24 Macfarlane, 110–14, 119–22, 126–7. Macfarlane was Britain's Minister for Sport at the time.

25 The 1981 tour proceeded and New Zealand went into a state of virtual civil war (Chapple; Richards). See Black & Nauright and Templeton for political histories of New Zealand and South African sporting relations.

26 The material following comes from Tatz 1981.

27 Colin Tatz covered political aspects of the games for the *Australian* and for ABC Radio from Brisbane. See his 'Politics and the games', *Weekend Australian*, 25–26 September 1982; 'The games really have been worth the candle', *Weekend Australian*, 9–10 October 1982.

28 Francis, 49.

29 Turner, *OCAS*, 240–3.

30 'Rebel' sportspeople were those who played in defiance of their code's national governing body, such as the Australian Cricket Board.

31 Francis, 129–40, 271–3.

32 Turner, *OCAS*, 243.

33 Gordon 1994, 339.
34 McKay 1991, 79.
35 Gordon 1994, 319.
36 Woodman, *OCAS*, 103.
37 Tatz 1995, 77–9. Bradman played for New South Wales in the 'duck' game; in the 1936 game he played for South Australia—the only time he batted at number four rather than his customary place at three.
38 Guttmann, 105.
39 Gordon 1994, 316–18.
40 Ibid., 398.
41 Turner, *OCAS*, 438.
42 Ryan, 41–58.
43 Semotiuk, 158–9; Armstrong, *OCAS*, 189.
44 The material following comes from Gordon 1994, 324, 325, 328–30.
45 The government paid the six individual athletes who withdrew $6000 each and the national sports federations nearly $70 000 (Stoddart 1986, 77).
46 Stoddart 1986, 69–70.
47 Inflation reached double digits in the early 1980s and unemployment jumped to 6.7 per cent in 1982, compared with 4.5 per cent in 1975 (Withers, 150; Clark, 322).
48 In the 1930s, English economist John Maynard Keynes argued that full employment is a prerequisite of a properly functioning economy and that the state should invest in economic activities (that is, state-owned enterprises) to employ labour not needed or wanted by the private sector. Keynesian economic policies underpinned the welfare state and guided economy policy in most Western countries after the Second World War until the early 1980s.
49 For a similar history of the NSWRFL, see M. Phillips 1998b.
50 The material following comes from Nadel 1998, 201, 207, 214, 215–16, 220–1, 222, 223–30. While we acknowledge Nadel's facts, we disagree with his interpretations. For elaboration see Booth 1999.
51 James, *OCAS*, 15, 27–8. See also James 1986.
52 Most of the material following comes from McKay 1991, 21–31.
53 In one well-documented period, he travelled to Perth 'to celebrate victory in the America's Cup, Melbourne for the Victorian Football League grand final,

Bathurst for the James Hardie 1000 touring car race and back to Melbourne for the final of the Davis Cup tennis' (Stoddart 1986, 69–70).
54 James, 28.
55 Gordon 1988, 468.
56 Alomes & Jones, 348.
57 Gallico, 70.
58 Like Bond, Christopher Skase, who at one point owned 79 per cent of the Brisbane Bears, found himself in trouble with the law after his Qintex Corporation collapsed with the stock market crash (Nadel 1998b, 228–30). Another failed entrepreneur discussed by Nadel is North Melbourne's Bob Ansett (Budget Transport).
59 Colin Tatz, 'Why sport should give politics the high jump', *Australian*, 18 February 1983.
60 Stephen Alomes, 'Suckers for a circus', *Herald Sun*, 8 May 1995; 'Out of the pits, macho premiers rev up', *Australian*, 8 March 1996.

Chapter 9—'Market Stakes'

1 6 June 1998, 18–19.
2 M. Phillips 1994, 209.
3 Stoddart, cited in Cashman 1995, 198.
4 Houlihan, 149–50. For full details of the WSC, see Haigh.
5 Booth 1991, 152–4.
6 Booth, *OCAS*, 223–4.
7 Rupert Murdoch, cited in the *Economist*, 6 June 1998, 14.
8 Colman. In 1995 Packer's Publishing and Broadcasting Limited and Murdoch's News Corporation engaged each other in a struggle to control rugby (see FitzSimons).
9 In February 1996, the court ruled in favour of Packer and accused News Corporation of mounting a 'meticulously planned operation, involving secrecy, suddenness and deception'. In October that year, a federal court reversed the decision and ruled in favour of Murdoch and Super League, deeming the latter a lawful enterprise restrained by the unreasonable actions of the ARL. A month later the High Court refused a further appeal by Packer, thus ending the legal saga (Rowe, 224).
10 Super League 1997 (10 teams): Adelaide, Auckland, Brisbane, Canberra, Canterbury, Cronulla, Hunter, North

Queensland, Penrith, Perth. ARL 1997 (12 teams): Balmain, Gold Coast, Illawarra, Manly, Newcastle, North Sydney, Parramatta, South Queensland, Souths, St George, Sydney City, Wests. NRL 1998 (20 teams): Adelaide, Auckland, Balmain, Brisbane, Canberra, Canterbury, Cronulla, Gold Coast, Illawarra, Manly, Melbourne, Newcastle, North Queensland, North Sydney, Parramatta, Penrith, South Sydney, St George, Sydney City, Western Suburbs. NRL 1999 (17 teams) St George and Illawarra merged, Gold Coast and Adelaide disbanded. Our thanks to Daniel Williams for these details.

11 Daniel Williams, 'Rugby league pigskin preview', *Inside Sport*, March 1997, 60.

12 We thank Murray Phillips for helping us unravel this saga.

13 During the Munich olympics, Palestinian terrorists, members of Black September, stole into the olympic village and took Israeli athletes hostage. Eleven athletes and three captors eventually died, most killed by West German police during a poorly organised assault on the terrorists and their hostages at a West German airfield (Guttmann, 138–9). Montreal, host of the 1976 games, incurred debts of US$1 billion.

14 Guttmann, 160–1; Hill, 138–60.

15 Six cities signalled their intent to bid for the 1996 Games, eight for 2000, and eleven for 2004.

16 Michael Hall defines hallmark events as 'major fairs, expositions, cultural and sporting events of international status which are held on either a regular or a one-off basis. A primary function of the hallmark event is to provide the host community with an opportunity to secure high prominence in the tourism market place' (C. M. Hall, 263).

17 Gordon 1994, 322–3, 340–1.

18 Hill, 187–91 gives a fascinating account of the political intrigue in the contest between Barcelona and Paris to host the 1992 games.

19 Gordon 1994, 366. For similar international examples, see Hill, 95.

20 Houlihan, 72.

21 Gordon 1994, 385–7, 390. The unsuccessful Melbourne bid did force a much needed restructuring of the state-based Australian Olympic Federation which subsequently became the sport-based

Australian Olympic Committee (Gordon 1994, 387–9).

22 The material following comes from Booth & Tatz, 8–9, 10–12.

23 The burial place of Shih Huang-ti, China's first sovereign emperor.

24 *SMH*, 8 March 1999.

25 Hess & Stewart 1998, 261; Deirdre Macken, 'You can't trust anybody these days', *SMH*, 10 October 1998.

26 M. Phillips 1998a, 141; M. Phillips 1998b, 33.

27 Gregor Salmon & Ewan Corness, 'Lost kingdom', *Inside Sport*, October 1998, 103–4.

28 *Sunday Age*, 28 March 1999.

29 Gordon 1994, 392–3.

30 Windschuttle, 177–8. See also Lawrence.

31 Daniel Williams, 'The future of sport', *Inside Sport*, October 1998, 30.

32 Nadel 1998a, 220–21, 224.

33 Stuart Rintoul, 'The unstoppable game', *Australian*, 23 March 1998, and personal correspondence with Stephen Alomes; also *Australian*, 15 April 1999. By comparison, the average game attendance at premiership rugby league matches was 10976.

34 'Swans' Brownlow memories', *Australian*, 17 July 1998.

35 Stuart Rintoul, 'The unstoppable game', *Australian*, 23 March 1998.

36 Letter, *Inside Sport*, December 1998, 8.

37 Salmon & Corness, *Inside Sport*, October 1998, 104.

38 Stuart Rintoul, 'The unstoppable game', *Australian*, 23 March 1998.

39 Fitzroy did merge, but with the Brisbane Bears, to become the Brisbane Lions.

40 Nadel 1998b, 233.

41 Most of the material following comes from Booth & Tatz, 4, 15–16, 19.

42 'Games secrecy excessive, says auditor', *SMH*, 15 January 1999.

43 'Tax doubts could leave $600m hole', *SMH*, 15 January 1999.

44 Cashman & Hughes, 217.

45 'Funding bolsters chances', *Australian*, 21 June 1997.

46 Cashman & Hughes, 220–21.

47 Houlihan, 71, 75. In 1985 the Hawke Labor government established the Australian Sports Commission to assume responsibility for managing developments, particularly relating to elite sport. While the ASC, which currently operates under the *Australian Sports Commission*

Act 1989, is technically independent of the federal government, the relevant minister appoints its board, which depends on federal funding.

48 Houlihan, 76–7.

49 Most of the material following comes from Kirk et al., 21–4, 27, 33–4, 40, 41–2. See also Thompson, 1999.

50 The material here comes from McCoy, 136, 140, 143–4.

51 Petlichkoff.

52 The material following comes from Taylor & Toohey, 279, 284–6.

53 Mosely et al.

54 Doumanis, 66.

55 Taylor & Toohey, 285.

56 Stell, 189.

57 Jaggard 1997; Jaggard 1999.

58 Bell, 49.

59 Ibid., 46.

60 The material following comes from Le Blanc.

Chapter 10—The Australian Way of Sport

1 K. Dunstan, 12.

2 Note that most have succeeded in obscure or minor sports, and that Australians have been singularly unsuccessful in the world's two biggest sporting events: men's athletic track and men's soccer. Australian men have won only four gold medals on olympic athletic tracks. By comparison, New Zealand, with one-sixth of the population, has won six olympic track gold.

3 Richard Hinds, 'Two stars fade but more will hit the sky', *SMH*, 13 March 1999.

4 Tatz 1995, 134.

5 Ibid., 276.

6 'Tears and cheers for two of our best', *Australian*, 5 August 1996.

7 Paul Sheehan, 'Fields of ire', *SMH*, 2 January 1998.

8 Gideon Haigh, 'The decider', *Inside Sport*, March 1997, 96.

9 Paul Sheehan, 'Fields of ire', *SMH*, 2 January 1998.

10 McLean, 97–8.

11 Bradley, 51.

12 Mandle 1982, 86.

13 Daniel Williams, 'The white thing', *Inside Sport*, March 1999, 66.

14 Warren & Tsaousis, 36. See also Tatz 1995, 155.

15 Warren & Tsaousis, 33.

16 K. Dunstan, 70.

17 Daniel Williams, 'The white thing', *Inside Sport*, March 1999, 66.

18 Booth 1995, 202.

19 By the end of the 1997 season, Aborigines made up 6 per cent of AFL players, nearly three times their numerical ratio in the general population (Gardiner, 7; Tatz 1998, 9).

20 Warren & Tsaousis, 38.

21 Winkler, 98–9; Tatz 1998, 21–4.

22 In February 1995 the ACB learned that an Indian bookmaker named (only) 'John' had paid Warne and Waugh substantially for 'pitch and weather information' five months earlier, and that Waugh remained in contact with the bookmaker. The public first learned of the affair late in 1998.

23 'QC attacks Warne, Waugh, ACB over bribery scandal', *SMH*, 25 February 1999; 'Waugh, Warne fine light on says inquiry', *Australian*, 25 February 1999. The ACB fined Warne and Waugh a token $8000 and $10 000 respectively.

24 Leser.

25 Most of the material following comes from Booth & Tatz, 10–13, and Sheridan.

26 Gerard Ryle & Gary Hughes, 'Breaking China: How Sydney stole the games', *SMH*, 6 March 1999.

27 'IOC suspect a "broker" in bid bribes', *SMH*, 9 January 1999.

28 'IOC reaffirms Sydney, orders investigation into bid', *Otago Daily Times* (Dunedin), 26 January 1999.

29 David Uren, 'At last OECD puts paid to bribery', *Australian*, 23 January 1999; 'Time's up for grace and favour dealings', *Australian*, 13 April 1999.

30 *Ad Hoc* Commission 1999a; *Ad Hoc* Commission 1999b; IOC press release, 12 March 1999. The six expelled were: Agustin Carlos Arroyo (Ecuador), Zein El Abdin Ahmed Abdel Gadir (Sudan), Jean-Claude Ganga (Congo), Sergio Santander Fantini (Chile), Lamine Keita (Mali) and Paul Wallwork (Samoa). The warnings were issued to: Louis Guirandou-N'Diaye (Ivory Coast), Willi Kaltschmitt Lujan (Guatemala), Shagdarjav Magvan (Mongolia), Anani Matthia (Togo), Un Yong Kim (South Korea), Austin Sealy (Barbados), Vitaly Smirnov (Russia) and Mohamed Zer-

guini (Algeria). In addition four other members resigned: Bashir Mohamed Attarabulsi (Libya), Pirjo Haggman (Finland), Charles Mukora (Kenya) and David Sibandze (Swaziland).

31 'Sydney 2000 "breached the spirit"', *Australian*, 25 February 1999.

32 'Legends support AOC chief', *Australian*, 25 January 1999.

33 'Chinese highway drove Coates into African bid', *Australian*, 25 January 1999.

34 Coates's fanatical devotion to the olympic movement in Australia reveals itself in his lobbying for the *Olympic Insignia Protection Act 1987* and the *Olympic Insignia Protection Amendment Act 1994* (designed to protect olympic symbols from unauthorised commercial use, and to give the AOC total marketing rights over olympic symbols), in the AOC's (highly questionable) decision to invest in the Reef Casino, Cairns, and in his blind determination to control the organisation of the games and to secure the long-term financial position of the AOC (Gordon 1994, 369; Crombie 1996, 41–3; Crombie 1999a, 1999b; 'Tough Coates still wears the pants', *SMH*, 25 January 1999).

35 Coles competed as a canoeist in the 1960, 1964 and 1968 olympics, was manager and coach of canoeing in 1972, assistant general manager of the Australian team in 1976, and general manager and *chef de mission* in 1980. Defying Prime Minister Fraser's proposed boycott of Moscow brought him to the attention of the new IOC president, Juan Antonio Samaranch, who appointed him a member in 1982. But the following statement, made after the AOF appointed him secretary-general in 1984, reveals that Coles subscribes more to self-gratification than the philosophy of olympism: 'Originally, I thought just one olympics would be enough but after marching in the opening ceremony, I was hooked forever' ('Gravy train derails man whose life is one big Games', *Australian*, 27 February 1999).

36 Board of Ethics, 29; *Ad Hoc* Commission 1999b, 19–23.

37 'Salt Lake's largesse: "Who could ask for more"', *SMH*, 27 February 1999. Interestingly, when asked, in 1993, in general terms about abuses, Coles insisted that IOC members were hard workers who abided by strong principles ('Sydney's golden touch', *Sunday Age*, 14 March 1993).

38 'Coles quits: "I've been careless"', *SMH*, 13 March 1999.

39 'Costigan tell IOC pair: it's time to go', *SMH*, 12 March 1999.

40 '7.30 Report', ABC television, 15 March 1999; 'Just walk away, Phil', *SMH*, 6 May 1999; 'Olympics: Coles accepted jewels', *Australian Financial Review*, 5 March 1999; 'Coles faces new five star claims', *SMH*, 11 May 1999, 'Secret high notes', *SMH*, 16 May 1999; 'Coles quits—but keeps perks', *SMH*, 15 June 1999; 'IOC executive board reprimands Mr Phil Coles', IOC press release, 14 June 1999; 'The end of the Coles affair?', *SMH*, 16 June 1999. Coles's first wife made the jewellery allegations. It seems that Coles's enemies in Melbourne, who accused him of supporting Atlanta against Melbourne in the race for the 1996 games, advised Georgina Coles to fax her allegations to the IOC! (Pamela Williams, 'Unforgiven, unforgotten in Melbourne', *Australian Financial Review*, 5 March 1999; Ferguson & Way). The ABC made the dossier public in early May. Coles and Coates have since fallen out.

41 'A hard sell message for our sponsors', *SMH*, 20 March 1999.

42 'Kissinger to help revive Olympics', *Australian*, 13 March 1999.

43 Cashman 1984, 138–9, 139–40; K. Dunstan, 100–2. The England team returned to play after staff cleaned the field.

44 Cashman 1984, 141–2.

45 Cashman 1988, 269.

46 'No time to mourn', *Mail and Guardian* (Johannesburg), 30 January 1998; 'Muralitharan deserves an apology, not idiots' jeers', *Australian*, 23 January 1999.

47 'Muralitharan will not return down under', *Australian*, 1 February 1999.

48 Tatz 1995, 156–7.

49 Tatz 1995, 154–8.

50 Warren & Tsaousis, 34, 37.

51 White, 168.

52 Lynch, *OCAS*, 126.

53 Booth & Loy.

54 K. Dunstan, 25.

55 Quotes from McKay & Rowe, and 'Olympic mud keeps flying', *Time*, 22 February 1999.

56 Headon, 80.

Bibliography

This bibliography contains only the sources cited in the text. It does not list individual items found in *OCAS* or newspaper articles.

Adair, Daryl (1994), 'Rowing and sculling', in Vamplew & Stoddart, 172–92.

Adair, Daryl & Wray Vamplew (1997), *Sport in Australian History*, Melbourne: Oxford University Press.

Ad Hoc Commission (1999a), Report of the IOC *Ad Hoc* Commission to Investigate the Conduct of Certain IOC Members, presented to the IOC Executive Board, Lausanne, 24 January.

Ad Hoc Commission (1999b), Second Report of the IOC *Ad Hoc* Commission to Investigate the Conduct of Certain IOC Members, presented to the IOC Executive Board, Lausanne, 11 March.

Alford, Katrina (1987), 'Women', in Aplin et al., 440–2.

Allison, Lincoln (1993), *The Changing Politics of Sport*, Manchester: Manchester University Press.

Alomes, Stephen & Catherine Jones (1991), *Australian Nationalism*, Sydney: Angus & Robertson.

Andrews, Ian (1998), 'Towards a conceptual framework for community', *Occasional Papers in Football Studies*, 1(2): 103–14.

——(1999), 'Redrawing "community" boundaries in the post-war AFL', *Football Studies*, 2(1): 106–24.

Aplin, Graeme, S. G. Foster & Michael McKernan (1987), *Australians: A Historical Dictionary*, Sydney: Fairfax, Syme & Weldon Associates.

Atkinson, Alan & Marian Aveling, eds (1987), *Australians: 1838*, Sydney: Fairfax, Syme & Weldon Associates.

Atkinson, Paul (1987), 'The feminist physique: Physical education and the medicalisation of women's education', in Mangan & Park, 38–57.

Bakhtin, Mikhail (1968), *Rabelais and His World*, Cambridge, Mass.: Massachusetts Institute of Technology Press.

Balibar, Etienne (1991), 'The Nation Form: History and Ideology', in Etienne Balibar & Immanuel Wallerstein, *Race, Nation, Class: Ambiguous Identities*, London: Verso, 86–106.

Barnes, Barry (1995), *The Elements of Social Theory*, London: UCL Press.

Bean, C. E. W. (1921), *The Official History of Australia in the War of 1914–1918*, vol. 1, Sydney: Angus & Robertson.

Bell, Glennys (1996), 'Playing the game', *Good Weekend* (supplement to the *SMH*), 16 March, 46–53.

Black, David & John Nauright (1998), *Rugby and the South African Nation*, Manchester: Manchester University Press.

Blainey, Geoffrey (1990), *A Game of Our Own: The Origins of Australian Football*, Melbourne: Information Australia.

Blair, Dale (1995), '"The greater game": Australian football and the army at home and on the front during World War I', *Sporting Traditions*, 11(2): 91–102.

——(1998), 'War and peace, 1915–1924', in Hess & Stewart, 114–39.

Board of Ethics (1999), Report by the Board of Ethics of the Salt Lake Organising Committee for the Olympic Winter Games of 2002, presented to the Board of Trustees, Salt Lake City, 8 February.

Booth, Douglas (1991), 'War off water: The Australian Surf Life Saving Association and the beach', *Sporting Traditions*, 7(2): 135–62.

——(1994), 'Surfing '60s: A case study in the history of pleasure and discipline', *Australian Historical Studies*, 26(103): 262–79.

——(1995), 'Ambiguities in pleasure and discipline: the development of competitive surfing', *Journal of Sport History*, 22(3): 189–206.

——(1999), review of Hess & Stewart, *Sporting Traditions*, 16(1).

Booth, Douglas & John Loy (1999), 'Sport, status and style', *Sport History Review*, 30(1): 1–26.

Booth, Douglas & Colin Tatz (1994), '"Swimming with the big boys?" The politics of Sydney's 2000 Olympic bid', *Sporting Traditions*, 11(1): 3–23.

Brabazon, Tara (1998), 'What's the story morning glory? Perth glory and the imagining of Englishness', *Sporting Traditions*, 14(2): 53–66.

Bradley, James (1995), 'Inventing Australians and constructing Englishness: cricket and the creation of a national consciousness', *Sporting Traditions*, 11(2): 35–60.

Bradman, Don (1950), *Farewell to Cricket*, London: Theodore Brun.

Brawley, Sean (1996), *Beach Beyond: A History of Palm Beach Surf Club 1921–1996*, Sydney: University of New South Wales Press.

Broome, Richard (1979), 'The Australian reaction to Jack Johnson, black pugilist, 1907–9', in Cashman & McKernan, 343–63.

Broome, Richard & Alick Jackomos (1998), *Sideshow Alley*, Sydney: Allen & Unwin.

Brown, David (1986), 'The legacy of British Victorian social thought: Some prominent views on sport, physical exercise and society in colonial Australia', in *Sport and Colonialism in 19th Century Australasia*, Adelaide: ASSH Studies in Sports History, 1, 19–41.

——(1987), 'Muscular christianity in the antipodes: Some observations on the diffusion and emergence of a Victorian ideal in Australian social theory', *Sporting Traditions*, 3(2): 173–87.

——(1988), 'Criticisms against the value-claim for sport and the physical ideal in late nineteenth century Australia', *Sporting Traditions*, 4(2): 150–61.

Burroughs, Angela, Leonie Seebohm & Liz Ashburn (1995), '"A leso story": A case study of Australian women's cricket and its media experience', *Sporting Traditions*, 12(1): 27–46.

Caldwell, J. C. (1987), 'Population', in Vamplew, ed., 23–41.

Carr, Edward (1964), *What is History?*, Harmondsworth: Penguin.

Cashman, Richard (1984), *'Ave a Go, Yer Mug!: Australian Cricket Crowds from Larrikin to Ocker*, Sydney: Collins.

——(1988), 'Cricket and colonialism: Colonial hegemony and indigenous subversion', in J. A. Mangan, ed., *Pleasure, Profit, Proselytism: British Culture and Sport at Home and Abroad 1700–1914*, London: Frank Cass, 258–72.

——(1995), *Paradise of Sport: The Rise of Organised Sport in Australia*, Melbourne: Oxford University Press.

Cashman, Richard & Tom Hickie (1990), 'The divergent sporting cultures of Sydney and Melbourne', *Sporting Traditions*, 7(1): 26–42.

Cashman, Richard & Anthony Hughes (1998), 'Sydney 2000: Cargo cult of Australian sport', in David Rowe & Geoffrey Lawrence, eds, *Tourism, Leisure, Sport: Critical Perspectives*, Sydney: Hodder Education, 1998, 216–25.

Cashman, Richard & Michael McKernan, eds (1979), *Sport in History: The Making of Modern Sporting History*, Brisbane: University of Queensland.

Chapple, Geoff (1984), *1981: The Tour*, Wellington: Reed.

Clark, Manning (1995), *A Short History of Australia*, Melbourne: Penguin.

Clarke, John, Stuart Hall, Tony Jefferson & Brian Roberts (1976), 'Subcultures, cultures and class', in Hall & Jefferson, *Resistance Through Rituals: Youth Subcultures in Post–war Britain*, London: Hutchinson, 9–74.

Colman, Mike (1996), *Super League: The Inside Story*, Sydney: Pan Macmillan.

Corris, Peter (1980), *Lords of the Ring*, Sydney: Cassell.

Crawford, Ray (1987), 'Moral and manly: Girls and games in prestigious church secondary schools of Melbourne 1901–1914', in Mangan & Park, 182–207.

Crombie, Ali (1996), 'A most unlikely foursome', *Business Review Weekly*, 2 September, 40–6.

——(1999a), 'Mr Olympics chases his own gold', *Business Review Weekly*, 16 April, 85–91.

——(1999b), 'Five rings, four stars, no conflict', *Business Review Weekly*, 23 April, 149–57.

Cumes, J. W. C. (1979), *Their Chastity was not too Rigid: Leisure Times in Early Australia*, Melbourne: Longman Cheshire.

Cunneen, Chris (1979), 'The rugby war: The early history of rugby league in New South Wales, 1907–15', in Cashman & McKernan, 293–306.

Curthoys, Ann (1987), 'Children, women and men', in Curthoys et al., 309–25.

Curthoys, Ann, A. W. Martin & Tim Rowse, eds (1987), *Australians: From 1939*, Sydney: Fairfax, Syme & Weldon Associates.

Daly, John (1982), *Elysian Fields: Sport, Class and Community in Colonial South Australia 1836–1890*, Daly.

Dening, Greg (1982), 'What's "local" in local history?', *Victorian Historical Journal*, 53(1): 73–7.

De Serville, Paul (1980), *Port Phillip Gentlemen and the Good Society in Melbourne Before the Gold Rushes*, Oxford: Oxford University Press.

Dheensaw, Cleve (1994), *The Commonwealth Games: The First 60 Years, 1930–1990*, Sydney: ABC Books.

Doumanis, Nicholas (1997), 'The Greek community', in Mosely et al., 63–72.

Dow, H., ed. (1966), *Trollope's Australia*, Nelson.

Dunning, Tom (1993), 'Convict leisure and recreation: the North American experience in Van Diemen's Land, 1840–1847', *Sporting Traditions*, 9(2): 3–15.

Dunstan, Don (1978), *Australia: A Personal Perspective*, Sydney: Kangaroo Press.

Dunstan, Keith (1981), *Sports*, Melbourne: Sun Books.

Economist (1998), 'Survey of World Sport' (supplement to the *Economist*), 6 June.

Epstein, Helen (1998), 'Life and death on the social ladder', *New York Review*, 16 July.

Espy, Richard (1979), *The Politics of the Olympic Games*, Berkeley: University of California Press.

Ferguson, Adele & Nicholas Way (1999), 'The fall guy'), *Business Review Weekly*, 3 September, 64–72.

Ferguson, Niall (1998), *The Pity of War*, New York: Basic Books.

Fischer, David Hackett (1970), *Historians' Fallacies: Toward a Logic of Historical Thought*, New York: Harper & Row.

FitzSimons, Peter (1996), *The Rugby War*, Sydney: HarperCollins.

Ford, John (1977), *This Sporting Land*, London: Thames Television and New English Library.

Francis, Bruce (1989), *'Guilty': Bob Hawke or Kim Hughes?*, Francis.

Fraser, Dawn, with Harry Gordon (1965), *Gold Medal Girl*, Melbourne: Lansdowne Press.

Gallico, Paul (1988 edition), *Farewell to Sport*, London: Sportspages, Simon & Schuster.

Gammage, Bill & Peter Spearitt, eds (1987), *Australians: 1938*, Sydney: Fairfax, Syme & Weldon Associates.

Gardiner, Greg (1997), 'Racial abuse and football: the Australian Football League's racial vilification rule in review', *Sporting Traditions*, 14(1): 3–25.

Geertz, Clifford (1972), 'Deep play: notes on the Balinese cockfight', *Daedalus*, 101(1): 1–37.

Gordon, Harry (1988), *An Eyewitness History of Australia*, Melbourne: Penguin.

——(1994), *Australia and the Olympic Games*, Brisbane: University of Queensland Press.

Grossberg, Lawrence (1997), *Cultural Studies, Modern Logics, and Theories of Globalisation, Back to Reality? Social Experience in Cultural Studies*, Manchester: Manchester University Press.

Grow, Robin (1998a), 'From gum trees to goalposts, 1858–1876', in Hess & Stewart, 4–44.

——(1998b), 'The Victorian Football Association in control, 1877–1896', in Hess & Stewart, 45–85.

Grundy, Denis & F. F. F. Yuan (1987), 'Education and science', in Vamplew, ed., 328–46.

Guttmann, Allen (1992), *The Olympics: A History of the Modern Games*, Urbana: University of Illinois Press.

Habermas, Jürgen (1998), *The Inclusion of the Other: Studies in Political Theory*, Cambridge, Mass.: MIT Press.

Hage, Ghassan (1998), *White Nation: Fantasies of White Supremacy in a Multicultural Society*, London: Pluto Press.

Haigh, Gideon (1993), *The Cricket War: The Inside Story of Kerry Packer's World Series Cricket*, Melbourne: Text Publishing.

Hall, C. M. (1989), 'The definition and analysis of hallmark tourist events', *Geojournal*, 19(3): 263–68.

Hall, Richard (1989), *The Black Diggers: Aborigines and Torres Strait Islanders in the Second World War*, Sydney: Allen & Unwin.

Hargreaves, Jennifer (1987), 'Victorian familism and the formative years of female sport', in Mangan & Park, 130–144.

Hargreaves, John (1986), *Sport, Power and Culture*, Cambridge: Polity Press.

Harker, Barry (1984), 'Competitive sports and moral education: an historical and philosophic analysis'. M.Ed. thesis, University of New England, Armidale.

Harms, John (1998), 'On the outer', *Inside Sport*, February, 42–9.

——(1999), 'Marked by faith', *The Australian's Review of Books*, February, 10–11.

Harvey, David (1989), *The Condition of Post Modernity*, Oxford: Basil Blackwell.

Hay, Roy (1994), 'British football, wogball or the world game? Towards a social history of Victorian soccer', in O'Hara, 44–79.

——(1998), 'Croatia: Community, conflict and culture: the role of soccer clubs in migrant identity', in Mike Cronin & David Mayall, eds, *Sporting Nationalisms: Identity, Ethnicity, Immigration and Assimilation*, London: Frank Cass, 49–66.

Headon, David (1991), '"A conflagration of conversation and preparation and anticipation and jubilation"—Great sporting moments and memories in Australian literature', *Sporting Traditions*, 8(1): 77–93.

Henniker, Garth (1989), 'Richard Coombes and the olympic movement in Australia: imperialism and nationalism in action', *Sporting Traditions*, 6(1): 2–15.

Herbert, Xavier (1975), *Poor Fellow My Country*, Sydney: Collins.

Hess, Rob (1998), 'The Victorian Football League takes over', in Hess & Stewart, 83–113.

Hess, Rob & Bob Stewart, eds (1998), *More Than a Game: An Unauthorised History of Australian Rules Football*, Melbourne: Melbourne University Press.

Hickie, Thomas (1993), *They Ran with the Ball: How Rugby Football Began in Australia*, Melbourne: Longman Cheshire.

Hill, Christopher (1996), *Olympic Politics: Athens to Atlanta*, Manchester: Manchester University Press.

Holmesby, Russell (1998), 'In a new league, 1925–1945', in Hess & Stewart, 139–64.

Holt, Richard (1989), *Sport and the British: A Modern History*, Oxford: Clarendon Press.

Horne, Donald, with David Beal (1967), *Southern Exposure*, Sydney: Collins.

Houlihan, Barrie (1997), *Sport, Policy and Politics: A Comparative Analysis*, London: Routledge.

Howell, Max (1994), 'Comments on "Swimming with the big boys?"', *Sporting Traditions*, 11(2): 31–5.

Howell, Reet & Max (1988), *Aussie Gold: The Story of Australians at the Olympics*, Brisbane: Brooks Waterloo.

——(1992), *The Genesis of Sport in Queensland: From the Dreamtime to Federation*, Brisbane: University of Queensland Press.

Hughson, John (1997a), 'Football, folk dancing and fascism: diversity and difference in multicultural Australia', *Australia and New Zealand Journal of Sociology*, 23(2): 167–86.

——(1997b), 'The Croatian community', in Mosely et al., 40–62.

Inglis, Gordon (1912), *Sport and Pastime in Australia*, London: Methuen.

Inglis, Ken (1979), 'Imperial cricket: Test matches between Australia and England, 1877–1900', in Cashman & McKernan, 148–79.

——(1993), *Australian Colonists: An Exploration of Social History 1788–1870*, Melbourne: Melbourne University Press.

Jaggard, Ed (1997), Forgotten members: women in Australian surf life saving, 1906–1980, paper presented to the North American Society for Sport History, Springfield.

——(1999), Welcome to the clubhouse? Women's entry to surf lifesaving in 1980, paper presented to the Australian Society for Sports History, Queenstown.

James, Paul (1986), 'The ideology of winning: cultural politics and the America's Cup', in Lawrence & Rowe, 136–47.

Jarvie, Grant (1993), 'Sport, nationalism and cultural identity', in Allison, 58–83.

Jenkins, R. (1960), *The Victorians and Ancient Greece*, Oxford: Basil Blackwell.

Jones, Roy & Philip Moore (1994), '"He only has eyes for Poms": Soccer, ethnicity and locality in Perth', in O'Hara, 16–32.

Jutel, Annemarie (1998), '"I can't! I've got my period": menstrual mythology and the production of feminine movement', *Avante*, 4(2): 72–91.

Kaplan, Mordecai (1934), *Judaism as a Civilization*, New York: Thomas Yoseloff.

Kirk, David et al. (1996), *The Social and Economic Impact on Family Life of Children's Participation in Junior Sport*, Canberra: Australian Sports Commission.

Lamont, Leonie (1997), '10 great moments in talkback', in Phillip Adams & Lee Burton, *Talkback: Emperors of Air*, Sydney: Allen & Unwin, 35–42.

Lawrence, Geoffrey (1986), 'It's just not cricket', in Lawrence & Rowe, 151–65.

Lawrence, Geoffrey & David Rowe, eds (1986), *Power Play: The Commercialisation of Australian Sport*, Sydney: Hale & Iremonger.

Lawton, John (1992), *1963: Five Hundred Days*, London: Hodder & Stoughton.

Le Blanc, Roger (1986), The 'pink dollar' in sport, paper presented at the Fourth International Congress on Sport Management, Montpellier, France, October.

Leser, David (1998), '"Don't you know who I am?"', *Good Weekend* (supplement to the *SMH*), 14 November, 16–27.

Lipset, Seymour (1979), 'Approaches to social stratification', in J. Curtis & W. Scott (1979), *Social Stratification in Canada*, Scarborough, Ontario: Prentice-Hall, 29–58.

Macfarlane, Neil with Michael Herd (1986), *Sport and Politics: A World Divided*, London: Willow.

Main, Jim & Russell Holmesby (1992), *The Encyclopedia of League Footballers*, Melbourne: Wilkinson Books.

Mandle, W. F. (1973a), 'Games people played: cricket and football in England and Victoria in the late nineteenth century', *Australian Historical Studies*, 15(60): 511–35.

——(1973b), 'Cricket and Australian nationalism in the nineteenth century', *Journal of the Royal Australian Historical Society*, 59(4): 225–45.

——(1982), 'Sports History', in Graeme Osborne & Bill Mandle, eds, *New History: Studying Australia Today*, Sydney: Allen & Unwin, 82–93.

Mangan, J. A. (1981), *Athleticism in the Victorian and Edwardian Public School*, Cambridge: Cambridge University Press.

——(1986), *The Games Ethic and Imperialism*, Harmondsworth: Viking.

——(1996a), 'Games field and battlefield: a romantic alliance in verse and the creation of militaristic masculinity', in Nauright & Chandler, 140–57.

——(1996b), 'Duty unto death: English masculinity and militarism in the age of the new imperialism', in Mangan, ed., *Tribal Identities: Nationalism, Europe, Sport*, London: Frank Cass, 10–38.

Mangan, J. A. & Roberta Park, eds (1987), *From 'Fair Sex' to Feminism*, London: Frank Cass.

Marcus, Greil (1996), *The Dustbin of History*, London: Picador.

Margan, Frank & Ben Finney (1970), *A Pictorial History of Surfing*, Sydney: Paul Hamlyn, 180.

Marshall, Thomas (1983), 'Citizenship and social class', in David Held et al., *States and Societies*, Oxford: Basil Blackwell, 248–60.

Martin, A. W. (1987), 'The people', in Curthoys et al., 59–75.

Matthews, Brian (1998), 'Hamstrung', *The Australian's Review of Books*, March, 3–4.

McAleer, Kevin (1994), *Dueling: The Cult of Honor in Fin-de-Siecle Germany*, Princeton: Princeton University Press.

McCoy, Damien (1997), 'The Vietnamese community', in Mosely et al., 136–48.

McGeogh, Rod with Glenda Korporaal (1994), *The Bid: How Australia Won the 2000 Games*, Melbourne: William Heinemann.

McGregor, Adrian (1998), *Cathy Freeman: A Journey Just Begun*, Sydney: Random House.

McGregor, Craig (1966), *Profile of Australia*, London: Hodder & Stoughton.

McKay, Jim (1991), *No Pain, No Gain: Sport and Australian Culture*, Sydney: Prentice Hall.

——(1997), *Managing Gender: Affirmative Action and Organizational Power in Australian, Canadian, and New Zealand Sport*, Albany: State University of New York Press.

McKay, Jim & David Rowe (1999), A short history of gender equity policy in Australian sport, paper presented to the Australian Society for Sports History, Queenstown.

McKernan, Michael (1979) 'Sport, war and society: Australia 1914–18', in Cashman & McKernan, 1–20.

McLean, Terry (1990), *Silver Fern: 150 Years of New Zealand Sport*, Auckland: Moa.

Mills, C. Wright (1953), 'Introduction', in Veblen.

Moore, Katharine (1989a), '"The warmth of comradeship": the first British Empire games and imperial solidarity', *International Journal of the History of Sport*, 6(6): 242–57.

——(1989b), 'One voice in the wilderness: Richard Coombes and the promotion of the Pan-Britannic festival concept in Australia 1891–1911', *Sporting Traditions*, 5(2): 188–203.

Moore, Katharine & Murray Phillips (1990), 'The sporting career of Harold Hardwick: one example of the irony of the amateur-professional dichotomy', *Sporting Traditions*, 7(1): 61–76.

Mosely, Philip (1994), 'Balkan politics in Australian soccer', in O'Hara, 33–43.

——(1997a), 'Australian sport and ethnicity', in Mosely et al., 13–42.

——(1997b), 'Rugby League', in Mosely et al., 199–209.

——(1997c), 'Soccer', in Mosely et al., 155–73.

Mosely, Philip, Richard Cashman, John O'Hara, Hilary Weatherburn, eds (1997), *Sporting Immigrants: Sport and Ethnicity in Australia*, Sydney: Walla Walla Press.

Mulvaney, John & Rex Harcourt (1988), *Cricket Walkabout: The Australian Aboriginal Cricketers on Tour 1867–8*, Melbourne: Macmillan.

Nadel, Dave (1998a), 'Colour, corporations and commissioners', in Hess & Stewart, 220–4.

——(1998b), 'The League goes national, 1986–1997', in Hess & Stewart, 225–55.

Nauright, John (1996), 'Colonial manhood and imperial race virility: British responses to post-Boer War colonial rugby tours', in Nauright & Chandler, 121–39.

Nauright, John & Tim Chandler (1996), *Making Men: Rugby and Masculine Identity*, London: Frank Cass.

O'Hara, John (1988), *A Mug's Game: A History of Gaming and Betting in Australia*, Sydney: University of New South Wales Press.

——ed. (1994), *Ethnicity and Soccer in Australia*, Sydney: ASSH Studies in Sports History, 10.

OCAS: Vamplew, Wray et al. (1994), *Oxford Companion to Australian Sport*, 2nd edn, Melbourne: Oxford University Press.

Organising Committee of the XVI Olympiad (1958), *XVI Olympiad, Melbourne, 1956*, Melbourne: Government Printer.

Petlichkoff, Linda (1996), 'The drop-out dilemma in youth sports', in Obed Bar-Or, ed., *The Child and Adolescent Athlete*, vol. 6, in *Encyclopaedia of Sports Medicine*, Oxford: Blackwell Science, 418–30.

Phillips, Dennis (1992), *Australian Women at the Olympic Games, 1912–1992*, Sydney, Kangaroo Press.

Phillips, Murray (1994), 'Rugby', in Vamplew & Stoddart, 193–212.

——(1996), 'Football, class and war: The rugby codes in New South Wales, 1907–1918', in Nauright & Chandler, 158–80.

——(1997), 'Sport, war and gender images: The Australian sportsmen's battalions and the First World War', *International Journal of the History of Sport*, 14(1): 78–96.

——(1998a), 'From independence to a reconstituted hegemony: Rugby league and television in Australia', *Journal of Australian Studies*, 58: 134–47.

——(1998b), 'From suburban football to international spectacle: the commodification of rugby league in Australia, 1907–1995', *Australian Historical Studies*, 29(110): 27–48.

Phillips, Murray & Katharine Moore (1994), 'The champion boxer Les Darcy: a victim of class conflict and sectarian bitterness in Australia during the First World War', *International Journal of the History of Sport*, 11(1): 102–14.

Price, Charles (1987), 'Immigration and ethnic origin', in Vamplew, ed., 2–22.

Raszeja, Veronica (1992), *A Decent and Proper Exertion: The Rise of Women's Competitive Swimming in Sydney to 1912*, Sydney: ASSH Studies in Sports History, 9.

Richards, Trevor (1999), *Dancing on our Bones*, Wellington: Bridget Williams Books.

Rickard, John (1988), *Australia: A Cultural History*, London: Longman.

Roderick, Colin (1972), *Henry Lawson: Autobiographical and Other Writings 1887–1922*, Sydney: Angus & Robertson.

Rowe, David (1997), 'Rugby league in Australia: the Super League saga', *Journal of Sport and Social Issues*, 21(2): 221–6.

Rowley, Charles (1970), *The Destruction of Aboriginal Society: Aboriginal Policy and Practice*, vol.1, Canberra: Australian National University Press.

Rutland, Suzanne (1997), *Edge of the Diaspora: Two Centuries of Jewish Settlement in Australia*, Sydney: Brandl & Schlesinger.

Ryan, Greg (1997), '"Extravagance of thought and feeling": New Zealand reactions to the 1932/33 bodyline controversy', *Sporting Traditions*, 13(2): 41–58.

Sandercock, Leonie (1987), 'Sport', in Gammage & Spearitt, 373–84.

Sandercock, Leonie & Ian Turner (1981), *Up Where Cazaly? The Great Australian Game*, London: Granada.

Semotiuk, Darwin (1987), 'Commonwealth government initiatives in amateur sport in Australia, 1972–1985', *Sporting Traditions*, 3(2): 152–62.

Serle, Geoffrey (1970), 'The Gold Connection', *Victorian Historical Magazine*, 41(1): 265–72.

——(1982), *John Monash: A Biography*, Melbourne: Melbourne University Press.

Sheridan, Tom (1999), Report of the Independent Examiner for SOCOG, Sydney: Deloitte Touche Tohmatsu.

Simmel, Georg (1971), 'The stranger', in David Levine, *Georg Simmel on Individuality and Social Forms*, Chicago: University of Chicago Press, 143–49.

Stell, Marion (1991), *Half the Race: A History of Australian Women in Sport*, Sydney: Angus & Robertson.

Stewart, Bob (1998), 'Boom-time football, 1946–1975', in Hess & Stewart, 165–99.

Stewart, Bob, Rob Hess & Chris Dixon (1997), 'Australian Rules football', in Mosely et al., 185–98.

Stoddart, Brian (1979), 'Cricket's imperial crisis: the 1932–33 MCC tour of Australia', in Cashman & McKernan, 124–47.

——(1986), *Saturday Afternoon Fever: Sport in Australian Culture*, Sydney: Angus & Robertson.

——(1987), 'The Ashes', in Gammage & Spearitt, 384–6.

——(1994), 'Golf', in Vamplew & Stoddart, 72–92.

Stokes, Geoffrey (1997), 'Citizenship and Aboriginality: two conceptions of identity in Aboriginal political thought', in Stokes, ed., *The Politics of Identity in Australia*, Cambridge: Cambridge University Press, 158–71.

Stremski, Richard (1986), *Kill for Collingwood*, Sydney: Allen & Unwin.

Tatz, Colin (1964), Aboriginal Administration in the Northern Territory of Australia, Canberra, Australian National University, doctoral thesis.
——(1981), 'Aborigines and the Commonwealth games', *Social Alternatives*, 3(1): 48–51.
——(1995), *Obstacle Race: Aborigines in Sport*, Sydney: University of New South Wales Press.
——(1998), 'Top marks', in *AFLs Black Stars*, Melbourne: Lothian Books.
——(1999), *Genocide in Australia*, Research Discussion Paper 8/1999, Canberra, Australian Institute of Aboriginal and Torres Strait Islander Studies.
Tatz, Colin & Brian Stoddart (1993), *The Royal Sydney Golf Club: The First Hundred Years*, Sydney: Allen & Unwin.
Taylor, Tracy & Kristine Toohey (1997), 'Women, ethnicity and sport', in Mosely et al., 279–91.
Templeton, Malcolm (1998), *Human Rights and Sporting Contacts: New Zealand Attitudes to Race Relations in South Africa 1921–94*, Auckland: Auckland University Press.
Thompson, Shona (1999), *Mother's Taxi: Sport and Women's Labour*, Albany: State University of New York Press.
Traikovski, Louie (1998), 'The importance of sport to students and headmistresses at four Melbourne private girls schools from 1900–1914', *Bulletin of the Australian Society for Sports History*, 28, 1–6.
Trollope, Anthony (1873), *Australia and New Zealand*, London.
Vamplew, Wray (1987), 'Sport and recreation', in Vamplew, ed., 378–91.
——(1994), 'Introduction', in Vamplew & Stoddart, 1–18.
——ed. (1987), *Historical Statistics*, Sydney: Fairfax, Syme & Weldon Associates.
Vamplew, Wray & Brian Stoddart (1994), *Sport in Australia*, Cambridge: Cambridge University Press.
Veblen, Thorstein (1953), *The Theory of the Leisure Class*, New York: Mentor Books.
Warren, Ian & Spiros Tsaousis (1997), 'Racism and the law in Australian rules football: a critical analysis', *Sporting Traditions*, 14(1): 27–53.
White, Richard (1981), *Inventing Australia: Images and Identity, 1688–1980*, Sydney: Allen & Unwin.
Wind, Herbert Warren (1960a), 'Visit to a small continent: over the rainbow', *Sports Illustrated*, 16 May, 84–97.
——(1960b), 'Visit to a small continent: the will and the way', *Sports Illustrated*, 23 May, 78–85.
Windschuttle, Keith (1988), *The Media: A New Analysis of the Press, Television, Radio and Advertising in Australia*, Melbourne: Penguin.
Winkler, Michael (1998), '1993–98: the AFL and the fight against racism', in *AFL's Black Stars*, Melbourne: Lothian Books, 96–108.
Withers, Glen, Anthony Endres & Len Parry (1987), 'Labour', in Vamplew, ed., 145–65.

Index

Numbers in bold refer to illustrations
n. refers to endnote numbers